Armchair Conversations
on Love and Autism

Armchair Conversations on Love and Autism

on Love and Autism

Secrets of Happy
Neurodiverse Couples

Eva A. Mendes

Jessica Kingsley Publishers
London and Philadelphia

First published in Great Britain in 2024 Jessica Kingsley Publishers
An imprint of John Murray Press

2

Copyright © Eva A. Mendes 2024

The right of Eva A. Mendes to be identified as the Author of the
Work has been asserted by her in accordance with the Copyright,
Designs and Patents Act 1988.

Foreword copyright © Mona Kay 2024

Front cover image source: Shutterstock®.

A CIP catalogue record for this title is available from the British
Library and the Library of Congress

ISBN 978 1 78775 913 8
eISBN 978 1 78775 914 5

Printed and bound by CPI Group (UK) Ltd, Croydon, CR0 4YY

Jessica Kingsley Publishers' policy is to use papers that are natural,
renewable and recyclable products and made from wood grown
in sustainable forests. The logging and manufacturing processes
are expected to conform to the environmental regulations
of the country of origin.

Jessica Kingsley Publishers
Carmelite House
50 Victoria Embankment
London EC4Y 0DZ

www.jkp.com

John Murray Press
Part of Hodder & Stoughton Ltd
An Hachette Company

Dedicated to all the couples who shared their stories in this book.

~

To my mentors, Daisaku and Kaneko Ikeda
Thank you so much for the example of your beautiful, lifelong marriage.

~

For my daughter, Arya, a ceaseless font of joy and inspiration.

~

With deepest gratitude,
Eva

Contents

Foreword

In 2017, when I first discovered that I was in a neurodiverse marriage, I found Eva's first book *Marriage and Lasting Relationships with Asperger's Syndrome* (autism spectrum disorder). That book became my anchor in a stormy sea and it helped me understand why my husband and I had been having so many challenges throughout our 30 years together. It also provided me with some valuable tools that I needed as I moved forward in our relationship.

Although my marriage ended in 2018, I took everything I learned about neurodiversity into my next mixed-neurotype relationship and it had such a positive impact on the way I saw myself and my then partner and the way we understood and accepted each other's different ways of experiencing the world.

Fast forward to 2020, in the middle of a global pandemic I decided that even though I had read every book I could find on neurodiverse relationships, watched every video and followed every social media account I could find, it still wasn't enough. I started the *Neurodiverse Love* podcast with one of my dear friends, so that we could both share the lived experiences and lessons we had learned in the love relationships we had had with autistic men. We knew there were others who needed this information and they also needed to know that there was hope for understanding how the differences in your neurodiverse relationship could become opportunities for more self-awareness, growth, and healing.

I have also learned that neurology isn't the only factor that impacts our relationships. Our family of origin, attachment styles, culture, trauma, sexual and gender identity, and physical and mental health issues also have a big influence on how we show up in our relationships. However, when you don't understand your own neurology and that of your partner, you can both cause each other so much "unintentional" hurt and pain.

Eva's third book is filling a gaping hole in the neurodiverse community, showing a full spectrum of love exploring multiple intersections from race, gender, and sexuality across mixed-neurotype relationships. They help us understand not only that our neurology can have an impact on our relationships, but also that recognizing and acknowledging that our cultural differences and our diversity in gender or sexual identity may help facilitate more patience, compassion and grace for the differences in our relationships. Whether these differences facilitate a slower pace in our relationships, or move us to have more grace and give more space to our partners, the couples in Eva's book repeatedly show us that by understanding, affirming, and accepting our differences they can be viewed as strengths and opportunities for healing and growing. In addition, by sharing the hopes, dreams, struggles, and strengths of being in a neurodiverse relationship the couples that Eva and her team have interviewed are giving all of us a glimpse into their lives that we have never had access to before. Sometimes this is all we need to know that we are not alone and that the experiences we are having with our partner are a reflection of the way other neurodiverse couples experience life together.

Some couples may repeatedly struggle with communication differences and not understand why one of them sees communication as an important part of connection on a variety of different subjects, while the other partner prefers in-depth conversations about a few subjects that they are most passionate about.

Other couples may not understand why one partner is more logical and rational and rarely shows emotion in conversation, while the other may repeatedly get emotional about lots of things. One partner may have a variety of sensory sensitivities and doesn't like certain foods, smells or sounds, or clothes, and the other loves loud music, lighting candles and is a foodie. In addition, both partners may have very different physical and sexual needs. One may be hypersensitive and some types of touch may actually feel painful, or they may be hyposensitive and need a more intense touch to feel pleasure.

While these are some of the differences I often hear about from partners in neurodiverse relationships, each person and relationship is unique and Eva's book shows us that. Each couple has to create their own unique blueprint for the life they want individually and together and then find the strategies and tools that are going to help them build the future they want.

As Maya Angelou once said "when we know better, we can do better." I believe we can all "choose" to do better and be our best selves and a better partner in our intimate relationships. Some of the most important lessons the couples in Eva's book teach us are these:

• Increasing your self-awareness and understanding your own wants, needs, values, and dreams is very important.

- Being able to share these with your partner so that you can work together to determine which can be met through your relationship and which can be met on your own or with friends, family, or outside groups or interests is critical.

- Knowing that many of the problems and conflicts we have in our relationships are due to "unmet" needs that we may want our partner to fill, but it may not be something they can do, or want to do, and it is important to accept that that is the reality.

- Understanding that the only person we can ever change is ourselves and accepting ourselves and our partner's strengths, challenges, and differences is the way we reduce suffering and create more peace for ourselves and our relationships.

- When we can forgive past hurts, focus on healing, and learn how we can grow and be the best partner possible, we can create a path forward that helps us live our best, most authentic lives.

While my 30-year marriage ended, I am so grateful for the years I spent loving and learning with an awesome man who has so many strengths. Together we have an adult daughter who not only has many of the strengths and gifts of both of her parents, she is also a role model and shows me daily how life can be lived when you fully acknowledge, understand, and accept the differences, strengths, and challenges that are a part of being in a mixed-neurotype family.

Eva's book provides the world with a glimpse into what makes a neurodiverse relationship work well and shows us that with love, understanding, and acceptance we can create a healthy, loving partnership where we can live our best, most authentic life. I am so grateful for Eva's books and the work she is doing to make the world a more neuro-affirming place. There is something for all of us to learn from the ten couples who share their lives with us through this amazing book. I hope that everyone exploring or currently in a neurodiverse relationship finds the information and stories shared in Eva's book as valuable and inspiring as I have.

Mona Kay, MSW, PhD
Host of the Neurodiverse Love *podcast*

The Interviews

DIVERSITY AND INCLUSION

Couples representing diversity in racial, ethnic, and religious identities, as well as interracial couples and those representing a diversity of sexual orientation and gender identity were intentionally chosen.

RECRUITMENT

The couples invited to participate in this book were primarily recruited from Eva's private practice. The couples were motivated to be a part of this book to add to the literature on successful neurodiverse relationships. Additionally, they wanted to be heard as a part of underrepresented minorities such as people of color and those with LGBTQIA+ identities as a way to inspire and give others hope for their own relationships.

INTERVIEW PROCESS

Participants had the option to complete a written questionnaire, or to sit with the author or her assistant for a recorded interview, which was then transcribed. Recordings were then destroyed following the transcription. Interviews were minimally altered and edited for the sake of clarity, brevity, or terminology. Once the final draft of the book was completed, both partners were given the chance to read their partner's and their own contribution and were satisfied with the information that was included as part of their narrative as a couple.

ANONYMITY

In order to ensure anonymity, the real names of all participants in this book have been changed to pseudonyms. Additionally, identifying information such as where they work, names of pets, and associated people have also been modified.

COMPENSATION

Each couple was asked to review an informed consent form, and was encouraged to comment on and express any questions about the book prior to their involvement. As compensation for the time and effort spent in sharing their stories, couples were presented with gift cards and a copy of the finished book.

Introduction

The young man slumped into his chair in my counseling office. Sounding dejected, he admitted, "I'm wondering if I should go ahead and break up with my girlfriend now."

"Why is that?" I asked, curious.

"Everything I've read online seems to indicate that our relationship is doomed because I'm autistic." He shrugged. "I bet I could save everyone a lot of pain if I just quit now." Arriving at my office for the start of another work day, I opened my email to get caught up before meeting my first client. One subject line snagged my attention. It read, "Is there hope?" I opened the email to find a message from yet another desperate wife of an autistic man.

"Don't 80 percent of autistic marriages end in divorce?" she wanted to know. "All the online forums are so depressing to read, and they make me feel hopeless. Is there hope for us?"

Her pleading tone tugged at my heart, making me sigh.

My phone rang. It was one of my therapist friends and colleagues who I consult with and offer supervision to on occasion.

Picking up the phone, I heard a deflated voice on the other end.

"Can an autistic person change?" The first haunting question was followed by a barrage of others. "Can they learn to be empathetic? Are all these marriages heading for divorce? How do these women stay in these marriages? What do you see in your practice?"

I took a deep breath and asked myself the same question. "What *do* I see in my practice?"

HOW THIS BOOK CAME TO BE

I've been an autism spectrum difference (ASD) specialist couples counselor for the past decade. Tragically, the mindset described in the above scenarios is not uncommon. Reading the various blogs, forums, online support groups, and even some books on the subject made me realize that most of them paint neurodiverse (ND) relationships to be either impossibly difficult or doomed for failure. The people writing on these forums express deep suffering, and it is very real. However, in my own practice as a couples counselor, I have long observed that each ND couple is utterly unique and while there are couples who are suffering greatly and really struggle to stay together, there are also couples who are in love, happy, and thriving in their relationships.

Regardless of what I was seeing in my sessions with my ND couples, I felt like the internet was flooded by negative stories. It shouted about the experiences of people who were deeply unhappy and enduring terrible suffering with their autistic partners. Every day, I would get emails from couples from all over the world asking me about the success rates for ND relationships. There even seemed to be some research papers floating around suggesting that the majority of neurodiverse relationships are basically doomed.

So, I decided that it wasn't enough that I as a couples counselor, who had the inside scoop on these relationships, knew that there were in fact hundreds and even thousands of successful ND relationships; I wanted everyone to know that ND relationships are not automatically doomed.

So I decided to interview some of the happy couples I knew and gather first-hand information and the best-kept secrets of what they do and how they make their relationships work. That way no one would ever have to wonder, "Are there any happy ND relationships?"

In my first book, *Marriage and Lasting Relationships with Asperger Syndrome*, I identified certain key strategies, tools, and best practices to making ND relationships work. In speaking to the ND couples in this book you will see how broad the spectrum of ASD traits is and how they can affect a relationship, but you will also learn that it's often the non-spectrum (NS) partner who has their own hangups and baggage and that often individuals come together with complementary needs and strengths. Additionally, many of these relationships have not just one ND individual, i.e. the autistic partner, but *two* ND individuals, with diagnosed or undiagnosed mental health or neurological differences—most commonly anxiety, attention deficit hyperactivity disorder (ADHD), other learning differences, or trauma experiences, which mean that accommodations, changes, and growth are needed on both sides. When couples are well-matched and enter the relationship for the right reasons—not due to trauma bonds or to escape or be rescued from their own lives—these relationships really work.

Therefore, my impetus for writing this book is to share positive, first-hand narratives of satisfying neuro-diverse marriages. More importantly, I want to show what these relationships really look like from the inside, from the point of view of each person in the couple.

These interviews were also undertaken against the backdrop of the Covid-19 pandemic, offering insights into the collective experiences of couples during this unprecedented period. Consequently, the interviews stand as a valuable record depicting the dynamics of ND relationships during the pandemic. They shed light on the challenges faced by individuals and couples and how they navigated through these unique circumstances, providing a glimpse into their coping mechanisms during this pivotal moment in our recent history.

WHO YOU'LL HEAR FROM IN THE BOOK

As I extended my invitation to participate in this book, I explained that I was looking for neurodiverse couples who were willing to share both their story and how they find happiness with each other, despite the challenges. For those couples who courageously decided to share, pseudonyms have been used in order to respect their privacy.

I also designed this book to be a diverse and inclusive voice amongst the books on neurodiverse relationships, which often only focus on stereotypical narratives. This book aims to present a diverse range of voices and so I have also intentionally shared the experiences of ra-cially and ethnically diverse couples—which include couples of color and mixed-race couples. Also, since I work with an increasing number of ND couples with identities ranging across the spectrums of gender identity and sexual orientation (as represented in my second book, *Gender Identity, Sexuality and Autism,* which I coauthored with researcher and psychologist Dr. Meredith Maroney), I wanted to include their relational experiences as well. After all, love is love. Additionally, the book is also enriched by the perspectives of couples with coexisting mental and physical health diversities.

WHAT QUESTIONS WERE THE COUPLES ASKED AND WHY?

The framework of the questions we asked the couples was designed to elucidate the various aspects of a couple's life together, such as how they met, how they came about their ASD diagnosis, and whether it was a formal diagnosis or they self-diagnosed. We also wanted to shed light on the support systems that the couples possess, be it financial or emotional, as it is the couples with such support systems who seem to thrive the most. We asked about their faith, as for many couples this can not only be a way to make meaning and provide them with some helpful tools, but also a way to unite the couple. We also wanted to reflect on the financial situation of the couples, as from my perspective as a couples counselor, I do find that this can have a tremendous impact on the marriage and the couple's marital success. As you will see, most of our couples are in financially secure positions, which definitely makes it easier to be with each other; however, you'll also see that these marriages are egalitarian in that even if one spouse is the breadwinner, they make a concerted effort to make sure that the power between them is balanced so that neither of them feels superior or inferior to the other. Another aspect we wanted our couples to talk about was their children and parenting challenges. And we made a point to have them discuss their pets as well, as for autistic individuals having a pet can often be a great boost to their mental health.

Another set of questions that we wanted to ask our couples was about the general awareness in society about ASD and ND relationships. As you will see, autistic individuals who are not visibly autistic, like so many of the individuals in this book, remain largely unseen and most people don't realize or understand the struggles that they have to face. We also asked about any advice that our couples might have for other couples in ND relationships, and they had a lot to say. What was universal in all of these answers was the importance of seeking help, becoming more self-aware, working on one's self, being flexible, and always keeping in mind the big picture that you're in the marriage for the long haul, which means constantly working on it.

Sex lives were also discussed as well emotional intimacy and marital happiness ratings. We wanted to use The 10-Point Marital Satisfaction Scale™ and ask the spouses to give us a number, as we wanted them to be as objective as they could be so as to encourage others. I created The 10-Point Marital Happiness Scale™ in my first book, *Marriage and Lasting Relationships with Asperger's Syndrome*, as a straightforward tool for evaluating marital happiness, using a scale from 1 (extremely unhappy) to 10 (extremely happy). This scale can help couples monitor their relationship's health, identify areas for improvement, and provide researchers like myself with quantitative data on marital satisfaction.

We did ask a somewhat controversial question of our couples which was whether they felt that they were in love with their partners, and almost all answered yes. I find this question to be important in proving my point that ND couples where one partner is autistic do deeply love each other and don't stay with each other out of financial or family compulsion, but because they are truly in love with each other. This of course can mean many things to many people, but for the purposes of this book, I wanted to see if they felt a passionate sort of love for each other. Many people seem to think that these types of feelings are fleeting and can only be experienced by those in the first blush of love, but I strongly feel that it's the ability to fall in love with the same person over and over again by focusing on and appreciating their positive qualities that defines a truly happy marriage.

WHY WERE THE QUESTIONS ASKED IN THAT ORDER?

We wanted to begin with a history of the relationship, and then focus on their ups and downs and strengths and weaknesses. We wanted to also ask couples about practical things like finances, parenting, division of labor, and support systems. And we wanted to end with the warm and fuzzy feelings that they had toward their spouses near the end of the interview so that we could really offer you, dear reader, hope that love and happiness in an ND relationship where one partner is autistic is possible.

WHO THIS BOOK IS FOR

This book is for the person who dares to hope that love wins. If you refuse to be intimidated by the voices that forecast failure, this book will strengthen your resolve. If you admit to being more than a little intimidated by the pervasive nature of autism and are grasping for encouragement, this book will lift your chin. If you can't deny that you dearly love an individual who happens to be on the spectrum—take heart! Others have found love on the spectrum; so can you and your loved one. These pages are filled with insights from individuals who are doing just that.

This book is made up of down-to-earth, living-room-style conversations. You'll soon feel that you've made a group of new friends who truly understand your experience in an ND relationship. If you've ever wondered how other individuals in ND relationships handle sensitive areas such as emotional connection, sex, co-parenting, families, spiritual practice, counseling, or finances, this is your chance to listen in!

You might even want your note-book or note-taking app nearby to record the best practices and relationship-saving secrets you pick up. As you identify with their successes and struggles, I am confident you will feel a bit less alone in your own relationship journey. I see any number of happy, successful neurodiverse couples who choose to be together, and now you will too. I'm sure that these stories will offer you a balanced and hope-filled view of autistic love and you will never again think that ND relationships are automatically doomed. So, grab your cup of coffee or tea, curl up in your favorite armchair, and join me for a chat with these trailblazers as they share their real-life ND love stories.

* * *

No, don't quit.
Yes, there is hope for you.
Absolutely—In my practice,
I see happy endings, too.

* * *

Terminology

AUTISM SPECTRUM DIFFERENCE (ASD): The acronym ASD in this book refers to autism spectrum differences, because the word "disorder" in ASD is disempowering and discriminatory, whereas the term difference implies that ASD is simply a different neurology, mindset, culture, and experience. You may read that some participants use the terms autistic or aspie to refer to themselves or their partners in their interviews as well. Additionally, a high percentage of autistic adults prefer identity-first expression (i.e. calling themselves autistic rather than "having autism") as that suggests that their autism is intrinsic and fundamental to their identity and not an accessory to it.

NON-SPECTRUM (NS) / NON-ASD: The term "non-spectrum" (NS) refers to those who don't have ASD. In the past, NS individuals were known as "neurotypical". However, even if a person isn't autistic, they often have neurological differences other than ASD that can include attention deficit hyperactivity disorder (ADHD), executive functioning issues, dyslexia, depression, anxiety, seizure disorders, etc.

NEURODIVERSE (ND) RELATIONSHIPS: Neurodiverse relationships are those where one or both partners might identify with having a neurological difference. In this book, an ND relationship refers to a couple where one or both partners are autistic or otherwise neurodivergent.

GENDER PRONOUNS: The pronouns people use to refer to themselves can include a wide variety of possible combinations. For instance, people may use he/him, she/her, or they/them, but they may also use he/they, etc.

CHAPTER 1

Evan & Sarah

Fewer Arguments and More Discussions
Married Six Years

INTRODUCING EVAN AND SARAH

*E*van and Sarah's story is an important read because both of them are ND, and both of them were diagnosed prior to their relationship. A majority of individuals in ND relationships are usually diagnosed after being in the relationship and, in some cases, years after being in the relationship. As we can see, this makes a tremendous difference. My hope is that the future will be populated by more couples with this advantage, given that many of those who were diagnosed as children are now coming of age. Sarah encourages us, "When you're both struggling together sometimes that can make your relationship stronger. I find that to be true."

Evan was officially diagnosed with ASD while in college. Sarah has had epilepsy and a seizure disorder since she was an infant, which is now in remission. Both were aware of their disabilities and limitations and were able to share this with each other before they even began their relationship. This allowed both of them to embark on this relationship with full awareness of what they were getting themselves into. Evan explains, "I would say that it provides a unique way of being with someone. It adds variables that might not be there with two neurotypicals and provides opportunities to grow a bit more."

Additionally, the couple engaged in premarital counseling with me for almost a year to make sure that they ironed out any issues that came up prior to the wedding. As we get to know them, we will see how their self-awareness, knowledge of ASD, and mutual understanding ensured that their relationship was honest right from the get-go. It has resulted in a beautiful and happy marriage for them. Sarah shares, "Well, we complement each other. We're opposite enough, so he has strengths where my weaknesses are and my strengths make up for his weaknesses."

This couple's story really sheds light on the fact that sometimes having two individuals with two different neurological make-ups can be an advantage. They can make fantastic partners, as they tend to have complementary strengths and weaknesses. They also tend to appreciate each other more. Neither partner feels like they're doing the other a favor by being with them; they both feel lucky to be with the other. Sarah affirms, "They say that difficult roads lead to beautiful destinations, and I can believe that." Also, as we will see, both Evan and Sarah focus on their own issues and challenges, rather than pointing fingers at each other.

Because of this, they have genuine confidence in their relationship and the prospect of being together long-term. Evan agrees, "I get the feeling that Sarah's always going to be there for me, and I'm always going to be there for her."

It doesn't mean we don't disagree—but knowing about ASD helps us have fewer arguments and more discussions. I think the diagnosis has probably helped with that.

MEET EVAN

Evan (he/him/his) is a 40-year-old, straight, white male. Evan has an ASD diagnosis which he received while he was in the Army. He has a bachelor's degree in history and works in IT support. He lives with his wife, Sarah, and their two kids, June and Jason. He and his wife got married in 2015.

Duration of relationship and marriage

Let's see, duration of our relationship and marriage... I'm trying to remember the anniversary date. I have a headache from today, and I'm not good with numbers anyway, so let's see. How many did she say? I'm going to trust her number right now. Her

answer sounds right; let's just go with that. Married 2015 to 2021.

Previous marriages and duration (if any)

None.

Please describe any short- or long-term past romantic relationships

I didn't have too many long-term relationships prior to Sarah. I dated someone for about a year and it was not a good relationship, so that's why I took a break after that.

Prior to these two, I didn't really have a lot of relationships. I certainly had short-term relationships.

ARMCHAIR CONVERSATIONS ON LOVE AND AUTISM

I'm a veteran, so in the Army I had two girlfriends I guess, but I didn't really understand what it meant at the time.

How did you meet?

So we initially met because our friend set us up at her birthday party. She was playing matchmaker, so we met then and we hit it off, but I was still dating someone else at the time, even though it was a difficult relationship. It didn't feel right for me to do that, so I explained that to everyone so that we were all on the same page, which was somewhat dramatic. Once that was all cleared up more or less, then I stayed in my relationship with that person for a while longer and then after we ended it, that's when I took the time off for a while. Then after that we met at Sarah's—I guess it was like a—Games Party. Our friends used to have these little meetup events at her flat, and I saw someone was hitting on Sarah. Seeing that just sort of...something inside of me said, "I don't like that, I want to hit on Sarah," so I did and chased him off. And then I think that restarted what we had originally started about a year, year and a half previously, and that's when we started dating more officially.

Diagnosis Journey

Did you receive any special education, support, or therapy while you were growing up?

No, because no one knew what it was. I was diagnosed much later in life, but not as late as some people. School was always a bit of a challenge and I was almost held back for my math skills but then was not in the end, and I kept going. I got mostly D's though, so I was never a stellar student, but I think if maybe I had more specialized care as they do now I would've done better. I did get extra time on my SATs though. So that was helpful in high school.

Do you or your partner have an official or self-diagnosis of ASD?

I was still in the Army when I received my diagnosis, so that would make it about 15 years ago. That's when the idea of being on the autism spectrum was introduced. I wasn't officially diagnosed until I came out of the Army and I came home. I think in 2005 or 2006 is when ASD was starting to get some more prominence. My parents had some doctor friends who knew more about it, and they had a conversation about it with them. Then it clicked with my parents that all the stuff I had exhibited when I was younger matched up with autistic traits. So they called me when I was still deployed in Afghanistan at the time and they told me about it. It just made sense to me as well, so viewing myself through the lens of autism helped to clarify things for me as a person in that moment and I could use it right away. When I got home, we then got the paperwork done for the official diagnosis.

My diagnosis was something like high-end, high-functioning ASD. What's the term for a high-functioning person with ASD? They've changed the whole spectrum since I got the diagnosis, but now it's something else. It's basically high-functioning whatever.

How accepting do you feel you and your partner are about the diagnosis?

I'll say one thing. For a long time prior to the diagnosis, I was always trying to figure out why things were different for me. Communication always seemed slower for me, or my brain was always humming, like, "Something is different, and why?" So the moment my parents told me about ASD, rather than feeling discouraged about the diagnosis, I could shift my brain over to, "Okay, that's fine. How or what can I do to get through situations that are harder for me than others?" as opposed to, "Why is this so difficult?" and getting stuck. In a nutshell, I was able to make an immediate mental shift, and that's helped out a lot.

I feel very accepting of my ASD. It's not a demeaning thing at all to me. I don't feel angry about it. I know that's one of the reactions some people get. They think it's some stigma or whatnot. I never felt that way about it.

I believe Sarah accepts it too, as it helps her to try and assess situations. In certain situations where my

ASD sticks out more, she doesn't immediately get angry. She just tries to think, "Oh, what is provoking this reaction and how can I use what I know about ASD to better it or help with it?" It doesn't mean we don't disagree—but knowing about ASD helps us have fewer arguments and more discussions. I think the diagnosis has probably helped with that.

> *I would say, figure out exactly where you are on the spectrum because then you can better define how much help you need...if you're here and you want a relationship, what do you have to do to get to that point?*

What advice would you give to someone who's just discovering either their or their partner's ASD?

I would say, figure out exactly where you are on the spectrum because then you can better define how much help you need just to be balanced. When you go to an autism event (like at the Association for Autism and Neurodiversity (AANE)), sometimes someone will be very focused on a very specific thing the whole night because that's what they do. And some people will be very social and walk around talking to others. So it's kind of like you just want to know where you stand and then figure out what support you need and then from there what goals you would want to set for yourself. So if you're here and you want a relationship, what do you have to do to get to that point?

Relationship Challenges

What are the main challenges in your relationship?

Firstly, communication can be hard sometimes. For example, getting the right information out at the right time. It's either not clear, or it's delayed. Often it's a situation with multiple people and it takes time to input information and assess it and then come out with the proper way of thinking about it. It's not an instantaneous process for me because I take a while to process that information.

I'm a lot better with one-on-one communication. Less delay because there are fewer opinions involved. I think that's generally true—the more opinions you have in the room the more information you have to process. Generally speaking, whenever there is a disagreement of some kind that means that someone is saying something for a reason and then someone else is saying something for another reason, so to me it's better to ask, "Okay, what is the root of what you're saying?"

Secondly, when there's a lot of stuff going on, my energy will run low toward the end of the day. So that means there's less time for me to spend with my wife. For example, on a day that I have a lot of meetings at work, I want to say to my wife, "I want to do things with you, but most likely I'm just going to fall asleep because I have to navigate so much." If I have what I call "talky days" which means I'm talking to people the whole day, at the end of that day I'm especially tired because I've been social the entire day. At the end of those days, I'm just mentally wiped, and I feel bad that I can't be as much with my wife.

Balancing everything is another challenge. You do too much of a couple of things and then you don't do enough of the other things. I'd say it's a tie between mental energy and communication.

Do you struggle with executive functioning, sensory sensitivities, communication problems, and/or social challenges?

EXECUTIVE FUNCTIONING: Time management has always been hard for me. Just keeping track of time. Keeping track of time has always been a challenge, and also being easily distractible. There are times when I feel more attuned and more focused and like I can do a lot of things. But I can get distracted, and often I'll go from small task to small task but don't get a big task done.

SENSORY SENSITIVITIES: I have sensitive hearing. But I don't really know how that impacts the relationship. Recently, we've had to transition our son into his sister's room because he would wake me up very easily with little noises. We now have a baby monitor, so that may still happen, but maybe it's just going to be for the bigger noises and not every noise, so we're experimenting with that. But it was interrupting our sleep and making us grumpy.

COMMUNICATION PROBLEMS: In the past, I haven't been as aware of things as the situation was developing in front of me. I was very passive, so I avoided getting involved, but then it would develop regardless, and the end result was that no one was happy. The wife wasn't happy, whoever else wasn't happy, and I was left with resentment as a residual effect. When I was single, it didn't bother me much. I was like, "It's fine, you have your opinion and I don't much care," but Sarah does care. So now I'm trying to be more aware of other people's feelings and those "gathering storm" types of scenarios. Through couples therapy, I've learnt that she wants me to support her not necessarily by being correct, but by showing that I'm on her side. So if there's a moment that's developing, I will just say, "Alright, something is happening. I don't know what the right thing to say is, but I want to support Sarah, so I'm going to say something here, and it's just going to have to be okay." That's all I can do to reduce the damage, versus saying nothing and leaving her to her own devices. That's kind of what I'm trying to do these days.

It doesn't always work, but I feel like Sarah appreciates the effort when I step in.

SOCIAL CHALLENGES: Sometimes there are times where there's nothing I can say to fix something. And it's already been told to me, and I've already offered my opinion on the matter, but then if Sarah's not satisfied, she still wants to talk about it. I tend to not want to repeat something if I've already said it. I feel like I've given you my opinion and made it clear (not in a mean way; it's often a very even-tempered delivery) but then it's brought up again. So I would just repeat myself and reference what I said before. In those moments what Sarah will do is she'll vent to one of her friends just to get a second opinion. Usually, I don't change my opinion unless there are new facts and because I want to remain true to my beliefs.

But then, I'm okay with her going to other people and having a discussion with them and them being a sounding board to her and hearing any new information she's learnt. That's where sometimes we have a difference of opinion, but then I still want to feel like I'm supporting her and listening to her point of view. So in those moments of communication, I feel weird to not know if she's expecting me to say more than what I have already said.

Have you encountered any difficult situations related to your ASD?

I got lost a couple of times in foreign countries. I went on a couple of team tour types of things. The purpose of that was to go to Israel, and on our way there, we stopped in Czechoslovakia to see all the old temples and stuff, and my group left me behind in this big square. I don't know how, but I found them again. Then the second time with this other tour group, we were in Costa Rica, and we were in this town buying something, and I got left behind. This time I knew some Spanish, so I could at least say, "I need some help. I'm with this tour group and we're in this small village." I was able to give enough information to get a ride back. I didn't know any Czech, though, so that would've been hopeless. This happened twice in a row. It means that my situational awareness just wasn't too great in traveling. I have a weird sort of luck, like weird situations happen to me but they work out.

I've never gotten into a car accident, but I could have. I've had these close calls a couple of times, but at the last minute I managed to hit the brakes. I feel like I have something watching out for me in these weird situations where it could be terrible, so I feel pretty lucky in that sense. I have this motto, "If things just don't work out, just try again. Just try again, it's okay." I think a big part of that is just the Army and having to overcome a mental shift almost to sense that there are going to be challenges, but they are achievable at the same time, and I think that's stuck with me.

What have been some of the low points in your relationship?

Well, one of the more interesting points in the relationship at the beginning was "defining love." I felt like I had to have a special definition of what love meant to me. So after going out with Sarah for a while, I didn't feel an emotional sense of love. Love had to be explained to me in bullet points. What does love mean to me? This, this, this, and this. And then someone who knew about ASD had to explain, "Yup, if you feel these things, it means you have loved that person," and then I had to look at it in that way. So, yes, it means I love Sarah if it follows these things. I feel like prior to that discussion we were at a low point, because it felt like she had expectations and she was clearly in love with me, but I didn't know how to arrive at that place of communicating to her how I felt. Those were some interesting times.

Another was that, early on, I had a condo (that's the one I didn't pay the mortgage on and the roof was also kind of caving in a little bit), so I kind of had to focus on that. At the same time, Sarah's parents were having some trouble, and I found out later that she was pretty much crying a lot during that period because she couldn't connect to anyone. One of the things about ASD is that you get very focused on one thing and not on others, so I kind of wish I had known that at the time, but I also might not have been as emotionally mature at the time either.

If you had a magic wand and could wish away one of your marital challenges or a partner's trait, what would it be?

Well, I wouldn't have married Sarah if, as a whole, I didn't like her the way she is. She is the complete package as she is. So I don't think I want to change that. I think for myself, though, if I could just not be so drained by the end of the day, I think that would make it better for everyone honestly. There could just be more done.

Relationship Strengths

What are some of your relational strengths and highlights?

I'd say birthing our kids was definitely the highlight. Then our wedding. We went on a couple of cruises together. The kind of times where we can get away just the two of us, those are the highlights.

What do you love most about your relationship?

I'd say that when we're together, Sarah and I are very good at being mellow together, especially when there are no distractions. We're getting better now at balancing out our tasks for kids and things. There's more to do these days, so it's like, "Alright, we have this list to do, so you're going

to take this, and I'm going to take this and you can do that" and that kind of thing. And then at the end of the day, what she typically likes to do is to snuggle with me before going to bed, so those are some nice moments when we get to do that as well.

I get the feeling that Sarah's always going to be there for me, and I'm always going to be there for her. I think there's no one else I would want to have kids with.

Intimacy

Is empathy or emotional reciprocity an issue in your relationship?

Empathy is not a challenge in our relationship. I think we're pretty empathetic toward each other.

Emotional reciprocity can be challenging sometimes. Sometimes Sarah feels that if she shares her emotions with me, I might get reactive. That's when she goes to a friend, but if it's something that I can help her with without being possibly offended, she'll go to me directly. Sometimes I don't always get as offended as her about a certain situation, and so that's when we have slightly different opinions on the exact same thing. I feel like she wants me to say, "Well, I was highly offended by that, too" but I can't always offer that. Maybe someone else, like a girlfriend, might be able to give her that validation. She feels better for having said it to someone. Before we had our son, we had more talks like that, but since then we're just more tired. Although it's important to keep an open dialogue in general, just to keep things flowing. You never want to have a situation where you stop talking because that's just a bad sign.

Does ASD cause challenges in the area of sex/intimacy?

Well, I would say that Sarah would probably appreciate it if I showed a bit more physical affection toward her. This just goes back to the whole energy thing sometimes. It's never been a huge requirement for me to be physically intimate. I know most guys are all about sex, and I've never been that way. So it's just been my characteristic, but I do know it's important for her so I'm just trying to balance those two things in general. I know that for her she feels like she is appreciated when she feels someone is intimate with her. Sexually or just cuddling or that kind of thing. It's been a while now just because of our schedule with Jason, but prior to that I would make an effort. I try to have a mental alarm like, "You haven't shown some intimacy in a while, you should do something," so we kind of keep mental track of that.

What makes you feel loved and cared for by your partner, and what makes your partner feel loved and cared for by you?

FEELING CARED FOR: Well, I'm just glad that we're together because we both have our challenges, and we complement each other. I feel like we can accomplish a lot together and it definitely would be very hard to have and raise a family alone. I would only really want to have a family with someone I really care about, so I feel like she is the right person for that.

CARING FOR SARAH: Well, I always try to be there for her. I'm usually the calm one in the relationship, and Sarah appreciates that I don't overreact and generally take things in my stride. Also I just really want to help out. I knew I wasn't ready to have kids until I knew that I was ready to help out with them. I didn't want to not be there to do things equally for the kids. We waited because I wanted to make sure that I could be part of the children's lives, and I wanted some things to be in place before that as well. So I think that a long-winded answer is that I have a certain manner toward things that is not overly emotional and that sort of helps balance her out as a person, and she knows that she can count on me for things when needed.

Finances

Describe your economic situation. Does your financial situation impact your relationship in any way?

Money is a stressor because we have a large-ish house, and part of the reason we have this house is because her parents wanted us to have a big place. In order to support our place, the work I have wouldn't cover it, so we have their help paying for certain things. I feel that Sarah wants to be more financially independent from them. I feel like that's sort of a burden to her. I've just come to accept it because that's the place we are in, but I feel like it bothers her. Going back to the question of what I bring to the relationship to make her happy, I think part of the reason why her parents do what they do is because they know that I bring some stability to Sarah's life, and that's why they offer a lot of support in order to help with that. Sarah has a multi-level cosmetics marketing home-based business that she's trying to grow so that she can be financially successful, and to prove to her parents and herself that she can make it.

We had a month where we were short on money. There were a lot of bills and stuff we were paying off, and it got a little stressful until we were able to figure out why we were low that month. It was that the water bill, the taxes, and all that stuff just came in at once. It did add negative stress to our relationship, but then we turned that around. We worked with her director at work, who helped us go over our stuff to see where we could cut down and figure out that if we made this much more, we would be fine. We kind of used that to strategize our finances. We tried to turn that around by getting to the root cause.

She does most of the bill paying because she does most of the numbers. Math isn't my strong suit, so I don't help as much with that part, but I do bring in most of the money with my work. Also for a time, I had this online game for which I kept on buying extras, and she brought it to my attention that I was spending a lot of money on there. At that point I said, "Okay, I'll stop doing that," and so having a discussion about that helped, and it hasn't been a problem since. So we reasoned through it and figured out a solution.

Support System

What support systems do you and your partner have?

Sarah's parents help us out monetarily, as I've mentioned. We have a handyman who helps us with the maintenance of the house. We have a mother's helper who comes to our place every day for a few hours, morning to afternoon, and she helps keep the place clean and helps with the kids. So those things help us out. We also have a couples counselor that we see once a month to kind of just talk about things. Usually Sarah does more talking than I do during those sessions. I just try to listen and express my thoughts and talk things out. So those are the main support things, and then we have our friends and whatnot.

Do you have friends individually and as a couple?

We have individual friends and mutual friends. Our friends tend to be people who share similar hobbies or interests as we do. Usually we all like playing games of various kinds, so before Covid we would have our meetups—for cards, conversations, and stuff like that. Some friends that we knew from school or prior roommates, that kind of thing.

Do you have a spiritual practice? Does that impact your relationship?

I used to practice Judaism more, but I haven't been as much lately. It didn't really influence my relationship with Sarah because she's not really spiritual. It was more for myself, and it helped before, I think.

Parenting

Tell us about yourselves as parents in this marriage.

My daughter is a daddy's girl, so she probably gets away with more stuff with me than she does with her mom, but I try to make sure it's not too much more, and try to moderate. For example, we got her some chocolate munchkins today, and she asked if she could have more and I said, "No, you've already had two." Sarah would've given her one more, so I try to keep it within certain limits. I will try to play the moderator, if you will.

For example, June was having a hard time transitioning from the crib to her new bed. One night, I found her sleeping on the floor with all her blankets and pillows and stuff, even though she had the new bed. So I sat her on the bed and explained to her why she couldn't sleep in the crib anymore. I asked her, "Where is your little brother's bed?" and she pointed to the crib. And I said, "Where is your bed?" and she pointed to her bed. And I said, "Do you know why you can't sleep there anymore?" And she said, "That's because Jason's going to sleep there." June is the type that if I just tell her to do something, she's less likely to do it, unless you try to explain why.

I'm good at explaining things at the level of the person without being demeaning. I'm better at that stuff. She did fall out of the bed, but it has a headboard built in so we just flipped it, and now she's happy with her bed.

Being in an ND Relationship

Do you feel that the challenges in ND relationships are unique?

I think that two ND people are going to share similar abilities. In ND relationships, there are communication issues, time management issues. However, even though someone may be very good at time management, they still might not make time for their wife because they're out doing other things. It's more about the want versus the ability, so I think that a lot of things are going to be similar problems across relationships. That's why people see counselors.

Based on your experiences, how informed do you find people are about ASD and ND marriage/relationships?

About ASD in general, I've only really disclosed it to a couple of people, and some people didn't really get it. They said, "No, that's not true." Some people guessed that I was on the spectrum, but this was in a work context, not really a relationship context. The only people I've really disclosed to have been a couple of managers. I know that in general the world is more tolerant of autism and people on the spectrum than before because of certain characteristics that work for certain fields like technology.

About ND relationships, I think that there's a lot of information out there, but a lot of it is mixed. There's no one place that you can definitely go, so I think that's the thing. I was doing research on ND relationships in the very beginning, and it kind of reached a certain point and then I stopped. It's a mix I would say.

What is your perspective on being in an ND relationship?

It's possible that you are more open to growth. I guess if you have a challenge, you're going to be working on the challenge and therefore you might be more open to change. But if you feel like you have everything well in hand, you might not feel like you have to change. Of course many people who aren't on the spectrum also embrace the fact that they're human and not perfect and work to adjust to any scenarios that come by. Say I come into a new relationship with the perspective that this is a new person and they may expect different things from me or vice versa. Hopefully, the other person will be open too, which I think is more of a personal characteristic than if you're on the spectrum or not.

What are the positives of being in an ND relationship?

I would say that it provides a unique way of being with someone. It adds variables that might not be there with two neurotypicals and provides opportunities to grow a bit more. I mean, no one really wants challenges, but if you have them you can use them. So I suppose that's the benefit. Take the challenges and use them to grow. You should use them to grow, otherwise you will always have a negative view on life. If you reject challenges, then you'll just always look at the negatives, and that's not good.

What advice would you give to people who are in an ND relationship?

Well, I think the best thing to do is to make an effort to be aware of the other person's general emotional state, even if they're not saying it. You kind of have to be aware. It may not be easy to do, but try to be attuned to your partner and what's going on with them. Just be in touch with their emotional side as best you can.

Couples Counseling

Have you pursued couples counseling? Was it useful?

I got involved with AANE when I came back. I had a LifeMap coach and they helped me focus on life tasks and job application stuff and whatnot. I worked with Eva for a while. I've had individual therapy, premarital counseling, and now marriage counseling, so I guess counseling and coaching really helped me out.

In the past, we saw Eva for premarital counseling for specific things that had happened with the parents and what not. But now we tend to just keep it as a way of bringing up anything that we haven't yet talked about. Things that we want to talk about, but aren't quite sure how to bring up. Or things we haven't had a chance to bring up regarding something that might have happened in our lives, in order to get emotional help with it. I know some people see counselors for specific things that need addressing, and I feel like we

had to overcome a lot of things to get to that point. Personally, I don't like drama. I'm not very good with it, so I've tried to adopt strategies to prevent it or get it to a manageable situation. Couples therapy helps with that.

Concluding Thoughts

10-Point Marital Happiness Scale™

Yeah, I would say 9 to 10. I'm happy with my relationship.

Would you say you're in love with Sarah?

Yes, I would say yes.

Do you think your relationship will go the distance?

I think that our marriage will go the distance because we try to take the time to understand when things need to be addressed and when to come up with solutions. So if something is clearly a problem then we both want to try to fix it so that we can move forward. I think there's going to be things that are difficult, but we don't want to let that prevent us from being together.

MEET SARAH

Sarah (she/her/hers) is a straight, 39-year-old, Caucasian female. She lives with her husband Evan and their two kids. She has earned her associate's degree and is self-employed. Sarah started dating her husband in

2012, and they married in 2015. Sarah does not identify as ASD, but had epilepsy and seizure disorder as a child.

Duration of relationship and marriage

We got married July 25, 2015. Ask Evan that question! I want to see if he remembers. It's typically the women that remember things like that. Got together Thanksgiving week of 2012.

Previous marriages and duration (if any)

None.

Please describe any short- or long-term past romantic relationships

That's an interesting question. They say you have to date a few frogs before you find a prince. I guess my first boyfriend liked me a lot better than I liked him. His feelings were so much stronger for me than mine were for him, to the point where it didn't seem fair to stay with him. We were only together for maybe four months.

My second boyfriend...we just weren't compatible enough. He didn't want to have kids, and I did. He lived really far away from me. We rarely got to see each other.

How did you meet?

It's a funny story. A mutual friend of ours introduced us at a birthday party, hoping to set us up. It turns out that she didn't know he had another girlfriend at the time. After that, at a Thanksgiving get-together, he saw these other guys hitting on me and it clicked in his head that he should be the one hitting on me. It's funny because we started out as friends, but we gradually started becoming closer and closer until we became a couple, so we're just one of those people—best friends that become a couple sometimes.

Diagnosis Journey

Did you receive any special education, support, or therapy while you were growing up?

Oh yeah, I've had plenty, but that too was a challenge. The socialization aspect of it was hard, but the work was too easy. I felt like some people mistook the words "learning difference" for "not as smart," which was sad.

I feel like every relationship is unique in its own way. Most of the time I don't even think about the fact that Evan's on the spectrum. It doesn't cross my mind. I don't know if it's because I'm used to it or if it's because I spent some of my time in school in special education, and I've just seen a lot of different disabilities.

I had special education from middle school all through high school. From grade 6 to 12. It helped me to see that I'm not the only one who has some kind of challenge and that we all struggle with something to an extent.

Do you or your partner have an official or self-diagnosis of ASD?

Evan is the one with the ASD diagnosis, but I have epilepsy, which was quite the challenge for sure. I got epilepsy from scar tissue left over from the meningitis that I had as a baby.

I had my first seizure when I was 14 months old. When I was ten and a half months old, the meningitis took my sight away. Fortunately only temporarily—some people thought I would never see again, but come Christmas Eve of 1982, I went from being completely blind to having 20/20 vision. A miracle for sure!

I always remind myself that if I didn't have all these seizures and those challenges, I wouldn't have moved to Boston, wouldn't have married Evan, nor would I have two kids. I wouldn't have had all these great and positive things happen. They say that difficult roads lead to beautiful destinations, and I can believe that.

I think that me having epilepsy has helped me have more compassion for people who have their challenges.

Evan has an ASD diagnosis which he received in 2007 or sometime around then. Eva was his test counselor through all of this; they've known each other for a long time.

How accepting do you feel you and your partner are about the diagnosis?

I feel fine with it. I can't speak for him, but I'm fine with it. It was something that was vocalized in my relationship when we were still just friends. It's gotten me to learn more about autism.

What advice would you give to someone who's just discovering either their or their partner's ASD?

To still be understanding of the other person's challenges, even if you're struggling. When you're both struggling together sometimes that can make your relationship stronger. I find that to be true. Don't give up so easily. I feel like one of the things that causes breakups and divorce is people don't try hard enough to make the relationship work.

Relationship Challenges

What are the main challenges in your relationship?

Getting Evan to understand how important it is to communicate with me when there is something on his mind. Emotions and also, for example, if clutter bothers him, just tell me and we'll clean it. It's that kind of thing. Speak up!

Also, being able to get enough sleep

with a newborn and a three-year-old in this house. Right now Evan is upstairs taking a nap because he is exhausted. I'm glad the kids are keeping us busy through this pandemic. It takes our mind off the isolation.

Helping him to remember things like numbers and dates and everything, like the important things on the calendars. I have to be the one to write things on the calendar so he can remember. I know that's a challenge for him, so I don't complain too much about it and try to help him as much as I can. Sometimes if I forget to write things down, then we both forget. This has been an ongoing thing for Evan, so that's the most common one.

Do you struggle with executive functioning, sensory sensitivities, communication problems, and/or social challenges?

EXECUTIVE FUNCTIONING: He's got those. He's got a lot of trouble with change, and I know that's common for people on the spectrum. But he definitely faces his challenges very well. With the whole "working from home" thing and having to log his time in 15-minute intervals that started almost a year ago (last March), with the whole isolation and everything—it was challenging for him at first, but since then he's gotten better at it. I reminded him that practice makes improvement. Even for people on the spectrum, they can still do things if they try. I'm finding that to be true with Evan.

SENSORY SENSITIVITIES: He's got really sensitive hearing. For example, our son has been sleeping through the night already, but he still makes those squeaky little noises, the stretching noises. He'll talk in his sleep kinda, and it will wake Evan up. I told him that part of that is probably the dad in him because other high-pitch sounds don't wake him up.

COMMUNICATION PROBLEMS: Communications issues, like him speaking up when there's a problem. Basically the way I put it to him is: "If you see something, say something." Like that announcement on the loudspeaker, *If you see something, say something.* It's gotten better. Our counselor helps us with that too.

SOCIAL CHALLENGES: That's a hard question to answer right now because everything is so isolated with the pandemic and everything, but generally we're both pretty social. I'm usually the one who plans events and having friends come over and that kind of stuff. Last time we had anyone come over was for our daughter's third birthday; it's been a few months. We definitely love hanging out just the two of us, and we also love having people over, so it's a mix.

My parents are dying to come here and see the grandkids, and I told them, "If you're going to come up here and see the grandkids, that also means you're babysitting and we're going out!"

What have been some of the low points in your relationship?

I don't know if having our son in the NICU could be a good example. That was really hard for both of us. He also failed the car seat test, and we had to get a car bed. We couldn't find anyone to help us install the thing at the last minute, and that was just rough for both of us. That was just a month ago.

We also had more conflicts with my mother-in-law, and Evan didn't understand how important it was to speak up and help with the situation.

If you had a magic wand and could wish away one of your marital challenges or a partner's trait, what would it be?

This applies more to his mother than to him. It's like, she's very difficult, so I try to keep my distance from her.

Relationship Strengths

What are some of your relational strengths and highlights?

Well, we complement each other. We're opposite enough, so he has strengths where my weaknesses are and my strengths make up for his weaknesses. He's very mellow, logical-minded, and I'm the absolutely crazy hardheaded one. He has trouble with numbers, and I remember numbers better. It's those kinds of things that are the reasons why I'm glad it was just Evan this time around

when we had our second baby because if his parents were here, I would've gone insane.

Our wedding day for sure. Having our daughter and our son. Becoming parents was a highlight. Watching our kids grow before our eyes and the fact that we're able to be parents to two kids.

What do you love most about your relationship?

The fact that we're each other's best friend along with being a couple. And the fact that we're just able to help each other in so many ways.

Intimacy

Is empathy or emotional reciprocity an issue in your relationship?

EMPATHY: Evan is pretty empathetic, to say the least. I think he understands better than some people how and when to be empathetic. He doesn't always understand every situation, but he can read me and I can read him. Lately it's been a little bit harder since I've been hormonal with mood swings and all that.

EMOTIONAL RECIPROCITY: For a while he had trouble speaking up about how he felt, and I had to push him. I still kind of have to do that—just remind him to tell me how he's feeling about something. It could also have to do with the fact that he's a guy, and women are more expressive of their emotions. Could be a gender difference. I have times when I want to get my feelings off my chest, but I don't want to put my foot in my mouth either. So it can be hard for me too. It depends on the situation I think. The most recent situation was with my mother-in-law complaining about how her son never calls her, and that's not true, and I reminded her that it's been pretty chaotic with two kids lately. She responded that she knows that, but then I wanted to say, "Well, if you know that then why do you complain about it."

Does ASD cause challenges in the area of sex/intimacy?

I haven't seen any challenges in that area, our sex life prior to me having our son was pretty good. I mean, it was recommended by my doctor that we not do anything like that for six weeks after having a baby, but other than that it's pretty good.

What makes you feel loved and cared for by your partner, and what makes your partner feel loved and cared for by you?

He's so helpful and supportive and so loving. It's just how he is. When we were in the hospital having our son, I was reminding myself like, "Oh my god, these struggles make our relationship grow stronger." Sometimes you just need a struggle in life to get reminded of how much you love each other.

That would be a question for him,

I think. But, since he has trouble remembering numbers, I take care of things like bills and anything number-related. I always make sure the meals are prepared, the bills get paid, and appointments are written down. I make doctor's appointments for him. I take care of him too.

> **Sometimes you just need a struggle in life to get reminded of how much you love each other.**

Finances

Describe your economic situation. Does your financial situation impact your relationship in any way?

Well, because he has trouble with numbers, he doesn't really know how to budget or manage money, and so he didn't realize that he had run up a huge bill on two of the credit cards. My parents found out about it, and we're helping him with that, to get the balance down. It's just money, but it's frustrating for him because he does have trouble with numbers and remembering them, and tracking what he spends money on and how much. It's a weakness for him. That's where I come in—I help with the numbers and the money management and all that stuff.

Evan is in IT, and I sort of had a small business prior to us having any kids.

Support System

What support systems do you and your partner have?

We have a couples counselor. We have doctors, and we have good friends that are local. We have family and all that kind of stuff.

Do you have friends individually and as a couple?

We have many friends. His friends became my friends and vice versa. That's just how couples work. Now that we're married with kids, we're finding that we know more people who are either married or together and have their own kids, and we have that mutual thing in common.

Do you have a spiritual practice? Does that impact your relationship?

I was raised Catholic, and now I would call myself a Christian. I believe in it a little bit; it helps me believe in miracles. We're an interfaith couple and we've figured out ways to incorporate both, like raise our kids as one practicing religion but incorporating part of the other.

Parenting

Tell us about yourselves as parents in this marriage.

Well, it's been fun to have a second baby in the house. I'm actually re-

lieved that our daughter's no longer our only child throughout all of the pandemic isolation, because she can't really interact with other kids right now and that's not healthy either. I was starting to get emotional from all that because it broke my heart to see our daughter try to play with other kids when she really can't.

Parenting, he takes over usually at night, usually with June while I am bathing and feeding the baby. Then he'll do more on weekends like he's doing now with taking the kids out.

Being in an ND Relationship

Do you feel that the challenges in ND relationships are unique?

I suppose they can be different, but I feel like every relationship is unique in its own way. Most of the time I don't even think about the fact that Evan's on the spectrum. It doesn't cross my mind. I don't know if it's because I'm used to it or if it's because I spent some of my time in school in special education, and I've just seen a lot of different disabilities.

Based on your experiences, how informed do you find people are about ASD and ND marriage/relationships?

More informed than they used to be, I think. I think nowadays people have gotten more knowledgeable about Asperger's and autism. When Evan was first diagnosed, some people had no clue as to what it was.

What is your perspective on being in an ND relationship?

Like I mentioned before, most of the time I don't think about the fact that he has ASD, I just go with it. I think knowing him well enough, I'm able to read him better than I would be able to read an aspie I don't know that well.

What are the positives of being in an ND relationship?

We both have our strengths and our weaknesses, and it's nice to be married to somebody who has had their fair share of hardships.

What advice would you give to people who are in an ND relationship?

Seeing a couples counselor definitely helps. It gives that extra support that puts my mind at ease. We've been seeing a counselor once a month.

Couples Counseling

Have you pursued couples counseling? Was it useful?

Couples counseling has been so helpful for us. It helps put my mind at ease to be able to talk about and cope with the challenges we have, and it's also helpful for him. Especially since our current counselor has a son who is on the spectrum, so she can really

relate. It's nice to have that personal experience along with professional knowledge.

Concluding Thoughts

10-Point Marital Happiness Scale™

I would say, well, I would give it a 9 for now just because of my mood swings and being so hormonal and us being so isolated.

Would you say that you're in love with Evan?

Yeah. Although I have to say having a baby boy has made me feel like I'm in love with another man. It's so unfair too. It's just like *dammit!*

Do you think your relationship will go the distance?

I think our marriage will go the distance because it helps to be married to your best friend and lover.

CHAPTER 2

Siddharth & Anisa

Knowing Our Differences
Married Nine Years

INTRODUCING SIDDHARTH AND ANISA

Siddharth and Anisa's story as a couple is especially significant for me, as they're South Asian and live in Mumbai, India, where I am from myself. I love that I'm able to work with couples from all over the world and learn how ASD presents in different cultures. Anisa explains, "In India in general, everyone lives within families. There's a lot of extended family, and there's a lot of these kinds of social relationships, which to Siddharth don't seem important, but are required." It's fascinating how couples develop their relationships in various environments. Often we think we know what neurodiverse married life is like within the context of our own culture. However, the whole reason I wanted to speak to a diverse range of couples was so that we could break stereotypes of ND marriages, broadening our perceptions of what they might be.

A turning point in Siddharth and Anisa's marriage was when he received his ASD diagnosis. Within a family of multiple generations of ASD individuals, one person receiving a diagnosis can completely change the paradigm in which the family comes to view themselves! Often, individuals who grow up in families with multiple ASD individuals don't realize there's another way of thinking until they marry someone who is neurologically different. In this case, Anisa is also a professional in the autism field. Her insight is particularly valuable for understanding both her husband and other members of her family. Hopefully, in the future, we will have more research on the multigenerational aspects of ASD, due to its genetic nature.

What is also remarkable about Siddharth is that he embraces, values, and is almost proud of his ASD. This makes the acceptance of his diagnosis very easy. Siddharth explains, "I've become more confident in myself. Getting the diagnosis has been very positive for me in terms of self-awareness." In so many cases, I see that the ASD individual is in denial or wants no part in thinking that they might be ND. However, in this case, we can see how accepting the diagnosis is a game-changer for the marriage. Also, we can see how both Siddharth and his wife take full responsibility for all of the aspects that they need to work on, as well as how they've grown and evolved in their marriage.

It's wonderful that, in this relationship, the struggles don't seem to be any less than in any other ND marriage. Yet they are happy to be together and express being in love with each other, which I think is pretty special. Anisa agrees, "There are so many great traits about ASD—for example, being honest and sincere."

MEET SIDDHARTH

Siddharth (he/him/his) is a 37-year-old, straight, South Asian/East Indian male. He has an ASD diagnosis, and he has earned his MBA and is a tech professional. He lives in India with his wife and two daughters, ages five and 11 months, along with live-in help. He has had no previous marriages, and dated his wife for three years before marriage.

> Sometimes we hate the differences, but I think knowing our differences, and at the same time being silly together and having some fun moments has been good—maybe not as many moments compared to a typical couple—but for me, that's what I love the most.

Please describe any short- or long-term past romantic relationships

I haven't had any short romantic relationships. They've all been long, relatively speaking. My first one was high school, which went on until freshman year of college. That was the hardest one because I was devastated when that ended because it was my first one.

How did you meet?

We met through common friends. We knew each other socially but ended up hitting it off at a common friend's wedding. One thing I hear a lot from her is that I was very different when we were dating compared to after we got married.

Diagnosis Journey

Did you receive any special education,

support, or therapy while you were growing up?

I did not receive any special education or therapies growing up. My wife is an autism professional and suspected it. That was kind of an informal diagnosis. I got a formal diagnosis from Eva. I was diagnosed a year after getting married with ASD. We saw Eva pretty consistently for a few years then, on and off, after that. Mostly together, but some one-on-one sessions.

How accepting do you feel you and your partner are about the diagnosis?

Totally. Initially I was skeptical. But after meeting Eva, she at once made me comfortable with it. Also, the fact that ASD is a lot more common than we realize or I had thought. I think that also played a role. My wife and I have been able to recognize it in other people now, and she knew that I might be on the spectrum way back, partially because of her professional background.

What advice would you give to someone who's just discovering either their own or their partner's ASD?

So a bunch of things. Read a lot! Get in touch with Eva. Basically, find a professional who understands ASD and can help you. There's no way you're going to survive without that, and both people in the relationship have to do that. The other thing is, I

think...it's a very long road. It feels like you're not making any improvement, and the standards keep going up.

One of the things I've spoken to Eva about (and I've told my wife this too) is, "My traits annoy you more today than they did eight years ago, but I've improved by miles from then to now on these traits." It's basically a moving goal post, which seems unfair. I think it sucks that the benchmark for a relationship is what typical relationships are, and there has to be some meeting in the middle where unfortunately, whether you like it or not, the neurodiverse person has to cover more distance. That's my perspective; I'm sure my wife will say the opposite of this.

Both people need to internalize that they need to go beyond the midline. I think it's hard for a neurotypical person to feel like the whole world is telling them they shouldn't need to go beyond the midline, or in fact the whole world is telling them that they don't even need to move. It's their own self-awareness that's bringing them to the middle, but both have to cross over and that's when it really works.

Anything else you'd like to say about the diagnosis?

A sense of relief. Everything made sense. Everything! My whole childhood made sense after understanding it. I've become more confident in myself. Getting the diagnosis has been very positive for me in terms of self-awareness. I feel more self-aware than I ever did.

In 2014, on Eva's recommendation, I saw a psychiatrist with my wife and started to take a small dose of an SSRI/anti-depressant. A super-small dose. I tried getting off of it, but according to my wife I was really on edge when I was completely off it. Also in the last couple of years, I've occasionally started smoking small amounts of marijuana, which has been amazing. Unfortunately, it's not part of the culture in India, but I've managed to get a hold of it on my trips to California. But it's rare for me.

Recently I transitioned to AANE's LifeMap Program for more pragmatic support which I've also found helpful.

Relationship Challenges

What are the main challenges in your relationship?

Empathy and perspective-taking is a big one. That's something I hear a lot. Being present and mindful. Screen time. Another way of putting it is me getting absorbed into my special interest. And my special interest happens to be tech-related (which is also my career), so it's like a black hole basically.

Do you struggle with executive functioning, sensory sensitivities, communication problems, and/or social challenges?

EXECUTIVE FUNCTIONING: I don't think I struggle with executive functioning, but my wife definitely feels like I do. Basically, I have no executive functioning issues when it has to do with something that I care about. For example, I'm obsessed with technology. Aviation is another interest, and—believe it or not—taxes is another. I read tax codes for fun. It goes without saying I'm the one on the spectrum in this relationship, in case that wasn't obvious. So when it comes to that, you can imagine our tax planning is impeccable, and our travel is impeccable. We have no issues going on holiday—everything will be beautifully laid out—but I find it difficult to pack a bag. One of the things we've done in our relationship is lean on each other for these things. We're very complementary when it comes to these things. All the stuff that I enjoy, my wife hates—so that works out.

SENSORY SENSITIVITIES: I don't have too many major sensory issues. There are two or three things that come up a lot. One is that I have digestive issues in general, and I think those tend to get in the way and my wife tends to get really annoyed. The second is a minor thing—initially I thought it was a quirk, but then we realized it was a sensory issue. I cannot handle a wet bathroom. It drives me crazy to the point that I don't like showering after my wife has showered. She comes out with her hair wet. We have more bath mats in the bathroom than any normal person would think necessary. It's not a big deal; we deal with it. We joke about it now. The third sensory issue is that I need silence. I don't need it all the time, but I definitely need to wind down. My wife also has sensory issues, but in a different way.

COMMUNICATION PROBLEMS: I definitely think I could do a better job communicating and doing small talk especially. I find it really tough to do small talk. Whenever I think I'm doing a good job making small talk, my wife reminds me that small talk is actually a volley of conversation, not like a barrage of questions that I ask and she answers. I do try to be aware of this. I have a few strategies that I use; one is to talk about my day. I don't use it always (when I'm mindful of it, I use it), but sometimes when I'm having my own issues I get self-absorbed. The kids are another nice topic. We might talk about family. The other thing that I do is I have a reminder list, like a to-do software that I use called *Todoist*, and nothing in my life gets done if it's not on *Todoist*.

SOCIAL CHALLENGES: We have tons of social challenges. I'm just comfortable being an asshole. I'm blunt. Direct. Sometimes I don't mean to be an asshole, but I'm told that I am. I fundamentally disagree with my wife on this. For example, when I say something and she's like, "That was rude," and I don't agree that it was rude. I guess we have a different calibration on what the definition of rude is.

If there's a situation—a social event—that I really don't want to go to, I just smoke a little marijuana before going. It takes the edge off things. Sometimes that's gone wrong as well because I've mis-calibrated how much I've smoked and I actually start feeling high...and that is also bad.

I think the other thing is the fact that she says that I should observe other couples and how they pay attention to each other even when they are independently socializing with other people in the same event. I guess I don't do that as well. I don't know how, but I try—I try to be more aware of it.

What have been some of the low points in your relationship?

Definitely once, before we got married, where I was confused about whether this was right for me or whether I wanted to be with my previous relationship. I think I was a little too vocal about that, so that wasn't good. I think also the first couple of years after we got married, before I got diagnosed, when we happened to be living with my parents, it was like hell (more for her than for me). However, because it was hell for her it became hell for me. That was bad. I think those two years were the really bad ones.

If you had a magic wand and could wish away one of your marital challenges or a partner's trait, what would it be?

I wish she would be a little more logical and less emotional at times. Just closer on the spectrum to me a little bit.

Relationship Strengths

What are some of your relational strengths and highlights?

I think the biggest strength is knowing that if shit hit the fan, we would be there for each other. I think that's the biggest thing. The fact that we're both looking out for each other's weaknesses, I think that's another big strength.

Definitely a lot of the travel that we've done, that's been a huge highlight. Obviously the kids, that's been a great highlight. Those have been the big ones.

What do you love most about your relationship?

We can just be silly together, and we can recognize our differences. Sometimes we hate the differences, but I think knowing our differences, and at the same time being silly together and having some fun moments has been good—maybe not as many moments compared to a typical couple—but for me, that's what I love the most.

Intimacy

Is empathy or emotional reciprocity an issue in your relationship?

EMPATHY: Yes. The refrain is that I don't understand her perspective and where she's coming from and how deeply stuff affects her. I think that's kind of what it is, what my challenges are. I think this is the biggest gap.

EMOTIONAL RECIPROCITY: Yes, emotional reciprocity is an issue too. I think these are the biggest issues. I think it's the root of all the other issues. All the other traits that drive my wife crazy I think wouldn't drive her as crazy if it weren't for these two things. I think as a result, her tolerance for ASD—for spectrum traits— has basically diminished over time because—let me put it this way—the rate at which I've improved in my empathy and emotional reciprocity has been slower than the rate at which her tolerance has decreased.

Does ASD cause challenges in the area of sex/intimacy?

Because of the empathy and emotional reciprocity, I think our sex life has been challenging. We talk about it, and she's like, "You know you annoy me so much in the day that by the end of the day, I don't want to be intimate." How do I cope with it? Mostly we don't have a way of coping with this. We've talked about it, and I guess we just do it when we do, but I've definitely expressed my concern about this.

What makes you feel loved and cared for by your partner, and what makes your partner feel loved and cared for by you?

She's very warm. I think that warmth kind of comes out.

When I read the book, *The Five Love Languages*, I realized that her love language was helping out or acts of service. I know I've done a good job there, but there's a physical layer to that and an emotional layer to that. I think I've done better on the physical layer than on the emotional layer. I hear this a lot: "I feel like you're not looking out for me."

Finances

Describe your economic situation. Does your financial situation impact your relationship in any way?

The fact that I'm not employed right now is a huge stressor for my wife. It's less of a stressor for me. I actually think that this is one area where I just completely disagree with her. She has a very emotional relationship with money, while I have a very rational relationship with money. I think that's the biggest issue socioeconomically.

Financially, we're doing pretty well. I have a very rational approach to money. I try to evaluate how much our lifestyle costs, how much we need to save, how much it costs to send our kids to college, and when I look at these parameters, I'm like, "We're done; everything else is greed." Which means I can take asymmetric career paths.

Having ASD does benefit our financial situation for a couple rea-

sons. One is that the kind of role I take at companies is very unique and I get paid highly for the work I do. As a result, I feel like I've been able to earn in two years what would regularly take me five or six years, maybe even more, I don't know. So I think it contributes positively to the relationship, because it enables me to take these asymmetric bets because I feel like our bases are covered. But I think it's also the biggest stressor in our relationship right now because she doesn't feel that way.

Both my wife and I are probably the most fortunate, privileged individuals that I can think of because we're—at least in India—at the top of the socioeconomic pyramid. I'm very grateful for what we have—and we want to work hard and do well and not lean on our families—but the fact is we have the family safety net and that safety net allows us to take asymmetric bets.

Support System

What support systems do you and your partner have?

We have our parents, but as I described to you, I don't think they're the best people from a social standpoint. However, her parents live down the road, and her sister lives up the road, so that's pretty good. It also helps that her mom's a psychologist, who now understands ASD. I don't talk about it, but I think her mom has talked to her a bit—has kind of been there for us—so that's definitely a good thing.

Do you have friends individually and as a couple?

We definitely have couple friends and individual friends. We socialize with these couple friends quite often. Some used to be individual friends that became couple friends on both sides. Most of my individual friends are not couple friends, as I know them professionally.

Do you have a spiritual practice? Does that impact your relationship?

I don't consider myself spiritual or religious. I don't have a practice, per se, but I do sometimes find myself trying to meditate to sort of calm down.

Parenting

Tell us about yourselves as parents in this marriage.

I think we're both great parents, but it depends on what comparison point you look at. From an Indian standpoint, I'm a very hands-on parent, but if you look at it from maybe a stereotypical Western standpoint, I'm probably less hands-on than average. I guess I can be checked out at times, which again ties in with the whole lack-of-mindfulness thing. The other thing I struggle with as a parent is setting the boundaries with my

daughter, and my wife says that that's probably because my parents never set any boundaries with me. That's an area that I'm working on. I think my wife is an amazing parent. She's like a professional parent!

Being in an ND Relationship

Do you feel that the challenges in ND relationships are unique?

Oh yeah, I do think ND relationships are different compared to typical relationships. I do feel the challenges are unique; I've always felt that way. I feel like I *know* they are unique now because I understand more. I think the biggest thing is basically that the way we process things is totally different. You just see things totally differently; you notice different things.

Based on your experiences, how informed do you find people are about ASD and ND marriage/relationships?

People don't really understand about ND relationships; that's part of the reason I'm doing this. I think it's become my wife's professional life's work and then, by extension, my life's work to educate people about ASD. We haven't openly talked about it with people. Well, we have openly talked about this, but only through the lens of my wife's professional pursuit as opposed to our own personal experiences. But yeah, people are extremely uninformed about ASD in general, and ASD in marriages people just don't know. India is miles behind the United States. Granted, my exposure to the United States is the East and West Coast, which is arguably the hub of people with ASD—the finance world and the tech world.

What is your perspective on being in an ND relationship?

At its core, being in a neurodiverse relationship is no different than any other relationship. It needs to work for both people. I just think that the stuff that makes a relationship work for the typical person, for the neurodiverse person to be able to deliver on that is a lot more work. I think that's the challenge, but it's like any other relationship. It's basically a social-emotional construct. That's how I see it.

> At its core, being in a neurodiverse relationship is no different than any other relationship. It needs to work for both people.

What are the positives of being in an ND relationship?

I am the diverse part of the neurodiverse relationship. I think that that diversity can bring a lot of strength if you can capture it well. It's very complementary. That's another positive.

Couples Counseling

Have you pursued couples counseling? Was it useful?

Yeah, I think it was really useful, and we did that for a few years with Eva. Then, Eva pushed me into LifeMap, as she said that I needed a more practical approach to keep implementing the behaviors I was working on. I actually wish my wife had continued to meet with Eva more frequently. Now, we do see her once in a while, maybe once every six months.

I think my wife needs Eva more than I do now to deal with the challenges that come with being married to me. It can feel lonely; it can feel tiring and exhausting being with someone on the spectrum. I think that it doesn't help that her work is in this world of autism. Eva framed it to her as, "Look, this has become your life's work."

I tend to need help with practical, behavior-driven advice. I'm like, "Okay, I get it, but tell me what I need to do. What should I say? What should I do? What does that look like? What does being more understanding look like?"

Concluding Thoughts

10-Point Marital Happiness Scale™

Definitely, yeah I'm happy. My instinct is to say 10, but I think that's too idealistic. I would give myself an 8, maybe 8.25.

Would you say you're in love with Anisa?

Yeah, definitely.

Do you think your relationship will go the distance?

Yeah, I think so. I think so more because of my wife's commitment to the cause, more so than mine. Even when we do have a blow out, at some point she will break it down and explain it to me, so I can understand. I think we will; time will tell.

MEET ANISA

Anisa (she/her/hers) is a straight, 37-year-old East Indian female. She lives with her husband Siddharth, their two daughters, and three live-in helpers. She has earned her master's degree and is now working professionally as a psychologist. Anisa and Siddharth were together for three years before getting married, and they've been married for nine years. Anisa does not identify as being on the spectrum.

Please describe any short- or long-term past romantic relationships

I've had no previous marriages. I've had three past romantic relationships that I'd say were pretty long term. Not *that* long term, but back then when I was younger it seemed long term. They were completely *not* on the spectrum, let's put it that way.

How did you meet?

We knew each other when we were both in the United States. He was studying, and I was working. We had common friends—that's how we knew each other.

> I really love that he is—as much as I think it's rude—I love that he is really frank and I'm not second guessing anything. I love that he is completely honest with how he feels, and about anything. I definitely love that he doesn't have any gender bias. There are no preconceived rules; there are no preconceived anything, which is great! It's really, really equal.

Diagnosis Journey

Did you receive any special education, support, or therapy while you were growing up?

No. My mom is a psychologist, though, so I don't know if I got anything at home without knowing. But not officially.

Do you or your partner have an official or self-diagnosis of ASD?

Siddharth was diagnosed a year after we got married with ASD. The diagnosis came from Eva.

I knew something was different, and I kept wondering about it. I work with a lot of kids with autism, but I never really knew what it manifested like for adults. It was always in my head, so I went to a lot of psychologists here in Mumbai and nobody believed me just because he was so smart and so put together. Everyone thinks autism is hand flapping and non-verbal, and they just couldn't believe it. So everyone said, "No your personality is ___, and this isn't this and this isn't this."

I looked up Eva when we were on a trip to visit a friend in the Boston area. So I looked for someone in Boston, and that's how we met Eva.

How accepting do you feel you and your partner are about the diagnosis?

Honestly, I feel like after he got the diagnosis everything made sense. Like *everything* made sense! Including his whole family, because it's completely in his family. As much as I have accepted it, it's not that it doesn't drive me crazy at times—of course it does. Of course at times, I'm

like, "I wish it wasn't there." But now that I know it and now that I know what it's like, I think I'm a lot more forgiving and I don't feel as hurt as I did early on in our marriage, because I just don't feel like it's directed toward me anymore.

Relationship Challenges

What are the main challenges in your relationship?

The most severe challenge that I've found from the beginning—that I told Eva on day one when I met her—was that I just find Siddharth's way of talking too rude. I find him really rude, even though he's tried to tone that down. He comes across as rude way too often to a lot of people, and even to me. He doesn't mean to; it's just the way he talks. But I guess because he's always pointing out the obvious, it's not exactly something you want to hear at that time. So that is definitely the most severe. Like if he could change the way he spoke, it would be great. He is very straightforward, and also there is absolutely no filter. You know he is saying it as he is thinking it, and again it's the most practical and maybe the most logical, but it's just...you don't want to hear it at that time.

I also think he has a hard time taking my perspective on some things.

The third challenge is with parenting. He's great because he wants to do a lot, but until I specify exactly what it is he needs to do, he's lost.

So it's that kind of real-time learning about when he needs to step in—he won't step in until I tell him to step in.

Does he struggle with executive functioning, sensory sensitivities, communication problems, and/or social challenges?

EXECUTIVE FUNCTIONING: He has a hard time prioritizing, and then he disappears behind his computer, saying, "This is really important and I need to send this email right now," or "I need to respond to this person right now." I have learned better now, obviously. Initially I would believe him, that everything was very important, because I had no idea and also because what we do is so different, I don't really get much of what he does. I didn't want to make a judgment call on something I know nothing about. Nine years into this marriage, I've learned that it's not that important. So he just disappears behind his computer and he just thinks it's a priority, but then a lot of these things that "are a priority" are not.

Managing our household, I kind of just take over. He's very good with financial planning and stuff, so I don't have to look at it at all. He does all of that. We just have our own areas.

SENSORY SENSITIVITIES: No major sensory sensitivities, nothing really. I mean, there are things that he prefers, but nothing that really comes in the way of the relationship. I mean, the temperature in the room...but I think most couples have that.

COMMUNICATION PROBLEMS: So one big communication issue is not having any small talk. He doesn't ask me anything, like if the question doesn't have a purpose, he doesn't bother asking. Again, if it doesn't have a purpose he doesn't really bother listening. So there's that.

And then other communication issues—I mean, sometimes I feel like when we're having an argument, we're on two completely different pages. He's viewing it completely differently.

The strategies that I use now are very different from what I used to use. I used to cry and scream and shout, and I don't do any of that anymore. I don't cry at all. I calmly tell him—I literally spell it out for him—that we are viewing this differently, so we need to take a step back and really listen as we talk. With the small talk bit, I point it out. I tell him, "I don't want you to tell me anything right now—just listen." But I mean, obviously sometimes I get irritated that he hasn't asked, and that he's not listening, so even though I say, "I want you to just listen now," I don't feel like talking.

SOCIAL CHALLENGES: In India in general, everyone lives within families. There's a lot of extended family, and there's a lot of these kinds of social relationships, which to Siddharth don't seem important, but are required. I think after having been through couples therapy and talking through this, he's become really good at it.

Definitely one big social challenge is that he tunes out in the middle of a social situation, and then he's on his phone. A lot of that is him, but I see my brother-in-law doing the same thing and my brother-in-law is not on the spectrum, so I feel like a lot of people just now escape behind their phones.

What have been some of the low points in your relationship?

So I think early on before his diagnosis—and even at the beginning right after he was diagnosed, especially when we were living with his parents—it was really hard. We lived with family for a while, and it was really, really hard because I think there were just way too many aspie people in that household for me to be able to take. I think ever since we moved and we have our own space, it's been a lot better.

Living with his parents was tough also because it was me getting married and coming from my parents' home into this home, and it was so completely different. The diagnosis was so new and I didn't know enough, so that was really hard. It used to get really volatile and ugly. Even now I just stay clear of this chaos, because things can become really abusive. Siddharth doesn't see the way I do, which is the hard part.

And then each pregnancy, just after the baby was born—both times were hard. Both times I delivered when there was so much going on,

and I was so tired all the time. Siddharth wanted to help, but he didn't really know what to do. It was basically before we found the rhythm. It was hard.

If you had a magic wand and could wish away one of your marital challenges or a partner's trait, what would it be?

Definitely his rudeness. Honestly, I didn't even think I would say that out loud, but that is how much it bothers me because I am not like that at all. But I am the other extreme. Siddharth has to keep pointing out to me that I need to be more firm when I say things.

Relationship Strengths

What are some of your relational strengths and highlights?

We're completely opposite, which is a great strength. We absolutely complement each other. I think I need the dose of practicality and boundary-setting that Siddharth brings. I would say complementing each other is our biggest strength.

In the last two years, things have been going really well. I feel like we're in a more stable place. There are no major ups and downs. There's no explosiveness. I definitely think Siddharth taking meds has helped too. I don't feel stressed. I don't feel on edge the way I see his mom feeling with his dad all the time, and I remember feeling like that in the beginning before he got diagnosed, when I didn't know what would cause him to lose it. That's not even a memory anymore. It's very, very stable. Definitely the last two years, and before when we were dating, would be the highlights of the relationship.

I'm more informed; he's more informed. We've both done the reading, we've both done counseling, and we're more in the rhythm. I don't think he was ever fighting what it is, but I'm not anymore. I'm very calm, and I know what his strengths are. I know what his weaknesses are, and I'm not constantly saying, "But why can't he, why can't he, why can't he?"

What do you love most about your relationship?

I really love that he is—as much as I think it's rude—I love that he is really frank and I'm not second guessing anything. I love that he is completely honest with how he feels, and about anything. I definitely love that he doesn't have any gender bias. There are no preconceived rules; there are no preconceived anything, which is great! It's really, really equal. Especially being in India, I see a lot of my friends around me, and I see a lot of their relationships being nothing like that and it's so great.

Intimacy

Is empathy or emotional reciprocity an issue in your relationship?

EMPATHY: Yes, empathy is huge. So I have to always talk about earlier and now. So earlier, Siddharth wasn't empathetic at all. He would listen, sometimes cut me off in-between and be like, "Whatever." Now he does listen and tries to be empathetic, but I know a lot of the stuff he says is stuff he's learned. It's very scripted—I know that. I appreciate that he's trying really hard, but he doesn't get it. I've made my peace with it, kind of. When I really just want someone to be empathetic, I call someone else. I call my mom, I call my sister, or I call a friend. I always tell Siddharth about it—it's not that I want to leave him out of the loop—but then I've gotten what I need, and then I tell him, and then it's okay.

EMOTIONAL RECIPROCITY: As far as emotional reciprocity, it's all me. I'm always sharing, I'm always expressing, and I keep doing it because that's just the kind of person I am. He doesn't do that as much. He listens now when I do. He has been trying, expressing his emotions more. The problem is it's not something I'd be that emotional about, so it can be a bit disconnected, but it's alright.

Also, I have these examples in the family of what I *don't* want our marriage to become. So I am very conscious about that. Sometimes, the non-ASD spouse takes the idea of reaching out to friends for support and leans on them so much that then you can have this whole life that doesn't include your husband at all. And also leaning on the kids too much, which can make a spouse overly involved in their lives, so I'm very conscious of that. So as much as I do reach out to my friends, I do include Siddharth. I do reach out to my friends, and then I get the practical bit from him, and I'm like, "Okay, I can work with this."

Does ASD cause challenges in the area of sex/intimacy?

No, ASD doesn't cause any challenges. You know, honestly I don't think it ever did earlier. I don't think it's ASD or having a more adult life. It's more about him not creating a mood at all and then expecting to have sex. So that is hard, which wasn't the case earlier.

What makes you feel loved and cared for by your partner, and what makes your partner feel loved and cared for by you?

So if I'm on Zoom calls in the afternoon and working, he'll make coffee and keep it behind me. So when he does stuff like that, these small gestures, that definitely makes me feel loved and cared for. When he checks in—when he checks in over a text message or whatever—and definitely when he takes over something for the kids without me having to tell him.

So I do all these things for Siddharth, but I don't think it matters to him. I think what matters, what makes him feel more loved and cared for, is when I agree with everything

he says. He's always like, "Why can't you view it this way?" and if I could view it his way, he would feel validated...if I could see things from his perspective.

Finances

Describe your economic situation. Does your financial situation impact your relationship in any way?

I work; Siddharth currently doesn't have a job. We are okay financially. Siddharth is very good with financial planning. He does that really well. Taxes are his special interest, so he's very good with that. He's pretty intelligent. It's not that he isn't going to find a job; he's had a lot of offers. It's more like, I don't know when he will want to take something that he thinks is worth his time. So that's the problem.

Again, I don't know anything about his field. He had a start-up, and then he had a job, and then was on paternity leave. He has still not found a job. He doesn't seem to be in any hurry to either, and that drives me insane. It drives me insane because, like I told you, in my family background, everyone works. We've always worked for ourselves, so I don't even know what it's like to have a job. I mean, I did have a job when I was in the United States, but I've never not been working. Through both my pregnancies—through everything—I've never not been working. Neither has my mom, neither has my dad, neither has my sister. We're always working, so it drives me crazy. And then he goes behind his computer and says he's doing something, but I don't know what it is. To me that's not work.

Support System

What support systems do you and your partner have?

We've been pretty financially independent, both of us. I mean, definitely our house where we live was bought by Siddharth's dad, so that was huge—there was no way we could afford it. He did buy the house, but with everything else we're pretty financially independent. If we needed to, we could lean more on my parents than on his, just because the money comes with no strings attached that way. The reason Siddharth's dad bought us this house is because I wanted to rent our own space, and he couldn't bear giving up control, which is why he went ahead and bought this house.

Do you have friends individually and as a couple?

My individual friends are mostly old high school friends that I'm still friends with. And then I have some mom friends because of my kids. Those are pretty much my individual friends. As a couple we made friends. We used to do a yoga class together, so we made friends there with dif-

ferent couples. A lot of Siddharth's school friends are now our couple friends because they're all married, so now we all kind of hang out.

Do you have a spiritual practice? Does that impact your relationship?

We're from different religious backgrounds, but I don't have a spiritual practice. I do yoga, but wouldn't say it's spiritual.

Parenting

Tell us about yourselves as parents in this marriage.

He's a very hands-on parent. Probably compared to someone in the United States he's just a regular parent, but compared to someone in India he's a very hands-on parent. In India we have a lot of help; everyone has a lot of help. So usually guys don't end up doing anything besides just playing with their kids, but he doesn't do that. He does a lot of the work bit.

So pretty much this whole year because of Covid, he's done the homeschooling with our older daughter. He's done a chunk of it, and I do all the art and the other stuff. Because he hasn't been working and is doing his own thing, he has flexible hours and can help with her homeschooling. He took on this responsibility on his own; it wasn't something I had to say. He has a great bond with my older daughter. The younger one is still a baby. The only thing he doesn't get with our older daughter is all the non-verbal things. Now she's much older, and she picks up on things in a second. She knows when we're both on different pages, and she plays that really well. He ends up getting bullied a lot by her.

I'm pretty much the one who has to deal with all the social-emotional bit with her. Siddharth is a great listener, so he listens to her about it. I'm glad that she's comfortable telling him all of it. He listens—he really listens. He puts her to bed every night, so they chat at bedtime, and she tells him all about whatever. Especially since we had a baby, she has a lot of sibling rivalry, and she talks to him about it. I'm definitely the parent that does all the remembering everything.

One thing I do want to point out is that because of Covid and because of school being online, Siddharth has been amazing. If anything is electronic, he's going to follow it to a T. If there's a Zoom class, it's in the calendar. Everything is there; it's all ready. He's amazing with it. It's when things happen in real time he's not.

Being in an ND Relationship

Do you feel that the challenges in ND relationships are unique?

Absolutely, I think they're different. I think the most unique thing about them is that when you're in a neurodiverse relationship, nobody gets how you feel. Nobody gets the lack of support you have versus in a typical relationship. An autistic person typically talks so well at work and they're so put together that you can't imagine what things at home look like. Nobody would guess that. Nobody gets it—nobody gets the loneliness, the feeling on edge. You can't see it, and it's so hard to quantify.

Based on your experiences, how informed do you find people are about ASD and ND marriage/relationships?

Nothing, people know nothing about ND relationships! And I see this so much. Many times, the parents I see micro-examine their kids and they can find all these ASD traits, and they can't see it in their partner. And I'm like, "How can you not see it? You know, your child lines things up but your husband lines things up in the bathroom and you can't see that?" Now that I know what to look for, I see that I have so many friends who have it. I have a close friend whose marriage probably ended because of it. She's the one on the spectrum, but she still doesn't realize anything.

What is your perspective on being in an ND relationship?

I was talking to a friend of mine about this because she is in a neurodiverse relationship too. She lives in San Francisco, and her husband is neurodiverse. You know, we were actually having this conversation about how she was very scared to have a second child. She said, "What if my child is on the spectrum?" and I said, "Well you know you can't guarantee any of these things, but honestly I would take being with someone on the spectrum over anything else in a heartbeat."

I just think that there are a lot of challenges, and the biggest challenge area for someone on the spectrum is social language communication, which impacts the relationship. There are so many great traits about ASD—for example, being honest and sincere. I think it's really good. But I definitely think having a diagnosis helps. All these traits are great when you are aware of both your strengths and weaknesses and you are not ignorant and saying, "I'm great at everything." The positives of being in a neurodiverse relationship are the honesty, being sincere, and wanting to work at it.

> **I definitely think having a diagnosis helps. All these traits are great when you are aware of both your strengths and weaknesses and you are not ignorant and saying, "I'm great at everything."**

What advice would you give to people who are in an ND relationship?

I would definitely, definitely say, "Research." Everyone kinda reads up and discovers it themselves, but I think it really helps to get a diagnosis. And then it really helps to work with someone who is trained in ASD-specific couples counseling. If not, I don't think this is something you can figure out on your own. I don't think you can because it's not the same as a typical relationship.

There's nothing worse than telling someone (I know because early on I would tell my mom or my sister), "Siddharth said this and Siddharth said this," and then they'd be like, "Oh but this one says this also." There's nothing worse than hearing that because you know it's completely different, and there's no way they get it. It really helps to speak to someone who is really trained in ASD and not just thinking you can manage it on your own because you can't. I've seen enough relationships where it's fallen apart because they're not getting the right help.

Get professional help even if you think you don't need it—you need it!

Couples Counseling

Have you pursued couples counseling? Was it useful?

Yes, absolutely. The diagnosis was helpful. A lot of this stuff that was there earlier, I don't think we could've worked our way around it if we hadn't gotten professional help for it.

Concluding Thoughts

10-Point Marital Happiness Scale™

I feel like 8 or 9.

Would you say that you're in love with Siddharth?

Yes.

Do you think your relationship will go the distance?

Yes. Siddharth's pretty much decided that this is what he's going to stick with. This is what he's going to work on, and he's very much like, "If I'm going to work on it, I will work on it." And honestly, the fact that he wants to keep working on it makes me feel like there's no reason to throw it away. He never seems to want to put his hands up and say, "No, this is it, I'm not going to do it anymore," so I mean if he's willing to work on it, then I'm willing to work on it.

CHAPTER 3

Tom & Mona

Deeper Than Just Saying You Are in Love
Married Nine Years

INTRODUCING TOM AND MONA

I love Tom and Mona's story and it was important to include for a number of reasons. They are not only an ND couple, but they are also interracial, as Mona is black and Tom is white. Tom was raised in a rural, closed, religious community, which was almost a cult. Mona, on the other hand, had an urban, modern upbringing, which was heavily African-American. Tom admits, "My life with Mona is totally against the way I was brought up, my dad would say."

Tom and Mona also met later in life, having had previous marriages and children. This means that they have had to figure out ways to integrate their families and dialogue about critical issues such as race, culture, privilege, microaggressions, values, and respect. Tom shares, "I always knew racism was wrong, but then when I married Mona, it was so much bigger than that. I mean, when I married her, I came in feeling like,

'I'm colorblind. I don't see race, and we're all a big loving family,' but it's not that simple." With all their differences, one aspect that unites this couple is their shared Christian faith, which serves to ground and renew their love.

Another notable aspect of this relationship (similar to so many others in the book, such as Siddharth and Anisa, and Amalia and Rajeev) is their love for travel. I find it truly wonderful that ND couples love to travel and experience the world as a way to reconnect with each other and recharge. As Mona says, "Our hiking. Our travels. Those are our highlights...we've traveled all over the world together. Eastern Europe, New Zealand—those were really big trips; they were awesome!"

You can also see how Mona is forgiving when Tom isn't able to meet her expectations in the relationship. On his part, Tom works hard to resolve the issues that come up for them. He explains, "Yes, we have challenges, yes we fight through the challenges, and yes here are some more rapids we're going to go through, but, 'Yes, let's do it!' As an aspie, that's not initially my response. I mean, usually when there's a challenge, I'll freeze. But when I get into it, it's like, 'Yeah okay.' I like our life. I definitely don't feel like we're living a mundane life."

This relationship is hope-inspiring for multiple reasons. First of all, people can find love again at any time in their lives, even after tragedy and loss. I say this because I regularly have autistic clients who are cynical toward finding love, due to bad past experiences and trauma. However, as you can see in Tom's story, he didn't let his past stop him from putting himself out there. He made a sincere effort with Mona and found a true life partner who loves and values him. Secondly, we see that skin color and cultural differences while posing some issues that need negotiating can be resolved and overcome in order to create a beautiful life and marriage. In any relationship, including ND relationships, if one is dedicated to problem-solving, introspection, and working on oneself, anything is possible. To quote Mona as she reflects on Tom, "He's not stuck. He's not afraid to try new things and to change and fix what he did wrong, and that's refreshing."

MEET TOM

Tom (he/him/his) is a 53-year-old heterosexual, white, cisgender male. He has earned a bachelor's degree and works as a manager of financial planning and analysis. Currently, he lives with his wife and their extended family, although usually it is just him and his wife. He has three children from a previous marriage of 13 years. He has been married to Mona for nine years.

Duration of relationship and marriage

What did she say? She said nine years of being married? There you go.

Previous marriages and duration (if any)

Yes. I've been married once before. This would be my second. I was married for 13 years to my ex-wife.

Please describe any short- or long-term past romantic relationships

My first relationship and marriage was based on me wanting to have sex. So, yeah, that's all it was, and I wanted to get married.

How did you meet?

I met Mona on eharmony. We met at

a coffee shop in the town where I was living at the time. I was actually living in a town that was in-between her work and her home, and so she could stop by. Leading up to the first time we met, I thought she was pretty cool. I mean, she had a cool profile, and we had good conversation. I felt like, "Okay, she's pretty, she's a pretty neat lady, and I'm just going to sabotage this relationship and tell her all my junk." I had had a very tumultuous past, so I let it rip and just gave her everything—all my dirty secrets and everything! And she kept wanting to talk, while I was very aware that we were at a coffee shop in the town I lived in.

She was also very youthful in her walk and in her appearance. I mean, she was wearing ripped jeans! She was very energetic and very youthful, and I really appreciated that. It was really neat, and she was really easy to talk to, so after the first meeting I was like, "Yeah, she's very cool."

Diagnosis Journey

Did you receive any special education, support, or therapy while you were growing up?

No. This wasn't invented back then. I'm surprised I didn't though. I remember being bored on my first day of school, and I remember walking out of class. Then I decided to walk, and home was like 15 miles away. I told my teacher I was leaving. I was like, "I'm out of here!"

Do you or your partner have an official or self-diagnosis of ASD?

I think it was like four years into our marriage because there were some rocky points in our relationship, so I started asking myself, like, "Why am I acting this way?" I started exploring the idea, but I think I brushed it off the first time. Then I decided, "You might as well take the online test and find out, just for kicks."

> She pointed out that we've been married for nine years, and I'm like, "Man, it has seemed like a lot longer than that," and I mean that in a good way because there are a lot of things that we came through. I have had a lot of self-doubts, and we survived that. We survived drama with my kids. We survived drama with her kids. And that's why I think our relationship is deeper than just saying you are in love.

I self-diagnosed with an online test; I don't even remember what test it was. The test explained the spectrum of autism and told me that I wasn't way up high. I wasn't totally, you know, autistic where you need help, but it was the functioning type.

How accepting do you feel you and your partner are about the diagnosis?

Do I accept the diagnosis? It kind of answers a lot of questions, and so it's like, I can't run from it. How does Mona feel about it? I think she's accepting. I hope so. She hasn't taken off yet, so that's a good sign!

Mona was struggling in our marriage to figure me out, and so then I went ahead and took the test that she pointed out. I was like, "Oh, this is surprising." And it made me feel like, "I'm not off or weird...well, I guess I am weird, never mind."

What advice would you give to someone who's just discovering either their or their partner's ASD?

Read all you can about it. Everyone talks about their aspie husbands, but there's more to it than that. Even if you don't embrace the ASD framework, you should be aware that there are differences between your non-spectrum wife and you. You can change the way you do things, but as a person with ASD, you can't wash your hands of it. So it's one of those things you embrace and learn how to cope with. Coping is a bad word...you just learn how to live with it. You do all you can to live successfully with it.

Anything else you'd like to say about the diagnosis?

I went into my yearly physical with my doctor and said, "My wife wants me to be diagnosed to get an official ASD diagnosis." He laughed and said, "Every woman wants her husband to do that." So that was before I took it seriously of course.

Relationship Challenges

What are the main challenges in your relationship?

I'm going to say race as I'm white and Mona is black and we were raised in vastly different environments. Communication or lack thereof, especially how I communicate. Socioeconomic differences—I was born poor white trash. It's communication we have to work on the most.

Do you struggle with executive functioning, sensory sensitivities, communication problems, and/or social challenges?

EXECUTIVE FUNCTIONING: No, I don't see us having that. With money, she doesn't like the way I wanted to set it up, so we don't mix our money. She has expressed wanting distance from it, so that's one less thing we argue about.

SENSORY SENSITIVITIES: Mona's going through menopause right now, and she likes things really cold and then really hot and then really cold again and then really hot! We don't have arguments about it, but when she has it really cold, I just put a blanket on. I keep a weighted blanket ready for when she does that.

I have hearing loss, and she doesn't. Sometimes she says that I don't hear her, and because of my hearing loss, I'm not sure if I'm not actually hearing her or if I'm choosing not to hear her.

COMMUNICATION PROBLEMS: Sometimes when Mona and I are talking, she'll be expressing her heart and saying something about her kids. In the back of my mind, I remember that I have a similar or even better experience than her, and just like that, all of a sudden I'll switch off what she's saying to remember what I have in the back of my head. So she'll pause, and then I'll say, "Well, I have this blah blah blah blah blah." There was this little snippet on a Ted Talk that was so perfect—it was about knowing how to listen, and I could relate because it's like, "My golly, there's something in the back of my head, and I'll tell you because I don't care what you're saying." So it's things like that. She'll find a different talk or article about communication, so she's always in this development and teacher mode.

SOCIAL CHALLENGES: We don't have any social issues because I've driven all our friends away. Yeah, I should have picked up on those things a long time ago, because now she feels awkward having her friends around. She'll say, "You are a white person. When my black friend comes to the house, you have to make an extra effort to say hi to them." So she says, "We don't have friends over because you've kind of chased them all off." And I'm like, "Okay." I like it when it's just Mona and me, and Mona likes it when she has this whole cluster of people and me. And so I know that's probably hurt her a lot. She's expressed her loneliness time and time again, "I don't have any close friends. I don't have anyone that I'm going to call for a barbecue."

What have been some of the low points in your relationship?

Honestly, initially when we first got married, I started building this wall right away. When we first met, Mona was this incredible lady. She was just totally awesome. But then the first summer my kids came to visit, she showed me a different side of her, like she was very strict with the children and expected them to be a certain way and it scared me. I was like, "I don't know who this person is," and it frightened me. So I started compartmentalizing her, and I guess a good way to do it was to start building a wall in the relationship.

If you had a magic wand and could wish away one of your marital challenges or a partner's trait, what would it be?

I don't want to wish anything away. I'm a better person because of these challenges. I think I'm actually learning to communicate. I mean in my family, when we have problems, we just like to sweep them under the rug. Since Mona's keen on communication, since I've entered this household, we talk out our problems. It's hard for me to communicate—I can't stand communicating—but this relationship has actually helped me communicate. The race thing, I wish it would be easier for me, but would I wish she was white? No, I don't. Again that's made me a better person; it's made me look at the world in a whole different way.

The socioeconomic difference, that would be one I might wish away. Her being successful—having money and all that—is awesome. She has her own job and career. The way she was raised, she didn't have to worry about buying generic brands. I mean, that's great, but she's like, "You always bring up being poor. You're not poor anymore; you make more money than me." And I'm like, "Yeah, but that's how I was raised." So I wish she could see us lower-class people sometimes.

Relationship Strengths

What are some of your relational strengths and highlights?

God first, that's definitely a strength. If she sees a problem, she'll research the heck out of it. If there's an issue with me, now I've come to the point where I'm pretty receptive to it, because with some of my issues I've been too closed off to the subject to

see what's wrong. So she's very informative and points them out. It's a good thing, and I'm willing to learn. I guess that's our ability to learn from each other, and that's a strength.

We've been to places I never thought I'd be able to go, being a poor kid from Montana. She always wears these fancy glasses, and she does that because that's her personality. It's always an adventure with her. Growing up, being the same was our thing. We would have pizza night—pizza was always Friday night—and we had these traditions. Ever since I met Mona, it's like, "Traditions?" She's such a breath of fresh air. I don't think we've done the same thing twice in a row, ever. I still watch movies on repeat, but not her. She'll watch them once, and I'll go, "Do you want to watch this?" and she'll go, "Uh, we already saw it." And I'm like, "Okay." So I guess I just watch it by myself.

What do you love most about your relationship?

I love that she's still here. I love that we're on this nice, slow river ride—you know, like in Disneyland, just flowing along. Yes, we have challenges, yes we fight through the challenges, and yes here are some more rapids we're going to go through, but, "Yes, let's do it!" As an aspie, that's not initially my response. I mean, usually when there's a challenge, I'll freeze. But when I get into it, it's like, "Yeah okay." I like our life. I definitely don't feel like we're living a mundane life.

Intimacy

Is empathy or emotional reciprocity an issue in your relationship?

EMPATHY: I have a hard time not bringing it back to me. I try to empathize with her. I try, but it's not easy. I just gotta spit it out.

EMOTIONAL RECIPROCITY: I'm going to say, yes, it is an issue with her. I have created an environment where she doesn't trust me with her emotions, and so it actually makes me feel just terrible because she can't come to me for comfort. It's like, I just can't do it. I guess, as a person with ASD, I have a hard time coming up with the right words to comfort a person. And so, over the course of our marriage, she has pulled back on that a lot, and it makes me feel terrible. I would love for her to tell me her issues. But then she says, "I'll just have to find someone else to help me with this." And it's like, "Oh my gosh, do you know what that sounds like?" She's like, "I'm not talking about that."

Does ASD cause challenges in the area of sex/intimacy?

To be honest, she was into scheduling sex, and I'm like, "No, sex should be random and sporadic and when the mood strikes you." And she's like, "You've been watching too many movies." It's the opposite of the aspie person, who should be rigid in that regard, but we're totally opposite. I like things to be spontaneous, and she likes them planned.

What makes you feel loved and cared for by your partner, and what makes your partner feel loved and cared for by you?

A lot of things. When she cares enough to actually research and try to figure out what's not working in our relationship, that makes me feel loved. She's a fierce defender of me, and she defends her kids and everything. She's a lioness when it comes to protecting people, and she protects me in the same way, even though I can't figure out why she would.

Good lord! From what I gather, she likes to be touched. Gifts mean nothing to her. I mean, I've tried several different gift-giving things, but they don't mean diddly to her. She loves communication. Oh, and she says she loves it when I love on her grandkids.

Finances

Describe your economic situation. Does your financial situation impact your relationship in any way?

We're in a position where we don't need anything. I'm at a point where, the older my children get, the more the child support keeps dropping off. Sometimes I go on a little shopping binge, and then Mona's like, "Okay, we spent way too much, Tom. You have to back down." And then

I become a saver for a little while. That's the thing about growing up poor, because I did grow up poor... I remember my mom made my clothes, and I would get new shoes once a year. We always ate corn flakes out of a white box rather than a box that said "corn flakes." Back in the day, generic things came in white boxes. It wasn't a brand; it was just generic, and it came in white boxes. So I grew up poor.

Mona pays all the bills, and I pay her a certain amount every month. I'm like, "You can handle it; do whatever you want" and I have my own money. If I see something the house needs, I'll buy it. But we don't have to come together to have a money meeting.

Support System

What support systems do you and your partner have?

In the past, my only support system was my spouse. I did rely on my parents a lot during my first divorce. After I put my parents on the "no-talk list," I no longer had that. Mona has friends. She talks to her colleagues a lot, texts them, etc. She's a great texter. She would prefer me to find some friends, too. I have started talking to my daughter again; we check in once a week.

Do you have friends individually and as a couple?

No. Her friends are my friends.

Do you have a spiritual practice? Does that impact your relationship?

Our faith has kept us together when things should've torn us apart.

Parenting

Tell us about yourselves as parents in this marriage.

Her kids are all grown up, and we have grandkids. We do have differences in parenting; our parenting styles are different. She always said my parenting style is so white. White kids always get away with stuff. But when I see the way she treats her grandkids, her grandkids get away with a lot too. So, it's like, "Why do you let them get away with so much?" I suppose she's kind of changed with the grandkids. When I was working, my mom used to watch my daughter when she was first born. Now she helps watch my daughter's kids and really spoils them, so I guess people evolve with grandkids.

Being in an ND Relationship

Do you feel that the challenges in ND relationships are unique?

I think ND relationships are unique; I'm sure that in neurotypical relationships they experience unique problems. I think that atypical relationships do present different problems, different challenges. I like to think in black and white; she likes to think in 3D color. A typical couple—they probably would see life pretty much the same.

Based on your experiences, how informed do you find people are about ASD and ND marriage/relationships?

I don't think people are very informed, actually, about ASD or ND relationships. That's why I wanted my son to get tested, to at least be aware of it, to know what's going on. Even if it's something he makes fun of and laughs at, at least that's something in the back of his mind that's like, "Yeah this is something that I'm going to have to deal with." Or at least have that communication if he's interacting with people, because people with ASD tend to communicate in a different way.

What is your perspective on being in an ND relationship?

Since I'm the neurodiverse person, I guess I have to be in it. I have to accept it. I don't know how else to say it.

What are the positives of being in an ND relationship?

It's challenging, I know some people aren't up for challenges, but some are. There are definitely positives. Life is never dull. I mean, I'm sure my

wife would love for me to be typical, but we have our positives. My rigidity regarding rules and numbers actually benefits us as a couple. I'm sure typical people have other things, but I like numbers.

What advice would you give to people who are in an ND relationship?

It's like the same thing—research it, do the work on it, don't let it just slide by. You have got to just embrace it.

> There are definitely positives. I mean, I'm sure my wife would love for me to be typical, but we have our positives. My rigidity regarding rules and numbers actually benefits us as a couple. I'm sure typical people have other things, but I like numbers.

Couples Counseling

Have you pursued couples counseling? Was it useful?

First of all, this isn't my first couples counseling. With my first wife, I had couples counseling, and we actually had this wonderful counselor who gave me this book that kept me grounded.

When we first worked with Eva—I mean bless Mona's heart—she read Eva's book, and it was like all this stress just melted. Mona was all wound up tight, and then with Eva's book and working with her on our relationship, it helped her relax. Discussing how there are other couples like us, it was like all these rubber bands just released, so couples counseling really has benefited the relationship.

Concluding Thoughts

10-Point Marital Happiness Scale™

How am I going to quantify that? Because I'm looking forward to the point when we are a 10. I think that we still have a ways to go getting to know each other. She is getting to know me. It's like, yes, I know we go through hard times (all couples go through hard times) and it's not all bliss. I think anybody who says a 10 is lying. That's how I feel.

Would you say that you're in love with Mona?

Yeah, this term "in love" has been used way too much in the broadest sense. In the weakest sense, sure, we have been in love with each other. She pointed out that we've been married for nine years, and I'm like, "Man, it has seemed like a lot longer than that," and I mean that in a good way because there are a lot of things that we came through. I have had a lot of self-doubts, and we survived that. We survived drama with my kids. We survived drama with her kids. And that's why I think our relationship is deeper than just saying you are in love. I'm trying to think of a deeper term.

I mean you see it in the movies and everything, like, "Oh, yeah, we're in love with each other blah blah blah." But it's like, "Yes, we love each other, but we're also going to go up to bat for each other. We're also going to fight for each other." I mean, we'd die for each other. It's that kind of thing, and I don't think that saying you are "in love" with your partner expresses that.

Do you think your relationship will go the distance?

I am surprised that we're still together. Every bump that we've encountered, I consider colossal. Huge bombs, and I was devastated over them. For Mona, the problem might be pea-sized or it might be ginormous, but when Mona sees it, it's always a pea-sized problem. And so she's looking at this tiny pea, and I look at it like, "Gosh the world is coming to an end!" And she's like, "No, it's only a pea-sized problem. Don't worry about it." And so when I view it that way, it's like, yeah, we're going to go the distance. Because I've got Mona, who sees the problem for what it is—not a world-falling-apart, run-for-the-hills type of thing.

MEET MONA

Mona (she/her/hers) is a 51-year-old, African-American (of non-Latino descent), heterosexual, female professor of political science. She currently lives with her husband, her daughter and son-in-law, and two grandsons, although usually it's just her and her husband. She has no children with her current husband but has two girls (ages 27 and 25) from a previous marriage.

> *If you're not willing to learn about the other person, it won't work. If the ASD person is not willing to try to learn about you, it won't work because they have some learning to do, too. They have to learn about the neurotypical brain. The two of you have to be willing to meet halfway.*

Duration of relationship and marriage

Married nine years.

Previous marriages and duration (if any)

Two previous. The first one was three years. The second one was nine years. The first one ended in divorce. The second one ended with widowhood.

Please describe any short- or long-term past romantic relationships

The first one obviously wasn't great, which is why I'm divorced. He's the father of my children. The second one—I knew him since high school, so there was a lot of familiarity with each other culturally, and it was awesome. I mean, it wasn't perfect, but it was awesome. We had broken up after dating in college, and then I married my first husband. I knew when I did that it was a mistake. And then some people said that my second husband was waiting for me. I don't know if that's true, but I ended up divorcing, and then three weeks later he was at my doorstep. Three years after that, we got married...except now it wasn't just me—it was two little kids that came with the package. He accepted the package. It was a nine-year marriage, and basically he raised the kids. Then he passed away from a heart attack at 41.

How did you meet?

eharmony. It was different from what it is now, where you had to actually talk via email for a while. Apparently they open it up much quicker now, but we did it ten years ago. I think you had to have at least four or five email exchanges only through eharmony. So that allowed us to get to know each other really well. I think getting to know someone via letters (I know it's old school) but it allows you to find out the true person, instead of when you go on a date and only the representative shows up. You might go on ten dates, and you still don't know anything about this guy. You can get straight to the matter in an email because you have nothing to lose. We were able to do that, and then we met probably a month later and started dating.

Diagnosis Journey

Did you receive any special education, support, or therapy while you were growing up?

No. I don't know if I'm gifted, is that considered special education? I was on the gifted program my whole life. It was great! I've always thought school was easy. You just have to breathe, and you'll get through it. It was great to finally be challenged and stay with a group of people, especially in high school where we stayed with this cohort the entire three years (high school for me was three years). It's just the way it was in LA, and it was great. I made great friends.

Do you or your partner have an official or self-diagnosis of ASD?

I don't know if Tom is officially di-

agnosed; he could tell you that. I know he did the online thing. Unless maybe he talked to a psychologist about it—he's been to the psychologist without me.

How accepting do you feel you and your partner are about the diagnosis?

I do. I don't know if he accepts his diagnosis, but I do. I think it's important that we know his brain works differently than mine, and I can work around that. That way I'm not so shocked by some of his responses or by his inclination to sometimes not be social. I kind of understand it now. I'm grateful. I feel like we get along better because I feel like now I understand not to take the things he does personally. I understand that his brain is just different from mine. I don't expect him to react like me anymore. Frankly, I did previously, and it drove me crazy. I was like, "What's wrong with this guy?" I would say that getting the diagnosis is important if people want to stay married.

What advice would you give to someone who's just discovering either their or their partner's ASD?

Don't be afraid of it; do a lot of research about it. Read Eva's book! I read her book, and it was really helpful right away. That's how she became our counselor. It said in the back of the book that if you need counseling to contact her, and I was like, "I'm calling her!" That was probably five years ago now. Read her book. Inform yourself. And don't be afraid to tell people what you're going through... but realize that you're going to have to educate them about what it is. The last thing I'd say is to put people in your space that love and care about both of you and want your success. If they don't, set up boundaries. I'd also say this, though—be careful of the social media chat groups because they spew a lot of nonsense about how unhappy they are. Not all of them—sometimes they can help you see you're not crazy—but if you spend too much time on them, they'll make you feel like there's no hope.

Anything else you'd like to say about the diagnosis?

Praise god that we know about it; otherwise, we wouldn't still be married. That's the first thing that comes to mind. I had no clue what was going on, and when I figured it out, it gave me hope. Even though he fought me for a year about it and didn't want to take the test. It just gave me peace because now I know what the problem is, and I know we can work it through.

Relationship Challenges

What are the main challenges in your relationship?

The challenges have changed and gotten a lot better over the years. What was initially challenging for us

no longer is. Initially when we got married, I was like, "Oh my god!" The first challenge would be social skills because that's what made me recognize there was a problem. He didn't have any friends when we got married, but we got married so quickly in six months that I didn't even have time to think about it. His social skills were not good then either. He acted like an asshole, but he's not an asshole—he's nice to me. But in terms of other people, it was this sort of possessiveness. I realize now that that was just him being unsure about the situation, or not knowing what to say.

Secondly, the emotional ups and downs. I guess not knowing how to regulate his emotions. So we have super happy times and then there are super sad times, so it always feels like a roller coaster. Up and down, up and down, up and down, and you have to kind of know when the up period is and when the down period is and know how to navigate it. That can be challenging, especially because I have a lot of emotions to deal with.

Another challenge, I would say, is his family. We come from really different families, and that has been a huge challenge, especially in terms of race. The kids have gone through a lot of traumas, so there's that. I just don't think they understand black culture, nor do they want to—and that's annoying. That's not Tom.

Do you struggle with executive functioning, sensory sensitivities, communication problems, and/or social challenges?

EXECUTIVE FUNCTIONING: He loses stuff almost every day, and then he asks me, "Where is it? Have you seen this? Have you seen this?" Then he finds it.

He also likes to do things a certain way. Almost like, if it's not done accurately, then it doesn't make sense. There are things that he'll take over and do because he wants to do them his particular way.

There used to be issues of him not understanding affection. So, like, we're in the airport or taking a walk, and he doesn't realize that he is always standing behind me. He doesn't understand that when he's with me, he should stand parallel to me because that shows that he's with me.

I think the last thing would be that he just moves slowly. Or maybe I move fast, I don't know. When we get out of the car, he's always the last one out of the car. I gotta get all my stuff, and he doesn't see a need for urgency in some things.

SENSORY SENSITIVITIES: He doesn't like loud noises, but it doesn't have any effect on our relationship. He doesn't have any sensory issues in terms of being touched. He likes being touched, and he touches me. He has to remind himself to do it, though. He has to remind himself to hold my hand, as these things don't come naturally to him.

COMMUNICATION PROBLEMS: Oh my gosh, this is the whole book! Tom expects me to read his mind,

maybe because his mind works so fast. He's a really smart guy. He will start the paragraph without the topic sentence. So he's thought of it in his head and thought he'd already talked to me about it. He's like yeah, "Let's go get that thing." And I'm like, "What thing?" Or he'll say, "I'm sure you don't want to do A, B, C," even though he hasn't talked to me about it. But he's worked it out in his head.

SOCIAL CHALLENGES: Some friends don't understand his ASD and aren't willing to, either. I mean, there are a few who do, but the majority of my previous friends wanted him to be neurotypical like them, and that's just not possible. And they're not interested in getting to know how his brain works. Just because they're lazy, to be honest.

I would say that's one way we deal with the challenges—and there ARE challenges. I'm really social, and I have tons of friends. After marrying Tom, I lost some of my friends. So that's been a bit isolating for me. I've been trying to nurture more girlfriends because that seems to work a little bit better.

When we're traveling (we travel a lot), Tom will say really blunt things to people, and they will respond as if he's an asshole. He's not trying to be one; that's just his style. That can be uncomfortable because then he wants to argue and fuss, and I'm like, "You started it," and he's like, "No, I didn't." He doesn't get it.

He's really worked on that, and I'm proud of it. For example, you go up to a customer service counter, and you say, "Good morning, how are you?" You know, he would just be like, "I'm here to get my car." So I might remind him, "You forgot all your hard work; you didn't ask him how he's doing."

What have been some of the low points in your relationship?

I would say the family drama that's impacted us in terms of race. It's been really hard for us. It's been the biggest problem.

If you had a magic wand and could wish away one of your marital challenges or a partner's trait, what would it be?

I would wish away Tom's low self-esteem. I think that would have such a big effect on his life, on the choices he makes, on the chances he's willing to take, and just on the bigger feeling of confidence he would have. Not being so afraid to always make mistakes.

Relationship Strengths

What are some of your relational strengths and highlights?

We like each other. It's not that I didn't like my first two husbands, but Tom and I have gotten to know each other so well that we really know each other. We like each other. That really makes a difference, especially when you don't see eye-to-eye, and you can still be like, "I like this person."

Trying new hobbies. He isn't afraid to try the things I want to do, and I'm not afraid to try the things he wants to do. He got me into cycling. I didn't like it, but we did it for a minute. We hiked on our first date, and now we're hiking in all 50 states. I facilitated that. He's not stuck. He's not afraid to try new things and to change and fix what he did wrong, and that's refreshing.

Our hiking. Our travels. Those are our highlights. Not just hiking, we've traveled all over the world together. Eastern Europe, New Zealand—those were really big trips; they were awesome! I think one of the biggest highlights is that both of us want to be there in terms of our marriage. We work hard at it, and we don't just take it for granted, and that's really nice.

What do you love most about your relationship?

I would say, I think most people would assume that we don't fit together. I'm black; he's white. I was raised in a city; he was raised in a rural community. He grew up poor; I grew up working/middle class. I'm really pro-black, and, again, he's white. I mean, like, rural white, never been around black people. And the assumption is that this can't work, but it does work because we do have the commonality of Christ.

Intimacy

Is empathy or emotional reciprocity an issue in your relationship?

EMPATHY: He's not good at that. He might feel it, but he's not good at expressing it. I have a funny story that explains that. We helped take care of my mom before she passed away. She had Alzheimer's. My sister had her half the week, and we had her half the week. Tom helped me, and he was really good at that. Because my mom had Alzheimer's, she used to think at a child's level, and Tom was good at staying at her level. But, anyways, she passed and we cremated her. I had to pick up her urn, and so he went with me. The lady was giving me the urn, and I was feeling really heavy because I was holding my mother. Tom was trying to ask all kinds of questions about the weight of the urn and how they got my mom's ashes in there and how long did it take? I had to tell him, "Just go sit in the car."

EMOTIONAL RECIPROCITY: Yes. I do it all the time, and he does it every now and then. I'm probably not as good as I should be with that myself. But if I ask him how he's feeling and prompt him to be honest about it, he'll do it.

Does ASD cause challenges in the area of sex/intimacy?

It's great. We don't have too many challenges. The only challenge we have is time management and timing.

If we're traveling, he can travel all day, see all these sights, spend eight hours walking eight miles, and then still want to have sex. But I'm exhausted. The timing is bad. Sometimes when he's kind of down, he's not interested. That's interesting because I guess it's part of the ebb and flow of things. But when he is, it's awesome, and then when he isn't, it's like, "Is it me, or what's going on?" But, really, most of the time, it's just timing. He's not good at reading the signs, but I think our sex life is great.

> Kindness—he's really caring. So for example, I worked out with my friends this morning in our backyard gym. He will get up and clean it and make sure it's ready for us. He does stuff like that all the time.

What makes you feel loved and cared for by your partner, and what makes your partner feel loved and cared for by you?

FEELING CARED FOR: Presence, not presents. Like not giving me stuff, but being there. Time, time spent together. And he's good at that. Probably because he doesn't have any other friends—he's all mine. Kindness—he's really caring. So for example, I worked out with my friends this morning in our backyard gym. He will get up and clean it and make sure it's ready for us. He does stuff like that all the time. If I say, "Aw man, my chair is killing me," he'll research a bunch of chairs and say, "Let's go get this one." He's really kind, and that's very endearing.

CARING FOR TOM: I think time, also. I also think sex. My initiating sex is really important to him. For him, it's me giving him as much detail about the things going on in our lives as possible. He doesn't like surprises.

Finances

Does your financial situation impact your relationship in any way?

We don't have any. Let me explain why. I make my own money, he makes his own, and we don't necessarily mix it. Sometimes I wish we would, but we don't. We take care of ourselves. He gives money to the household, and I pay what I need to pay. It's just not a factor, to be honest. I think because we're both working professionals.

ASD has benefits for him, as he is good at his job. He is compensated well for it. He makes more money than I do. We always compete. It's been a benefit. I've read stories where it isn't this way for everybody, so I'm grateful. He keeps a job; he doesn't get fired. He's pretty regular at his job.

Support System

What support systems do you and your partner have?

We have our children, my adult children, and my sister lives nearby. We have good friends that we have dinners with. We've got a great church. I have colleagues at work that we get together with. We use Eva every three years! We do five sessions every three years.

Do you have friends individually and as a couple?

We don't have any friends that are his. We have friends that were my friends that are now our couple friends. We have friends that we've made together at church, but none that he's brought into the relationship. We did have one of his friends from his old home town come visit recently, and that was really nice. But it was more of the other guy initiating it. Tom doesn't really initiate it.

Do you have a spiritual practice? Does that impact your relationship?

Yes, we are Christian. It absolutely helps. The prayer. The Bible studies we do together. They help us realize that it's not about us. They make us move, be more of a servant to one another, which is refreshing.

Parenting

Tell us about yourselves as parents in this marriage.

Well, my parenting style is more culturally black, meaning up-front, aggressive, loving, demanding of respect, and communal. He is more culturally, what I would call, white. I don't know, I could be stereotyping. I'm stereotyping myself, too. He is more permissive, more individualistic. So, for example, he had teens, and they could shut their doors. And in my culture, you don't shut a door in your parents' house because you don't own the house. We just had a lot more rules. They were lovingly structured rules—nobody's getting beat—but it was, "You're a member of the community, and we want to embrace you as a member of the community." Whereas they were raised as, "You're more of an individual; be all you can be."

Being in an ND Relationship

Do you feel that the challenges in ND relationships are unique?

Well, everybody has problems, but they're unique in that, in a neurotypical relationship, you don't have to explain to people what the individual problems are between you.

But, for example, if we go to dinner with friends, I might have to explain ahead of time to them, "Look, he's cheap, so he's not going to pay for everyone at the table." But if I was in a neurotypical relationship, that situation might not come up, and I wouldn't have to share our interpersonal issues like that with others. Or I might have the conversation that, "He might not talk much, but that doesn't mean that he's not having a

good time." Or "He might not smile, but that doesn't mean he's not enjoying himself." So the things that you would assume as a neurotypical don't always work in social environments. You have to figure out how to navigate them. Sometimes that means you talk them over ahead of time, or sometimes the couple you're going out with already knows and they can be like, "Oh that's just him." So those are different challenges.

I mean, couples go to dinner, and they act like everything is okay and one of them's beating the other and nobody says anything. You don't have to have that all out on the table. I mean, sometimes you should. It's healthier, but, anyway, I have to vocalize some of these things so they don't assume that his brain works like theirs.

Based on your experiences, how informed do you find people are about ASD and ND marriage/relationships?

The general public is horribly uninformed and not willing to learn. There's no curiosity, and they don't ask me about it. I usually just have to say it. Even my own children don't ask a lot of questions about it, but I want us all to understand each other. I just think it's so foreign to people; I don't think they're informed about it at all. And even in my community, some people are ashamed of it. They want to hide it, which is so silly, like, "Oh he's on the spectrum? Don't tell anybody." There's a sense of shame about it, but I'm like, "This guy can out-think you. He can run circles around you!"

What is your perspective on being in an ND relationship?

If you're not willing to learn about the other person, it won't work. If the ASD person is not willing to try to learn about you, it won't work because they have some learning to do, too. They have to learn about the neurotypical brain. The two of you have to be willing to meet halfway. There's just no other way for it to work. But I don't think the issues are different from any other more typical relationship issues. Everybody has issues. I guess maybe it would depend how far on the spectrum they are, if they're high-functioning or not.

What are the positives of being in an ND relationship?

We have three brains helping to conquer the world. It's like being in a superhero movie. You have one superhero that's good at one thing and the other superhero who is good at the other, instead of two superheroes who are doing the same thing. You have less power that way. When I don't know how to do something, he does.

What advice would you give to people who are in an ND relationship?

Figure out what you do well together, and do it. If there are some things you can't get from each other, try to find them outside of the relationship—and I don't mean sex or anything like that. I mean like, "Oh, I want to learn how to roller skate." Go do it with your girlfriend, and then come back home and love your husband. He doesn't have to do everything with you. Find people who will support you.

Couples Counseling

Have you pursued couples counseling? Was it useful?

Oh my gosh, the first three counselors we had were horrible. Not because they were horrible counselors, but because they were horrible for us. Because these counselors were pre-ASD diagnosis, they were counseling him to do things that maybe he didn't know how to do. Working with Eva, the difference was like night and day! After our sessions with her, it was fabulous.

Concluding Thoughts

10-Point Marital Happiness Scale™

I'd say an 8.5. There's room for improvement.

Would you say that you're in love with Tom?

Yes! Definitely! I might not always feel it, but, yeah, it's there.

Do you think your relationship will go the distance?

Yes, because if we were going to kill each other, we would've done it in the first five years, and now we've invested in each other instead. Not that I'm staying just because I'm invested. I love Tom, and we've figured out the road bumps. So when we come to them, we know to slow down and take caution, but we're still going to go over them together.

CHAPTER 4

Ellie & Beth

Each Other's Number One Cheerleaders
Together Ten Years

INTRODUCING ELLIE AND BETH

Ellie and Beth are a lesbian couple, and *both* are neurodiverse. Ellie is autistic; Beth has ADHD. Their love story is of vital importance, not only for the autistic, ND, and LGBTQIA+ communities, but also for society at large. They offer a valuable model of a deeply emotional and intellectual bond, while also supporting each other's ND and spiritual orientations. Faith is fundamental to both of them, even though one of them is Jewish and the other Episcopalian. Layered over their other differences is also their religious variation, but they are able to harmonize their lives and passions in a way that is most definitely a role model for all couples, be they ND or otherwise. Beth shares, "The moment of realizing what our individual callings were and how they melded together so beautifully was a highlight."

Additionally, in reading this beautiful love story, we will see how much effort and energy they both put forth for each other and their relationship. They bring a "never give up" spirit to resolving the issues that their differences present. They are also very honest about their feelings and expectations with regards to the future. For example, they have decided together that they do not want to have biological children, so as to avoid the perils of pregnancy and childbirth. They would rather adopt. This is something that many people often feel, but aren't always honest about. This is a stunning example of doing things differently for the benefit of the relationship, even if they deviate from the societal norm.

Also, the depth and range of dialogue that they are able to have with each other is nothing short of astonishing. This exchange of information leads to the obvious deep connection they share. For example, Ellie explains, "Since my diagnosis, I've also started to learn how to unpack some of my masking behaviors that have prevented me from communicating authentically in the past. Beth has been a huge source of support during this learning period."

The love Ellie and Beth share is nothing short of transcendent. Beth tells us, "Even being able to talk through some religious or social questions together, coming together and harmonizing with our unique perspectives from the two different traditions. That's when I feel, 'How did I get so lucky?' I could never have imagined this." Ellie adds, "I feel loved and cared for by Beth when she hugs me and cuddles with me, when she stims with me, when she listens to me info dump, when she asks about my special interests, when she does a task she knows I'm dreading, when she comforts me, when she encourages me, when we sing together."

MEET ELLIE

Ellie (she/her/hers) is a 32-year-old, cisgender, lesbian, white female. She was diagnosed with ASD in 2019. She has earned her master's degree and works as a teacher, musician, and prayer leader. She lives with her fiancé, and they have been together for ten years. They have no children.

Previous marriages and duration (if any)?

None.

Please describe any short- or long-term past romantic relationships

I didn't date in high school. I dated my first girlfriend for my first two years of college.

How did you meet?

I met Beth my senior year of college.

We are deeply committed to each other, we care deeply for each other's well-being and personal growth. We support each other as we change and grow, we are each other's number one cheerleaders, and we laugh and have fun together.

We both studied with the same voice teacher and sang in the chamber choir together. A mutual friend set us up on a choir tour in Italy, and we had our first date under the stars in a Sicilian olive grove. A few months later, I graduated and moved away for graduate school, and we continued to date long distance for several years before moving in together.

Diagnosis Journey

Did you receive any special education, support, or therapy while you were growing up?

No.

Do you or your partner have an official or self-diagnosis of ASD?

I received my ASD diagnosis in March 2019.

How accepting do you feel you and your partner are about the diagnosis?

My diagnosis had a huge impact on my life. It allowed me to understand why I have always felt different from most people and allowed me to have more self-compassion. It also connected me to the online autistic community, which has been an incredible source of support. It's amazing to know that there is a whole community of people who share similar experiences.

I'm proud to be autistic! I spent a lot of my childhood and young adulthood suppressing the things that made me different, but now I realize that my struggles have made me more empathetic, creative, and resourceful. I love that I think differently than a lot of other people, and I have learned how to surround myself with people who don't merely tolerate my differences, but also celebrate and value them.

My partner is my number one cheerleader—she affirms my strengths and supports me in my struggles.

What advice would you give to someone who's just discovering either their or their partner's ASD?

My advice would be to connect with the autistic community. There is power in solidarity. Look for organizations led by autistic people, read blogs and books that amplify autistic voices, listen and be willing to challenge your assumptions.

Relationship Challenges

What are the main challenges in your relationship?

Sometimes our sensory needs conflict. At other times, I need more alone/quiet time than my fiancé does. Also, historically, I have had a hard time being forthright with my needs because of ingrained masking behaviors, but I've become better at advocating for myself since my diagnosis.

Do you struggle with executive functioning, sensory sensitivities, communication problems, and/or social challenges?

EXECUTIVE FUNCTIONING: We both struggle with executive functioning in different ways. I have a lot of trouble returning emails, phone calls, opening mail, and staying on top of certain household tasks. However, I am diligent about always making sure we have balanced meals and a clean kitchen.

SENSORY SENSITIVITIES: I am sensory avoiding a lot of the time, as I'm extremely sensitive to loud noises and overlapping sounds. Beth is sometimes sensory seeking and needs to listen to loud music to keep track of time and stay motivated. We've solved this by having her listen to her music with headphones when possible. When that's not possible, I use my ear defenders. Beth is also more extroverted than I am and enjoys hanging out in restaurants and bars, while I get overwhelmed by the noise and crowds. This hasn't been an issue during Covid, but we used to compromise by seeking out quieter bars and restaurants with outdoor seating areas, or sticking to a time limit.

We've also negotiated the overlapping sounds issue effectively—if she needs to talk to me and there are other sources of noise competing, she will turn down the music or find a quieter place to talk.

COMMUNICATION PROBLEMS: I tend to shut down and repress my feelings when I'm in distress, and I don't always show strong emotions on my face. Beth has learned to read me pretty effectively, and therapy has really helped me understand my strong emotions better. I used to hold onto anger, sadness, or resentment until it would all spill over in a huge meltdown, but now I'm able to express myself more effectively. Since my diagnosis, I've also started to learn how to unpack some of my masking behaviors that have prevented me from communicating authentically in the past. Beth has been a huge source of support during this learning period.

SOCIAL CHALLENGES: We have a really wonderful circle of friends. We met most of our friends through music and religious communities, so we connect over these aspects of our identity. I also suspect that many of our friends are neurodivergent too. Most of our friends have intense special interests or unique areas of expertise in music, language, and/or religious studies, and we feel safe being quirky together and info-dumping!

In the past, I have had trouble opening up to people and sharing my true self because of a fear of boring people or standing out too much. In my childhood, I was very bubbly and open and became a target for bullying; in my teen years and early adulthood, I overcompensated by withdrawing. I thought that I could protect myself from rejection by hyper-censoring all the parts of myself that distinguished me from my peers. I've come to realize that friendships are so much more meaningful when I just take the leap and allow myself to be vulnerable. I've learned that this also helps other people feel safe enough to be vulnerable with me.

I still struggle in large groups of people, especially in noisy environments. I'm much better with smaller groups.

What have been some of the low points in your relationship?

We struggled in the early years before Beth's diagnosis with ADHD. Neither of us understood why she was so irritable and angry sometimes, and I was often frustrated by her difficulties with completing tasks. She would often get frustrated with me for withdrawing in social situations with large groups or getting irritable seemingly inexplicably. Now we understand how I am affected by sensory overload.

If you had a magic wand and could wish away one of your marital challenges or a partner's trait, what would it be?

I would wish away our social anxiety! We both have bad anxiety, and sometimes we end up in a bit of an echo chamber.

Relationship Strengths

What are some of your relational strengths and highlights?

We are deeply committed to each other, we care deeply for each other's well-being and personal growth. We support each other as we change and grow, we are each other's number one cheerleaders, and we laugh and have fun together. We have disagreements, but we always work them out by respecting and listening to each other.

I treasure the time we spend together making music, learning, and helping people, and I treasure the time we spend together with our family and friends.

What do you love most about your relationship?

I love that Beth gets me and loves me as I am. I can be 100 percent myself around her, and she can be 100 percent herself. She has seen me at my best and my worst and still loves me. I love that we can have companionable silence together, or have long conversations about theology, or sing in the car for hours. I love nerding out with her about our favorite fictional characters, learning new things together, praying together, cuddling on the couch and watching *Star Trek*.

She's also incredibly caring and nurturing, and my heart bursts whenever I watch her caring for a baby. She is going to be such an amazing parent. I can't wait to have kids with her. She's going to be such an incredible priest and make a huge difference in the world. I'm just so grateful for our life together and I know that whatever challenges life throws our way, we can handle them.

> We have disagreements, but we always work them out by respecting and listening to each other.

Intimacy

Is empathy or emotional reciprocity an issue in your relationship?

EMPATHY: We are both extremely empathetic, sometimes to the point that it's painful. I absorb emotions from people around me, and I feel other people's pain, sadness, and embarrassment keenly. I consider this one of my strengths, but I recognize that it is sometimes overwhelming. One way that my empathy affects our relationship is that I want to make Beth feel better when she is suffering, and I automatically jump to problem-solving mode. Sometimes, she just needs me to listen and comfort her or give her space, instead of immediately jumping to action. I also sometimes go into a spiral when she is irritated at me and end up making things worse. I've gotten better about accepting that I can't control how other people feel.

EMOTIONAL RECIPROCITY: Beth is highly expressive and shares her emotions easily. I sometimes don't know that I'm feeling a strong emotion until a few days later. Early in our relationship, she would sometimes become frustrated with me when she would ask me how I was feeling and I would respond that I didn't know. She thought that I was refusing to communicate, but I often really didn't know how I was feeling in the moment. Now I know that I sometimes need extra time to process how I'm feeling, and Beth

gives me the space and time to process.

Does ASD cause challenges in the area of sex/intimacy?

We still have a great sex life, even after ten years! We've gone through some rough patches, but we've been able to negotiate them with time, patience, and communication. For me, one struggle has been that I have trouble verbalizing my wants and needs during sex. This posed a major problem for us for many years until we figured out what the problem was, with the help of couples counseling. We came up with a system for me to communicate non-verbally or with minimal speech. We use a green-yellow-red system to check in with each other, which takes a lot of the pressure and guess-work off of both of us. We also have a non-verbal system that we can use: we tap each other on the shoulder once, twice, or repeatedly to communicate different needs.

What makes you feel loved and cared for by your partner, and what makes your partner feel loved and cared for by you?

I feel loved and cared for by Beth when she hugs me and cuddles with me, when she stims with me, when she listens to me info dump, when she asks about my special interests, when she does a task she knows I'm dreading, when she comforts me, when she encourages me, when we sing together.

Beth feels loved and cared for

when I process with her, when I listen to her, when I bring her coffee, when I stroke her hair, when I help her stay on routine, when I cuddle her.

Finances

Describe your economic situation. Does your financial situation impact your relationship in any way?

Beth is currently in graduate school and is not working full-time. She will be receiving some income from a teaching assistant position, tutoring, and babysitting. I have four different jobs currently. I work as a prayer leader, synagogue administrator, and Hebrew school teacher, and I teach voice and piano online through two different studios. ASD doesn't negatively impact my employment situation. I am proficient in multiple languages and musical instruments, and I have found steady part-time employment teaching these various subjects. In a way, ASD has helped me because my special interests turned out to be marketable.

Money is often a source of stress, since we both have historically had multiple low-paying, part-time jobs. We are lucky to currently have our rent paid for by Beth's graduate program, so this burden is currently lower.

Support System

What support systems do you and your partner have?

We both have therapists, and Beth

has an ADHD coach. We receive support from our rabbi and cantor, and Beth has an advisor, spiritual director, and senior mentor in her graduate program.

Do you have friends individually and as a couple?

Because we've been together for so long, most of our friends are mutual friends. We both have a few individual friends, but many of those friends have become couple friends too.

Do you have a spiritual practice? Does that impact your relationship?

I am Jewish and my fiancé is Christian. When we first met, one of the first things we connected about was our deep relationship to our respective religions. Although we have different faith traditions, we find abundant joy from praying together. We have many commonalities, and over the past ten years, we have developed a combined prayer practice that encompasses elements of both Judaism and Christianity. Our spiritual life has been one of the great blessings of our relationship—we both struggle with anxiety that can overwhelm us at times, but we find peace and wholeness when we pray together. We are both pursuing callings to the clergy, and our relationship helps us discern, grow, and support each other. Even being able to talk through some religious or social questions together, coming together and harmonizing with our unique perspectives from the two different traditions. That's when I feel, "How did I get so lucky?" I could never have imagined this.

Parenting

Tell us about yourselves as parents in this marriage.

We aren't currently parents, but we are hoping to adopt in the future. We have a cat currently.

Being in an ND Relationship

Do you feel that the challenges in ND relationships are unique?

No two brains are alike, so I'm sure that every relationship has challenges. I think that communication, care, and flexibility are critical for any relationship. The two of us probably have more challenges than a neurotypical couple would have, simply because we are in a neuro-minority, and society tends to privilege neurotypical people.

Based on your experiences, how informed do you find people are about ASD and ND marriage/relationships?

I have unfortunately found that most people have very little education about ASD. Most people's knowledge seems to be limited to stereotypes and TV characters.

What is your perspective on being in an ND relationship?

I love being in a neurodiverse relationship. Even though Beth and I have different traits, we can understand and empathize with each other. We are more patient and compassionate with each other because we understand what it's like to be neurodivergent in a neurotypical world.

What are the positives of being in an ND relationship?

We (neurodivergent folks) see the world differently and have valuable perspectives to offer. We are often deeply concerned with equity and justice, and less concerned with social hierarchies. We often dedicate ourselves to unique interests and passions and love sharing knowledge with the people we love.

What advice would you give to people who are in an ND relationship?

Spend time on self-reflection and practice self-compassion. Learn about yourself so you can explain your needs to your partner. Seek out the help of a neurodiversity-aligned counselor or therapist to help guide you on this self-exploration. Acknowledge that both of you will change and grow throughout your lives together, and be willing to support each other through these changes. Remember that your partner has needs just like you, and try to listen without judgment or defensiveness. Make time to just relax and goof off together!

Couples Counseling

Have you pursued couples counseling? Was it useful?

Yes. Couples counseling helped us unravel some miscommunications and establish healthier patterns of communication. It helped us understand each other's perspective better.

Concluding Thoughts

10-Point Marital Happiness Scale™

Yes 10!

Would you say that you're in love with Beth?

Yes!!

Do you think your relationship will go the distance?

Yes, we have been through a lot in our ten years together, and we continue to get stronger. We love each other, and we are committed to continuing to build a life together.

MEET BETH

Beth (she/her/hers) is a 29-year-old, white (predominantly Anglo-Irish-German) musician and administrative professional. She identifies as gender fluid and queer, and she currently lives with her fiancé and their cat Kenzi. She is in graduate school for her Master's of Divinity and is in formation to be an Episcopalian priest.

Duration of relationship and marriage

Eleven years plus. Engagement: It's been two years, and our wedding was planned for May 2020, but it was postponed due to the pandemic.

Previous marriages and duration (if any)

None.

> They're not necessarily holding back from you, they're not keeping a secret from you, it's not that they can't trust you, or talk to you—it's that they're still trying to figure out what the heck is going on. So if you can approach it with the sense of like, "We're going on an adventure, kids!" then that kind of takes a lot of the pressure off of this constant process of self-discovery.

Please describe any short- or long-term past romantic relationships

One boyfriend in middle school, dated two to three months and we both later came out. One casual relationship with another boy in high school for a month. One intense female friendship with romantic overtones, ages 11–15, ended with traumatic separation and estrangement, later tentative reconciliation followed by gradual dissipation over time (ages 17–19). A handful of dates with two or three girls during the first year of being an undergraduate.

How did you meet?

We attended the same college, were in the same voice studio and high-level choral group; she was a senior and I was a first year. I admired her singing immensely and made a point of attending her performances, but I had very little social contact with her and was not considering her as a romantic prospect (only because the thought never crossed my mind). While on a choir tour to Italy and Sicily, we were set up on a date by a mutual friend, which surprised us both, but we both went into the date with a sense of, "Why not?" The date ended up being a late-night walk through a Sicilian olive grove in view of Mount Etna, on the grounds of the farm where our choir was staying. We both found conversation easy and engaging, a great deal of common ground in our background, identities, and interests, and most importantly, comfortable silences and easy physical proximity. The next morning, I overslept (typical!) and rushed to make it to the tour bus in time. When I arrived, I found her waiting for me with a roll, cheese, jam, and fruit rolled up in a napkin!

One of my clearest memories of the day was how gently she held my hand as we sat together on the bus. When we returned to our college, we decided to take it one day at a time, and to enjoy our time together without putting any pressure on the future, which we did for about two months until she had to make a decision between two graduate schools. One was quite close, but her preferred program was several states away. We realized that we were already more committed than we had admitted to ourselves or each other, and we talked through the decision to give long-distance a try, because the first priority was for her to attend the best program for her. We made it through three–four years of long-distance (at various distances), moved in together after I graduated, and have lived together ever since.

Diagnosis Journey

Did you receive any special education, support, or therapy while you were growing up?

Therapy from age seven to nine for

uncharacteristic/sudden anxiety attacks during sleepovers. Therapy from age 16 on for symptoms of anxiety and depression.

Do you or your partner have an official or self-diagnosis of ASD?

I have an official diagnosis of ADHD, predominantly inattentive type, which I received at age 24. Since then, I've been in continuing psychotherapy, cognitive behavioral therapy, and on stimulant medication. I began work with an ADHD coach in September 2020.

I had no real awareness of ADHD, nor had I ever considered it in connection to myself, until my long-time therapist brought it up in November 2015 (she herself only thought of it then). Upon evaluation and diagnosis (and subsequently, treatment), it provided so much clarity, self-acceptance, and momentum for self-improvement that I would say it was life-changing. Conversations with my family led to my father and sister eventually pursuing evaluation and obtaining diagnosis.

ELLIE'S ASD DIAGNOSIS: Ellie has an official diagnosis of ASD. I would not say that she had fully self-diagnosed, but she had been researching ASD with increasing intensity over the two years leading up to her formal diagnosis.

How accepting do you feel you and your partner are about the diagnosis?

Ellie's diagnosis (and the research that led up to it) was an incredibly positive and clarifying moment for her and in our relationship. It would not have previously occurred to me, but once she showed me her research and shared her thoughts with me, it made a great deal of sense, as my own diagnosis and learning process had for me. I was very accepting and encouraged her to pursue whatever evaluation/treatment she thought would be helpful to her.

We have both found each of our diagnostic journeys to be largely positive experiences that helped us to better understand the ways in which we are created in the image of God—as both of our religious traditions teach the ways in which our neurodiversity is a small sliver of the reflection of God's infinitely diverse nature reflected throughout humankind.

What advice would you give to someone who's just discovering either their or their partner's ASD?

Seek out autism self-advocates, in particular women, because female presentations of autism have historically been overlooked or just misdiagnosed. I've found the perspectives of autistic women to be super helpful for myself for learning not only about ASD, but also just about neurodivergence. I've found writing by autistic women to be super helpful and delightful, as I've found a lot of humor, good grace, and creativity in it.

Relationship Challenges

What are the main challenges in your relationship?

Our most severe challenge is definitely our shared/overlapping executive dysfunction. Secondly, differences in communication style—me hyper-verbal, her sometimes non-verbal. Differences in family culture, the "ask versus guess" thing can get in the way.

Do you struggle with executive functioning, sensory sensitivities, communication problems, and/or social challenges?

EXECUTIVE FUNCTIONING: One of us has ADHD, the other ASD, so we can both struggle with task initiation, transitions, and hyperfocus. So this would be a good place to say this—Ellie asked me to tell Eva this. Sometimes she has some auditory processing difficulties. Maybe three months ago, I was sort of clattering around getting stuff together, and I was not in a very good mood and she said, "What's wrong, is everything okay?" And I said, "Executive functioning!" and for some reason she heard me say, "Backhoe has pedals!" This is now our code word for executive functioning challenges!

We also say, "Your autism is poking my ADHD or your ADHD is poking my autism," which is something we got from an autistic occupational therapist we follow online. Because sometimes we're both having our "backhoe pedals" at the same time. But often I could be having a good executive functioning day and she's not, so it can be frustrating when I'm on a roll and she's not, as she might not be going at the same speed as me at that particular time.

SENSORY SENSITIVITIES: I'm generally sensory seeking. She is generally sensory avoiding. But we have major exceptions to that—sometimes I do get really overstimulated if she's verbally stimming a lot. She always did before, so when we discovered the term "vocal stimming," we were like, "Oh, that's what you do!"

Her verbal stims are a combination of vocal and verbal stims. This includes tongue clicks or little snippets of vocal exercises that have been given to her in the past, and she'll just randomly do this—not because she's actually warming up for anything but because she is stimming and so uses those exercises to stim. Sometimes if she has found a word that she really likes, she plays with it, by repeating it over and over again. It's like watching a bird, singing in different tones and registers. Sometimes she's not aware of it, and sometimes she's clearly delighting in it.

Sometimes I'm overstimulated, having sought out a lot of sensory stimulation earlier in the day, and need a break. At these times when she is vocally or verbally stimming, it kind of cuts into the flow of things, so that can be a point of friction. So I go into another room or ask her, "Can you physically stim, instead of vocally?" Since the diagnosis, we're able to navigate that much more easily.

COMMUNICATION PROBLEMS: Over the course of our relationship, we've navigated a lot of communication issues. We have different communication styles. We are constantly meeting each other in the middle, like peeling back layers of an onion. Things that used to be major issues with communication just aren't anymore. Because we were both diagnosed as adults, we're still discovering ways that we were masking, and particularly for Ellie.

She very often does not ask for what she needs and sublimates what she needs to a point where she is irritated and cranky and can't hold back anymore, and then it comes out as passive aggression. For example, I was recently on a Zoom call, and after I got off the call, she was like, "Can I eat my breakfast now?" And I was like, "What?" And she said, "You were glaring at me!" I said, "I was not glaring at you!" I wouldn't say it turned into a full fight, but it got very emotional. She felt like I had been glaring at her and scolding her, trying to say, "You can't eat because I need the quiet for my call." That's not at all what I was saying, so we can cross our wires sometimes.

SOCIAL CHALLENGES: I'm more generally extroverted than she is, and I need more interaction with people. Not so much that I need to be going to parties or need to be seeing friends all the time, but I need to be out and moving around in the world and be bouncing off of other people's energy. Due to Covid, I haven't been able to go to church or outside of the house or on campus or to in-person classes. It is really dysregulating for me. Ellie does miss some things, like teaching in person, being able to see her students and friends, and being in the synagogue, but she doesn't experience it like me, where I feel like a whole part of my life is missing and I'm not fully able to be myself.

What have been some of the low points in your relationship?

When we were long-distance, well before either of us were diagnosed, when I was in undergrad and she was in graduate school. We met up fairly regularly, but felt like the visits could go either way. We felt alienated from each other on some visits, and then the other visits were just like, "Okay, glad everything's well again."

The year that we moved in together, it was a staggered move because I joined her in the place where she was living with roommates. I was commuting on the weekends to be with her, and so the process of moving in together was drawn out and there was just a lot of transitional stress. Looking back at the situation, I think we were both really struggling with executive functioning. With moving, changing jobs, figuring grad school tracks, vocations, changing circumstances, and for the first time being adults, I'm pretty amazed that we made it through all of that.

When I look back on those times, I always feel like we were mutually supportive, and we got a lot of comfort from our time together. But there were a lot of really stressful situations and emotional dysregulation for both of us, and yet our relationship always felt solid.

If you had a magic wand and could wish away one of your marital challenges or a partner's trait, what would it be?

Oh my gosh. I was initially going to say that usually there is a flipside to our challenges, where it gives us some kind of benefit or super power or whatever you want to call it, so I couldn't wish that away. That said, even though she has well-grounded self-esteem, there's a really deep devaluation of self and her body image issues, which can cause communication problems. This aspect is so powerful that it really torments her sometimes, and she does struggle with intrusive thoughts, and she has talked to her therapist about that. I do wish that I could wave a wand and take that away. It really is painful for her, and for me.

Relationship Strengths

What are some of your relational strengths and highlights?

RELATIONAL STRENGTHS: I would say humor. Communication—I mean, with all of its twists and turns, I think that we've done well with it over the years. Our particular communication style as a couple, as we've told you, is song. When we go to bridal showers and they request the guests to write down advice to the bride on an index card, this is what we write down: When you get into a situation where you are tempted to tell your partner, "I told you so," instead you sing, "You were right, you were right, you were right right right" and the B section goes, "I was wrong I was wrong I was wrong wrong wrong I was wrong." So a combination of music and humor for defusing emotionally intense situations is definitely a strength of ours.

And the willingness to ask for help. We came to Eva for couples therapy when we needed to. I've been in therapy since I was 16, and I had been pleading with her to get back into therapy until she went.

HIGHLIGHTS OF THE RELATIONSHIP: One of the concerts we did together for sure. The moment of realizing what our individual callings were and how they melded together so beautifully was a highlight. Also, when we lost our respective grandparents, being able to be present with each other was just really profoundly affirming of the relationship. Kind of like, "Yeah, this is who I want to be supporting me in the worst times of my life. The way that this person is supporting me, this is how I want to get through life."

What do you love most about your relationship?

Our shared vocations. As musicians, and as spiritual and religious people, and as people who feel called to be spiritual and religious leaders. Leadership in the way of service, as our traditions tell us that being a leader is really being a servant first. There are moments when I get goosebumps or just start crying when we're making music together, or when she's working on a sermon and it just so happens to bump up against something I'm studying in my Biblical representation class.

Intimacy

Is empathy or emotional reciprocity an issue in your relationship?

EMPATHY: We are both highly empathic people, to the point that we do have to be careful to discern what is actually empathy and what is projection with each other, and sometimes with other people too. Ellie's so attuned to non-verbal cues in people's emotional expressions that her brain will take whatever data is given and fill in a bunch of information around it that may not be the obvious reality. So I would say if empathy is an issue, it's sometimes an excess of empathy—it never felt like a defect.

EMOTIONAL RECIPROCITY: There has always been some dissonance rather than disparity. We're just in two dif-ferent keys, if you're talking musically. I process my emotions and communicate my emotions verbally, and I prefer that in others too. Like I told you earlier about the stimming and how thrilled she was when I reciprocated her little stim, and she likes to be able to snuggle when she's feeling in need of comfort.

I get overheated in the summer really easily, so we've developed language around that. All I have to say is, "I'm a bear," and she knows that I'm not rejecting her snuggles, that I love her deeply, that I'm just way too hot. So there's a whole glossary on the ways we've developed to communicate, and we're constantly discovering more of what she needs to hear to fully believe something. When she says something to me, I'll say, "Okay, taken and received, thank you."

Does ASD cause challenges in the area of sex/intimacy?

I don't know what would be helpful because I feel like I've talked to Eva so much about this. I don't even know where to start. Scripting causes an issue with our intimacy and still occasionally pops up. For a long time, she would enter any situation of intimacy relying on a script to help her navigate any areas of insecurity, or not knowing how to communicate what she wanted or guess what I wanted.

To cope with the ask-guess culture, she would rely on scripts to try to get her through that. Before I knew what scripting was or that she was doing it, something about it felt inauthentic to me because she was not allowing herself to be vulnerable and was relying on these scripts instead.

Sometimes, in our moments of intimacy, her face would be blank and I would perceive that she was checking out. It took us talking to Eva to realize she's not checking out, that's just her not masking like she usually is; it's actually her being vulnerable. So there was the crossing of wires on all of those levels, combined with a sense of devaluation of self that is present in her, particularly manifesting through body image.

Also, because of my ADHD and chronic illness, I am hypersensitive to the pain response and fatigue. So I get tired or feel pain much more quickly than probably a lot of folks do. Or even if they do, they can sort of push that to the side, but with me I can't turn the volume down. I want to prioritize her over what I am feeling, but I just cannot turn down that volume button. Our different sensitivities and neurodivergence are all thrown together, and it can get complicated.

What makes you feel loved and cared for by your partner, and what makes your partner feel loved and cared for by you?

FEELING CARED FOR: A lot of stuff. One of the first things I remember from our first date is how we had this lovely conversation, we felt very comfortable with each other very

quickly, and we were able to be in silence together. And then I was late the next morning, and she got me breakfast. And then we sat together on the bus, and I remember her taking my hand for the first time. I remember thinking, "Oh my god, this is the most gentle that any human being has ever touched me that I can remember." In my family, we give each other strong, firm touches, and she just took my hand like it was a baby bird. It was the sweetest thing, and I was like, "Oh my god, she's just so tender." That just made me feel like— it's no judgment on other forms of physical contact—but like, "Oh I feel really special. She's treating me tenderly." So the combination of feeding and gentle touches has persisted.

We make music together. We sing together for hours. I will sing a melody, and she will improvise a harmony over my melody. Then something about the fact that she lets herself be vulnerable enough to compose on the spot with me feels very special to me. It's a very vulnerable thing to do with another musician. And the feeding thing—feeding people is one of her very, very central love languages. And you know, when I'm sick or when I'm upset, she's just very solicitous. She's always more patient with me than I am with her, and she spoils me, she coddles me. It makes me feel very loved.

CARING FOR ELLIE: Responding to verbal stims. I am not kidding, you should see the change in affect for her when I participate in a stim in any way.

After we found out about stimming, Ellie realized that's why she liked braiding my hair so much. So now she'll ask, "Can I stim on you?" and she'll tap my hand while we're talking, or she'll play with my hair or play with my clothes or something. Giving enthusiastic consent to her stimming on me, it makes her feel really safe and validated.

I very rarely cook for her, but reciprocating any of her love languages, even if they don't come naturally to me, she takes that as, "Oh you really like me!?" My love language is getting things done for her. Like having laundry done, having the house clean, organizing things, decorating.

She's been leading a lot of services for the community over Zoom, and she gets paid for that. I run all the tech for her and sing melody with her so she can sing harmony.

I did her website, and I fix things or make things run. Sometimes one of us will do something and, after doing it, be overflowing with love and be like, "I'm doing this because I love you."

Finances

Describe your economic situation. Does your financial situation impact your relationship in any way?

Her family is slightly more well-off than mine, and so her parents have been paying for voice lessons for years, which I haven't been able to afford. Her parents helped her with her student loans. My parents are in a bunch of debt, as well as me for my student loans.

I don't have good financial hygiene, I guess you could say. It's something I've been actively trying to work on and develop and improve over the years. Ellie, coming from more of the "guess culture," doesn't like to talk about it readily, and she's kind of uncomfortable talking about it. So that combination of circumstances has created issues that have kind of put us in a financial bind in the past. Prediagnosis, we had racked up enough consumer debt that we were looking at years of minimum payments and a lot of interest and that kind of thing. She finally expressed her level of discomfort, and then I was the one who did the research on debt management programs and got us signed up for the green path debt management program. I did all of the administrative leg work to get us to that place, but I probably just would've kept going if she hadn't been the one to say, "No, this is not working."

Support System

What support systems do you and your partner have?

Lots, fortunately. I come from a large family. We're both very close to our families of origin. I have a broader network of family of origin. Hers is very nuclear. There are lots of estrangements on her side of the family. So she grew up kind of with an open awareness of being cut off from relatives that she never got a chance to know because there had been estrangements in the generations before her. So she was sort of simultaneously overwhelmed and overjoyed at the size and noise level of my family. We're very, very social.

I have a ton of family friends from multiple generations—my parents' and grandparents' generations that we address as family. You know, people who are absolutely not blood-related to us but we call grandma or grandpa or aunt or uncle and are actively in contact with. We had a joint bridal shower with church and musical friends, and her mother was delighted to be there and everyone was delighted to have her mother there. That's kind of how that tends to balance out. Her family does have a few intimate friends that she doesn't call aunt or uncle, but when I look at those relationships, I see a parallel of those in my family.

Do you have friends individually and as a couple?

So Ellie tends to have smaller support networks than I do, but they're very deeply rooted for her. And then, we have sort of dug into and created support networks in our faith communities. Having two faith communities comes with a bonus of having more support networks. We have lots

of professional and spiritual mentors that we both can reach out to rely on, and we both regularly remind each other during situations of stress like, "Hey, you really should call Rabbi Bobby," or she'll be like, "Hey, do you need to go to your spiritual director?" We're very fortunate to have diverse support networks, and we're familiar with each other's support networks, so we're able to prompt each other to reach out and take advantage of them.

We each sort of have one very long-term friend (for me from high school, for her from college) that we would each describe as our best friends outside of the relationship. We have a certain amount of joint interaction with these friends and their spouses, but it is also the sort of thing where, like yesterday, my best friend called me and we talked for like an hour. It was a conversation between the two of us, and we can talk about our relationships to each other, and I know Ellie does the same thing with her close friend.

Do you have a spiritual practice? Does that impact your relationship?

Ellie and I are both clergy-in-training. I am Christian (Episcopalian), and she is Jewish. Not only our individual spiritual practices, but also the intersection of our faith identities, have been both individually and mutually supportive and transformative throughout our relationship. Our relationship has also strengthened and clarified our understanding of our own traditions and our commitment to them, as well as nurturing our individual vocations. We pray together, we sing together (this is central), we are in constant conversation about scripture and other traditional texts, and we actively participate in one another's faith communities, observances, education, and other aspects of spiritual formation.

Parenting

Tell us about yourselves as parents

So, our cat Kenzi is very much her baby. He is our baby, and she really benefits from having a cat. It's interesting because we are not parents, but when we met she thought that she wanted to give birth and I knew that I do not want to give birth ever. But I want to be a mother, and I've been aware of that for a long time, so I want to adopt. I've been doing childcare since I was very young, and so I've never had any doubts that I could love a child I hadn't given birth to.

Ellie also didn't have a lot of exposure to pregnant women or to infants. I was doing childcare because I came from a large family and a very close church community where there were always babies being passed around and always someone pregnant. I just had a lot more exposure to the reality of that. Once she started reading the *New York Times* pregnancy columns and learning what happens to the body through pregnancy, she real-

ized that maybe pregnancy wasn't for her either. Even when we would be near an infant at a party or on a visit home, she would never feel confident enough to hold them. She would get a little wild around the eyes. And so I was like, "You'll be fine, you just need to build up your comfort level. We'll just have to find a baby to hang out with!" Low and behold, we have a baby to hang out with, and I bring her back here more than half of the time. The parents bought us a pack-and-play that I keep in the bedroom, and so Ellie has been working on holding her and feeding her. I still do the heavy lifting when it comes to the changing and the burping and the discerning as to why they are crying.

> Not only our individual spiritual practices, but also the intersection of our faith identities, have been both individually and mutually supportive and transformative throughout our relationship.

Being in an ND Relationship

Do you feel that the challenges in ND relationships are unique?

I can't speak to anything about neurotypical relationships, but I would say there's a unique challenge and benefit to being in a doubly neurodivergent relationship. And there's benefit because we're not both ASD, and we're not both ADHD. The kind of blessing and curse of double consciousness that you can get from being neurodivergent in the world is amplified when you're in a relationship because there are things that I can talk to her about that I don't need to explain. She gets it immediately, even though she doesn't experience most of the traits, and she has a lot more empathy for me.

I feel so unbelievably supported to have a partner who is also neurodivergent and then also sometimes like, "Okay, I wish someone in this house was typical or whatever." But ultimately, I would not trade anything. I think it makes us more mutually supportive of each other, and I think it's only going to be a strength for what we want to do in the world. Because you really don't know what people are dealing with, and often they don't know what they are dealing with. So just going in with a whole lot of empathy and room for grace is going to be the best way to move forward for all involved, and I think we've gotten a lot of that from being in a doubly neurodivergent relationship.

Based on your experiences, how informed do you find people are about ASD and ND marriage/relationships?

I don't find people to be informed about ASD at all, and I don't find

them to be informed about ASD relationships either. Yeah, it's pretty frustrating and heartbreaking, actually. They don't know anything about it, their parents don't know anything about it, their teachers don't know anything about it. You feel like you have some insight, but it's absolutely not your place to insert yourself or diagnose or refer or anything like that. It's really frustrating because you see people either suffering or being dismissed for no good reason.

What advice would you give to people who are in an ND relationship?

Read other peoples' writings, and listen to your partner. Be curious with your partner! That's one of the big things we learned from Eva. I thought I was being supportive. I thought I was being curious, but I was still making a lot of assumptions. Ellie often doesn't know what is going on with her. She is still discovering all this stuff about herself. Even when she's figured out the shape of something, she sometimes can't name the color or the texture of the particular experience that she's having. Especially for some people, and their particular presentation of ASD, language is a barrier. Being curious and patient and working on humility like, "No, you can't assume what your partner is thinking or feeling; they don't even know what they're feeling half the time." Being willing to be a detective with them and kind of letting it be an adventure. They're not necessarily holding back from you, they're not keeping a secret from you, it's not that they can't trust you, or talk to you—it's that they're still trying to figure out what the heck is going on. So if you can approach it with the sense of like, "We're going on an adventure, kids!" then that kind of takes a lot of the pressure off of this constant process of self-discovery. A past therapist once said to me the process of self-acceptance is self-improvement.

Couples Counseling

Have you pursued couples counseling? Was it useful?

Ellie did a lot of research, like two years of research and at high levels, because she initially found out about this stuff through a master's-level course. This was not just her poking around on the internet; she was reading a ton. She was seeking out autistic self-advocates, and she was really well-educated about ASD. But when it came to couples counseling, we just needed a third person who was knowledgeable about ASD to sit with us and hear the gaps in our communication, reflect them back to us, and poke at both of our assumptions. We both came into conversations with Eva carrying a lot of assumptions.

For me, everything is verbal and can be articulated, but for Ellie a lot of it is preverbal. She'll have a deeply held belief that she won't necessarily be able to articulate. A lot of the work that was really helpful to both

of us was that Eva started asking Ellie questions that started to draw out some of those preverbal assumptions. It's hard, slow work, but she was able to eventually put some of that into words, and that sort of unlocked a lot going forward. And again, I think it's not accidental that Eva herself is a woman and that she specializes in working with women with ASD, because I think autistic women have been sidelined or brushed off in the past.

Concluding Thoughts

10-Point Marital Happiness Scale™

Yeah, I would say somewhere around 9 or 10 because you know (this is my Christian theology coming out), nothing is perfect. And I think saying that something is perfect puts pressure and, frankly, falsehood on it that is just unhealthy and unnecessary, so somewhere in the high 9s. Some days it might go to an 8. I am very grateful for her and everything I've articulated here.

Would you say that you're in love with Ellie?

Yes, but not in a way that I would've imagined being in love to be like when I was younger.

Do you think your relationship will go the distance?

I do. I do, because I think—I'm not

saying that this is a paradigm for everyone else—but I think in our particular circumstances, the fact that we are an interfaith couple and the way that we navigated that from the beginning made for a very strong foundation for doing the work of marriage and relationship. We're not yet married, but we're pretty much married and have been for years.

We always understood and recognized that, while we have individual differences, there's also an overlay of shared experience and shared language, so even when we just understood ourselves as an interfaith couple, there was our musical language that connected us.

CHAPTER 5

Oscar & Hope

What I Love the Most

Married 15 Years, Together 18 Years

INTRODUCING OSCAR AND HOPE

Oscar and Hope are Mexican, and they work and live in Mexico. Latino couples are often underrepresented in ND couples literature, as are other people of color. For this reason (and many others), this couple's perspective is a treasure. Hope explains, "I would say that being in a neurodiverse relationship helps promote an inclusive and diverse world. We complement each other. We are also breaking stereotypes about this image of what the 'perfect couple' or the 'perfect relationship' looks like."

This chapter provides a glimpse into Oscar's experiences of being autistic in Mexico. Additionally, his artistic and romantic personality reveals a different side of ASD. He explains that gender roles in Latin American culture are fairly rigid. These expectations conflict with their neurodiverse marriage, which is, by definition, anything but typical. For example, the fact that Hope makes more money than Oscar can be a tender subject. Oscar has found his community to have very little understanding of ASD, but he has learned that when he is direct about it with his students or coworkers, they tend to respond supportively. "It's hard work. I think it's even harder when you're neurodiverse and come from different planets," explains Oscar. "It's basically a cultural thing. It's like being married to someone who comes from a completely different country, with a completely different language, with a completely different set of beliefs. That's how I see it."

As is common in many neurodiverse marriages, the NS spouse (in this case, Hope) shoulders a lot of the important responsibilities in the house. These include keeping track of Oscar's sleeping and eating habits, paying Oscar's credit cards, and managing the family's finances. Smaller aspects also require her attention—

details such as keeping the light dim due to Oscar's photosensitivity and cooking food to the texture Oscar tolerates. Still, because she values Oscar so much and has come to understand how his ND brain works, she's able to accept him as he is, while working hard to keep their life as a married couple going.

Hope's perspective offers encouragement to spouses who feel ready to quit the ND relationship because she was able to reconcile with Oscar after a nine-month marital separation. She also found that having an official diagnosis made a massive difference in her ability to connect with Oscar. Hope demonstrates how communicating explicitly about her emotional needs is a strong coping technique in ND relationships. "I try to tell him in a very direct, assertive, clear man-ner how I'm feeling and what I want," relates Hope. "I have to be very, very specific."

Oscar and Hope model a relationship of lasting love. The qualities that contribute most to this longevity are humor, loyalty, and resiliency. Oscar admits that his sense of humor may be a bit odd, but because his wife understands it, they unite around the laughter. Both spouses are confident in the commitment of the other; they do not question each other's faithfulness. Through their perseverance, Oscar and Hope have arrived at a place where they can say, "Our mantra is, 'You have what I am missing, and I have what you are missing.'" Their story encourages ND couples, no matter their struggles, to embrace a learner's mindset and welcome their differences.

MEET OSCAR

Oscar (he/him/his) is a 50-year-old, straight Mexican male. He went to college and is now a college professor, visual artist, photographer, translator, and freelance style corrector. He lives with his wife, they have no children, and they've been married for 15 years.

Previous marriages and duration (if any)

None.

Please describe any short- or long-term past romantic relationships

I'm a romantic at heart; I'm an artist. The problem is that most of my emotional education comes from other sources. I have to intellectualize most of it, so it comes from pop culture, movies, and books. I tend to idealize women, so in that way, I was in love several times in my life, starting in my early teens. But it was all so complicated to deal with. I found these love affairs overwhelming, especially because my brain isn't wired in the same way as everyone else's. So it's like, "Okay, this is the way women think, and this is the way it makes sense to me." But in the end, the relationship doesn't work, regardless. I tend to be very intense, I've been told that more than once.

No relationships as long as this one. This is the longest relationship—and the most successful one—that I've been in. Romance is overrated, definitely. There's more to a relationship than romance. I didn't get that when I was younger, but now I do.

> We're very loyal to each other. I'm not a saint, but still I try to be loyal and to be there for her as much as I can, regardless of my shortcomings. I know that I'm not fun to be with or to be around because I have a different sense of humor, but my wife gets me.

How did you meet?

It's a cliché, but we met on a blind date and hit it off. We started going out, and eventually we fell in love. We were together three years before getting married, but I asked her to marry me during the first year of our relationship. She was not only my type, but she's also very kind and

loving. People (including her) ask me this question, and I always answer that she has what I don't. In many ways, she's my better half.

Diagnosis Journey

Did you receive any special education, support, or therapy while you were growing up?

Yes. I was diagnosed with ADD when I was ten years old. I was hyperactive, and I was diagnosed when I went to some therapy sessions. Nothing heavy. The therapist's advice was, "Well, he's got a lot of energy, so keep him busy, keep him tired."

So, I did a lot of physical activity when I was younger. Karate, music (I learned to play the guitar really well), and languages. My mom did all she could to keep me busy, and she also asked my siblings to leave me alone.

Do you or your partner have an official or self-diagnosis of ASD?

Next year, it will be three years since I received my diagnosis.

Once I was diagnosed with ASD, it made all the sense in the world. It explained to me why my brain works like this. I was always aware of my thinking differently, but then it all made sense. Especially to my wife, it was like, "Oh that's why you did this, and that's why you behave this way and that." It was liberating in many ways.

We're in couples therapy, but most of the time it's just my wife during the sessions. She's not only in couples therapy, but in individual therapy also. I join the sessions every once in a while when I think I have something to say or to add to it. To be honest, I think therapy only works if you believe it works, and I have my doubts about it. But it's very individual, and in my case, I've got my photography and my music and everything else that sustains me.

How accepting do you feel you and your partner are about the diagnosis?

As I mentioned before, it all makes sense. I was absolutely accepting of it. I was very curious about it, so I started my own research. I've this knack for neurosciences. I mean, as a teacher you learn how the brain works, so it's interesting to make sense of it all.

What advice would you give to someone who's just discovering either their own or their partner's ASD?

Get some professional help as soon as possible. Do the work. Do the reading. Read the books. Go to therapy, couples therapy if that works for you. If not, do it on your own, but do it. Forget about your expectations. Just take the good with the bad, the sweet with the sour. That is something I have learned. Be brave.

Don't give up on it. Don't give up on it until you realize that you've done everything in your power. I know that sometimes it's unhealthy to stay together. I do think that especially today, younger people tend to be not as resilient. Whenever trouble arises, they tend to give up very soon. I think that this is all a matter of not giving up too soon anyways.

Anything else you'd like to say about the diagnosis?

This happened because Hope works at this huge global company, and she's in charge of events. So they had this inclusion-based company event, where they tried to address many important topics. One of them was diversity, including neurodiversity. There was this lecture, and when my wife listened to it, she was like, "Hey, I'm married to that guy!" My wife had this small conversation with the speaker, and she suggested that I take the test and do the diagnostic interview and so on.

Relationship Challenges

What are the main challenges in your relationship?

I'm this stubborn, stubborn SOB. Oh man, I never give up, for good or bad, so it's exhausting. Of course, it's not only exhausting for myself, it's exhausting for everyone around me. I never let go.

I'm a creature of habit, so I have this very clear routine. I'm stressed out most of the time, 90 percent of the time. My mind is racing, and I have described this in therapy as "always being in the red." Always. I sleep very badly. Maybe four hours or so every night since I was a teenager, because of my obsessions. That's probably the third thing.

I'm very obsessive. If I find something interesting, I will go for it—all in. I'll pursue it to the ultimate consequence. Of course, that's very difficult for the people around me. Especially my wife, who has to deal with it. I tend to zone out to just get in the flow of the stuff I find interesting, and I tend to ignore everything else and everyone else. I forget to sleep; I forget to eat. So that's why I need a routine because if I don't have one, it's a mess, it's a disaster.

Do you struggle with executive functioning, sensory sensitivities, communication problems, and/or social challenges?

EXECUTIVE FUNCTIONING: I'm very bad at paying bills. Very, very bad with finances...basically the small, nit-picky things. I don't have a smartphone. I always make the joke that I want to be the smart one. Really, I don't have a smartphone because I find it overwhelming. The WhatsApp thing, going back and forth, the whole mechanics of it all, the politics of it all...it's too much.

That transcends into other areas of my life, also. I'm always challenged by the small things. We live in this apartment where we're surrounded by neighbors, but I don't really care

or am not interested in them in any way. I tend to ignore people, so when my wife talks about something that's going on in the building, it's like, "I don't know what you are talking about. Who's that person? There was a problem in the opening of the garage door with the remote? What are you talking about?" But that's me. And of course, paying taxes, filling out forms, insurance paperwork—it's a nightmare for me.

SENSORY SENSITIVITIES: My wife, she's tried to make this home ASD-friendly. I appreciate that, even though I probably don't tell her that as often as I should. For example, I've been photosensitive since I was a child. Light hurts my eyes all the time, and I have to keep the curtains or drapes closed all the time. I'm very distracted by noise. And I have a very good ear—I am a musician, too, or I used to be.

Interestingly enough, I'm never cold. Never, ever. My wife, on the other hand, she's always shivering. So that's been interesting, especially during bedtime. I'm also very sensitive to textures when I eat, so if I don't like the texture of something in my mouth, I don't eat it. I love to cook, but I tend to cook only in ways that I like. For example, I like to not cook my carrots too much. My wife finds them difficult to chew, but I find them perfect. So that sort of stuff was an issue early on in our marriage, but we've learned to compromise more now.

COMMUNICATION PROBLEMS: It's all been about negotiating. I'm sure the diagnosis helped my wife realize that I don't have the mirror neurons in my brain, so I can't read people very well. I don't get sarcasm, which I think is very common for those with ASD. Sexual innuendo and that sort of thing, I'm very challenged with that. And, of course, if my wife doesn't tell me exactly what she wants or what she needs from me, it's impossible to guess because I don't get her signals. She finds it challenging to tell me exactly what she wants and needs from me. If she tells me explicitly, I can understand it perfectly well, and I can empathize with her. But if not, I'm lost.

That's why it was so exhausting for the first 13 years of our relationship because she wanted me to read her mind, and I can't. Now that I look back in time, I realize that it's always been me because I just don't get it. That was probably the most important thing for me to internalize and understand.

We try not to be mad at the same time. We used to fight a lot, and I found it very tormenting. I try to be a romantic because I had this model that I'd gotten from pop culture that relationships are supposed to be intense. But now, let me put it this way, I've learned to pick my battles. That's the best way to put it. In the past, I used to fight about everything and anything, especially because I'm so stubborn. That's the best way we've been able to deal with it.

SOCIAL CHALLENGES: I fake it. That's basically it. I tend to fake interest in stuff like sports or chit chat among my colleagues. If they're watching a certain movie or series on Netflix or whatever, then it's like, "Oh really?" to get into a conversation. The less time I spend talking about subjects that don't interest me, the better it is for me.

Another thing is I tend to be very blunt, and people don't like that. So I'm always either asking permission to be blunt or asking for forgiveness because I was so blunt. But still, I have the respect of my colleagues, I think. I have very few friends among my colleagues. I have a few friends among my ex-students. I think that if there's mutual respect, there is always something interesting to find about the other person. There's usually enough to build a relationship on, whether it's professional or personal.

What have been some of the low points in your relationship?

It's always up and down. It's never been perfect, and I don't expect it to be. One of the low points was when my wife wanted to have a baby. We tried, but it didn't happen. We even considered adoption and surrogacy, but it didn't make sense to us in the end. One of the specialists we consulted with said, "Well, you want to have a baby with the person you love because you love that person." If the point is to have a baby, then there's a dozen ways to do it. If you focus on it and you have enough money and patience, you will get a baby. But the point is—do you want a baby by any means or because you love your partner and that's why you want to have their baby specifically? Processing it this way made sense to us, and we stopped. We just stopped. I think it's been a lot more difficult for her, and I think that was one of the lowest points in our relationship.

When her dad died, that was also a low point. That happened like nine years ago or so, and it was hard. Really hard, because she is the youngest in her family, and she was very close with her dad. He was very ill, and he passed away after a bad accident. I think that was extremely difficult for her, and it was very difficult for me to be there for her. I have to intellectualize all of it, as it doesn't come naturally to me to be there for people. I'm always in my head, and that's a big place. That's a very big place, and kind of lonely.

I'm a diabetic. When I was diagnosed with type-2 diabetes, that was a challenge, but we've been able to deal with it over the years. Sometimes I just don't care and don't take care of myself. That's why she's always worried about me, and she should be.

A few days ago, she fell in the shower, and nothing really bad happened, but it could've been very bad. It was difficult for me to empathize with her. I really don't know how she feels unless she describes it to me.

If you had a magic wand and could wish away one of your marital challenges or a partner's trait, what would it be?

The bickering. I would get rid of it right away. That exhausts me.

Relationship Strengths

What are some of your relational strengths and highlights?

Loyalty—we're very loyal to each other. I'm not a saint, but still I try to be loyal and to be there for her as much as I can, regardless of my shortcomings. I know that I'm not fun to be with or to be around because I have a different sense of humor, but my wife gets me. When we laugh, which is not often because I don't tend to laugh very often (and, I mean, really laugh), it's so good.

Getting married was awesome. I hate weddings, except mine. It was a good one. I know that I probably wasn't the perfect groom. I always tell her that the best wedding I've ever been to is ours. I'm good at what I do, so I've earned certain recognition, especially as a photographer, so I'm at a very good level. We've shared the successes as a couple. My best friend from childhood passed away suddenly a few years ago, and my wife was there for me. She's my rock.

What do you love most about your relationship?

I love that we have learned to love

ARMCHAIR CONVERSATIONS ON LOVE AND AUTISM

each other better. Not more, but *better*, especially by learning about ASD. It was eye-opening.

Intimacy

Is empathy or emotional reciprocity an issue in your relationship?

EMPATHY: Totally. We're always, always challenged by it. I can't be empathic if I don't understand it in my head. So, yeah, it doesn't come naturally to me. Not sure how neurotypical couples deal with it, but we're talking about my marriage, so yes.

EMOTIONAL RECIPROCITY: Yes it is. My wife's a giver in that way. She always gives more, and I appreciate it and tell her that all the time. But I also tell her, "I don't want to fake it with you. I could have been faking empathy with you, but that's exhausting, so I don't wanna do it at home. If you give me the chance to understand what's going on and explain it to me in the clearest possible way, I'll be able to be there for you. Probably not in the way that you expect me to, but I will." So sometimes she tells me, "I just want you to listen me out and hold me." And I do it, even if it doesn't make sense to me. I'm working on being more aware, and I think it's working. Not aimlessly, but working in a way so that I become more aware and present, as often my mind tends to drift away. Especially when I don't find something interesting. Sometimes the conversations I'm having with my wife are not interest-

ing for me. Sometimes I just realize that I'm nodding, but I'm not really listening.

Does ASD cause challenges in the area of sex/intimacy?

Let's just say it hasn't been a walk in the park. It's been very challenging. I think that we've made our peace with it, at least on my side, but it was always, always challenging. Intimacy is difficult for me, not just sexually, but on all the other levels too. To be intimate, you have to be relaxed and stress-free. But as my natural state is usually so tense, it's very difficult for me to get intimate.

What makes you feel loved and cared for by your partner, and what makes your partner feel loved and cared for by you?

FEELING CARED FOR: Wow, that's easy—basically everything she's done and everything she does for me! She tries to be as understanding as she possibly can. She tends to my basic needs because, as I told you before, I forget to take care of myself because of my obsessions. So she's always worried about if I'm getting enough sleep or if I'm eating well.

Being with other autistic people, people from my planet, I've heard all the stories. I'm just like, "Oh man, this guy is only eating potato chips and drinking coke because his wife or his partner gave up." My wife, she always cares, even if she's mad and even if I drive her crazy, she always cares. She's so understanding and the

108

opposite of me. I mean, if she can cope with *this*...

CARING FOR HOPE: The small things, I think it's so much of that. The little things count more. The problem is that, being a creature of habit, if she tells me, "I like blue," then it all turns blue until she tells me, "Now it's red," and that throws me off balance. If she doesn't tell me anything different, it will be blue forever. That's frustrating because I'm always stuck in the previous moment, so I need directions all the time.

I need insight and guidance all the time. Regarding stupid things like the household chores or the way she likes her carrots to be or to let her sleep in late. I'm an early bird because I don't sleep a lot. Four to five hours, then I'm good to go. It's all about negotiating, as I always need directions. I need her to tell me what she wants from me. Sometimes I don't do it because I don't want to do it until I understand why, and then when I understand her reasons, it's like, "Oh, it totally makes sense." Then I do it. But then, of course, something else pops up, and we have to deal with that all over again. It's exhausting being myself, but it's definitely more exhausting for her to deal with me.

Finances

Describe your economic situation. Does your financial situation impact your relationship in any way?

Now she makes a lot more money than me, because I'm a teacher. As I told you, I'm an expert in the admissions process and so on. But that's been frozen for almost a year now, as we've lost a lot of students who've dropped out of college, so I don't have enough classes to teach. Being a freelancer has been a real challenge and stressful because my wife wasn't happy with me not making enough money. Even today, things get out of hand, and we start fighting if that comes up. That is one of the issues, even though I think of myself as a very good house husband, and I don't have any issues with that. However, sometimes I do the household chores my way because I think it's better that way when she was always at the office. Now that we share the same space 24/7, she realizes why I do things my way, but our differences are hard. We're doing well, but I was doing much better a couple of years ago. A lot better, but that's how things are now.

Yes, but I don't make enough money, even though I'm working more these days. As a teacher, I find the digital platform more challenging. My wife understands my work situation, but it's all about the way we were raised. It's not as bad as it used to be, but the gender roles in Latin America are still polarized, so it's difficult.

I also suffer when I don't find the work I do interesting. I can go through the motions, but it's draining in every sense. In the past, I used to work on stuff that I didn't really like, and even though I tried to make it interesting to me, it was very difficult. My wife feels that the job you do is the job you do, but I'm like, "No, if I don't understand why I'm doing it, then I'm not going to do it."

She saves as much as she can, and I try to give her all the money I'm able to because she's a lot better at administering that money than I am. I trust her totally. She pays my credit cards on time because I tend to forget those things. She's aware of many other issues that I tend to ignore. She's a lot more organized than I am in that regard.

Support System

Do you have friends individually and as a couple?

I have very few friends. I have a lot of acquaintances because of the work that I do. People know me and my work. I'm not famous in any way, but I'm very good at what I do. Over the years, some of my friends have become her friends, too, but not the other way around. Maybe because I don't tend to find my wife's friends interesting. Perhaps my crowd is more colorful in a way, and that keeps me motivated. So that's the way things are.

Do you have a spiritual practice? Does that impact your relationship?

Definitely. I was raised a Christian. My wife, she wasn't, but she became a Christian in her early twenties

I think. It's worked for us in many ways because we have this common ground to build on. Even though I'm not a religious person, I think that religion is interesting for me in many ways. Psychologically for example. Anthropologically, I think it's interesting also. My grandfather was a pastor, so in a way that's what we learned from the crib. Then you start asking questions, but still many things make sense. I find that interesting and valuable of course, especially in times of distress when you have something to hold onto. I think that's interesting and important too.

Being in an ND Relationship

Do you feel that the challenges in ND relationships are unique?

Yeah. It's coping with the unexpected. Our brains are wired differently, so differently that I know that we'll never ever be able to understand each other in the same way that neurotypical couples do. However, I think hard work has made us better people—better versions of ourselves—not only for each other, but also more understanding of other people. I think that's probably the best thing that we've gotten from the diagnosis.

Based on your experiences, how informed do you find people are about ASD and ND marriage/relationships?

They don't have a clue! They don't

have a clue because they base most of their knowledge on pop culture like the *Big Bang Theory* or *Atypical*. So they think if they watch Sheldon Cooper that they get us, and they find it cute, like, "Oh, that's so funny! He's so cute." But if they really knew what's going on in my head, they would be scared.

I haven't come out of the closet—the autism closet—with lots of people, including my mom, but I did it with some very special friends. I disclosed, not to make amends, but to let them know that it wasn't their fault in many ways. I have these two girls who were my assistants at different times when they were my students in college. We did excellent work together as photographers, but I know I was a nightmare to work with. It must have just felt crazy to them. I apologized to them and said, "I know I was a nightmare, and I'm sorry for that, but it's because of ASD." I found that very liberating, too. I don't do it with everyone.

In therapy, it was suggested that I tell my college students from the start. So I started disclosing a year ago, very casually and not going into any details, but explaining that this is how my brain works. I say, "It doesn't mean I don't have a sense of humor, but I don't tend to fake it. If I think that something is interesting or funny I will tell you, but I'm not the joking type of teacher. That doesn't mean I'm angry all the time or that I'm boring, but just be aware that my brain is different. It's wired differently."

It has worked like a charm in many classes. My students are very accepting of it because they realize, "Hey, he's not really angry all the time; he just doesn't really laugh that much." It's a matter of being respectful of each other. I don't joke in any offensive way with my students, especially my female students. I find it sad that that happens in classrooms, and I think it's a kind of bullying, in a way. I was bullied as a child, so I know how it feels. I think that's very common for those with ASD. So I think my students appreciate that. I don't make fun of them or mock them even though lots of teachers do that. Even though they find me a little bit awkward and geeky, they tend to respect me because I respect them too.

Ah, well, if my wife doesn't smother me with a pillow in my sleep and if she keeps on forgiving me and loving me despite my flaws, I think we can be together forever. But, again, that's the romantic in me.

I think that lots of them have even started to learn more about ASD. They tend to identify some characteristics in themselves or others. They're like, "Hey, maybe that's why it's like that. That's why we've got this problem. That's why we relate to him in that way." I always tell them, "When in doubt, get diagnosed." It's the best way to do it because people tend to Google everything. "Go to a professional, take the test, do the interviews, and it will make your life easier." I have noticed some of my students being on the spectrum. I think it makes me a better teacher because I know how to treat them better now. I think they appreciate that.

What is your perspective on being in an ND relationship?

Ah, well, if my wife doesn't smother me with a pillow in my sleep and if she keeps on forgiving me and loving me despite my flaws, I think we can be together forever. But, again, that's the romantic in me. So far, we've been doing it for 15 years—18 actually, so maybe there is a good future. You can only do this one day at a time. Even though it's a cliché, it's really like one hour at a time, one waking hour at a time. That's the only way to do this.

What are the positives of being in an ND relationship?

It's never boring. It's never boring. We're always dealing with new stuff, and I'm always discovering new things to obsess with. My wife, she's interested in more things too because of that. We're always learning from each other, and it's been fun. Not like fun haha, but interesting.

Couples Counseling

Have you pursued couples counseling? Was it useful?

I think couples counseling has been useful because it helps my wife understand what's going on in my head. And realize that it's not her fault, that it has nothing to do with her. Because even though I think that I have this way with words sometimes, it's not easy for me to verbalize what's going on in my mind. Therefore, going to therapy and doing the readings is important for me to gain insight.

My wife is also in a spouse support group, which I call Desperate Housewives. They're all married to ASD, and they just realize, "Hey yeah, that's happened to me too. How do you deal with it? How do you cope with it?" I'm not like that. I'm very self-contained in that way. I find many of the ASD traits are interesting, but not interesting enough for me to belong to an ASD support group where everyone is on the spectrum. That doesn't make sense to me. I'm not sociable. I think that therapy works only if you're willing to do the work.

Concluding Thoughts

10-Point Marital Happiness Scale™

I think that there's a twist to this question. It's never fixed. The number is not fixed. So we go from 10 to 0 and from 0 to 5 and from 5 to 7, depending on multiple aspects and details and circumstances. So I don't think that I can put a number to it. It's all very relative. But there's this verse in the Bible (and I'm paraphrasing, of course)—it says something like, "Love will cover most flaws." It makes sense to me. Sometimes we're not in the mood for it; sometimes, especially now, it's very challenging. I would love to say that we're going to be together forever, but I know that it's very challenging. My wife is not happy with me and with the situation all the time, and neither am I, so I don't think that I could put a number to it. Especially at this point in life, at this point in our relationship after 18 years of knowing each other. If you're 15 or 16 years old and fall in love for the first time, I think that you're living in another world.

Would you say you're in love with Hope?

I am in love with my wife in my flawed autistic way. I know that my wife had a lot of expectations when we got involved romantically, and I know that I probably haven't met most of those. So she's been coping with it forever. For me, it's basically realizing that life is not something out of a movie or something out of a novel. It's hard work. I think it's even harder when you're neurodiverse and come from different planets. It's basically a cultural thing. It's like being married to someone who comes from a completely different country, with a completely different language, with a completely different set of beliefs. That's how I see it.

Do you think your relationship will go the distance?

I think it has already gone the distance. And we've been in this for, I don't know, for 15 years, without knowing what was really going on. So now that we do know, I think that we have better tools to deal with it. I think that if we love each other not only enough but better, I think that we can still go the distance, wherever that is. But, again, it's all a matter of both wanting to. We have this expression in Spanish, and it's basically, "If one doesn't want to, then two can't do it."

MEET HOPE

Hope (she/her/hers) is a 51-year-old, heterosexual, Caucasian female who lives with her husband. She has a BA in marketing, and she works as an associate manager.

Please describe any short- or long-term past romantic relationships

Two years before I met my husband, I had a six-month relationship. At the beginning, it seemed like a fairy tale because I was living in California for a short period at the time. He said he wanted to propose to me and come back to Mexico with me, but he never did. I did return to Mexico. Unfortunately, he never fell deeply in love with me, and that was so sad and disappointing for me.

> I would say that being in a neurodiverse relationship helps promote an inclusive and diverse world. We complement each other. We are also breaking stereotypes about this image of what the "perfect couple" or the "perfect relationship" looks like.

Diagnosis Journey

Did you receive any special education, support, or therapy while you were growing up?

Yes, I received some therapies due to some learning issues in the fifth grade.

Do you or your partner have an official or self-diagnosis of ASD?

My husband was diagnosed with ASD in February 2018 at Asperger México by Tessy Villalobos, and we started couples therapy with her.

How accepting do you feel you and your partner are about the diagnosis?

For me, it was very liberating and healing to know about the diagnosis.

At the beginning of the diagnosis, Oscar found it very liberating. But after a while, it was a bitter-sweet experience—a loss or grieving process I would say.

What advice would you give to someone who's just discovering either their or their partner's ASD?

I would say, read a lot of books about ASD. Couples counseling is very important. Finding a specialized therapist/counselor in ASD is a blessing! Unfortunately, in Mexico, it is so difficult to find a therapist that knows about ASD. Love and care for yourself first—your body, mind, and heart. Have moments only by yourself that you really enjoy and that make you happy. For emotional breakdowns/meltdowns, the best way to cope is: run! He/she/they will recover when you come back.

Anything else you'd like to say about the diagnosis?

The diagnosis equipped us with the correct way to deal with our marital problems. He decided who to share the diagnosis with—basically some friends, his brother, and his sister.

His brother had a bad reaction when my husband told him two years ago, but now they have improved their communication, so it's better. My family doesn't know about it yet.

Relationship Challenges

What are the main challenges in your relationship?

I would say that our main challenges are communication, attending parties, and family gatherings. Other social events can also be major issues. And I would say Oscar's meltdowns—those are painful.

Do you struggle with executive functioning, sensory sensitivities, communication problems, and/or social challenges?

EXECUTIVE FUNCTIONING: Yes, I take care of all of the administrative tasks in our family. I manage our money and take care of household service payments. So, yes, there's definitely an issue with executive functioning for him in a major way.

SENSORY SENSITIVITIES: Oscar has auditory hypersensitivity and experiences sound overloads. Noisy environments easily make him desperate and angry. We deal with it by avoiding going to crowded and noisy places. Also visually, his eyes are extremely sensitive. Sunlight affects him, and how do we deal with it? When we go outside, we don't walk under the sun, and at home, we close the blinds.

I would say, read a lot of books about ASD. Couples counseling is very important. Finding a specialized therapist/ counselor in ASD is a blessing!

COMMUNICATION PROBLEMS: Our communication issues are mostly due to the fact that I assume that he knows how I am feeling all the time. So the main strategy I use is to try not to do that. I try to tell him in a very direct, assertive, clear manner how I'm feeling and what I want. I have to be very, very specific. Another issue is that sometimes I perceive his speech to be very direct and rude, and I feel offended. But he tends not to understand why I might be irritated or offended by him. So I have to explain very clearly why and how what he said has affected me. That helps him understand my point of view and why I'm thinking the way I am.

SOCIAL CHALLENGES: The social challenges of ASD are hard for Oscar. Being invited to social events like weddings, parties, family meetings, etc. is difficult because they make him feel very anxious. Social interactions with people who he doesn't consider either interesting or intelligent or with whom he doesn't share a common passion or hobby make him feel bored and disappointed, which then makes me feel very uncomfortable.

One strategy that we use to cope is that we try to prepare for these events in advance. We will discuss the event we've been invited to in great detail, which may be considered odd by other people's standards. We try to figure out the place, number of estimated attendees, number of hours it will go on, etc. We discuss the best way to go there, whether that's together or separately, in order for both of us to be happy, enjoy the event, and be comfortable. We mostly try to only say yes or organize social events as a couple with people that we both find interesting. When that's not fully possible, he has to fake interest.

What have been some of the low points in your relationship?

Our emotional breakdowns have been very difficult. Also, another low point is the relationships and communication with my family. He doesn't like my family, and it makes me feel disappointed. Our communication skills challenge us both. And also, he has a hard time with changes in the daily schedule.

I had to really deal with not having children, which for me especially was so challenging. Also, our separation from each other in 2013, when I left our home for nine months as I just couldn't cope in the relationship.

Dealing with mid-life crisis is something else we've had to deal with as well.

If you had a magic wand and could wish away one of your marital challenges or a partner's trait, what would it be?

Definitely the emotional breakdowns.

Relationship Strengths

What are some of your relational strengths and highlights?

I would say loyalty, fidelity, deep love, honesty, and our full commitment to each other.

The ASD diagnosis was a highlight in our relationship, as learning about it has transformed our relationship for the better. It's been life-changing for us.

What do you love most about your relationship?

I feel very confident, knowing that he is honest with me. For that reason, I think that he is the most secure person in the world for me.

Intimacy

Is empathy or emotional reciprocity an issue in your relationship?

EMPATHY: He can be empathic with me based on his own personal past experiences. For example, when my dad passed away 12 years ago, he was able to comfort and accompany me lovingly because when he was 24 years old, his dad passed away. So he had that experience to relate to and could draw on it in order to understand what I was feeling. If it's a new situation or something he does not have any experience with, he is not empathic. He gets angry and sometimes even has emotional breakdowns.

EMOTIONAL RECIPROCITY: I think that in the past, emotional reciprocity on both ends was definitely missing. Before the diagnosis, I didn't tell him about my troubles or situations, thinking that I didn't want to trigger his anxiety, which in turn would cause me to feel overloaded, tired, and alone. Now, after counseling sessions, I've learned to share emotions with my improved communication skills. For example, I ask him for help in specific tasks, establish expectations, and set responsibilities.

Does ASD cause challenges in the area of sex/intimacy?

Labels and romantic expectations make him feel nervous, so we did set our own way to express and share intimate life.

What makes you feel loved and cared for by your partner, and what makes your partner feel loved and cared for by you?

FEELING CARED FOR: I would say his genuine interest in my things. Being listened to and feeling supported by him.

Also, his unconditional loyalty and him being completely faithful to me. When he tells me, "I love you," or "You are so beautiful."

CARING FOR OSCAR: In some situations, literally, I need to leave him alone! Also, it's important that I tell him about my specific needs and my expectations because he can't read my thoughts. Being loving and spending time with him doing things that we both enjoy is also something that makes him happy.

Finances

Describe your economic situation. Does your financial situation impact your relationship in any way?

We both work. I have worked for 13 years in a company with a stable salary, and my income is higher than his. He is a professor and a photographer, and he gets a different salary each semester depending on the schedule. The pandemic and the emergency situation that has evolved because of it has been very difficult and stressful for him, especially adapting to the new online class format. Also, my husband, his brother, and his sister provide financial support to his mother (my mother-in-law). So we've definitely coped with some economic issues during our relationship. Sometimes it's caused conflicts, but fortunately we have improved on understanding how to manage the money. We also have learned to communicate better than in the past.

The economic and money issues have been problematic in our relationship. Each of us has a job, but sometimes I feel all of the responsibility of economic life. This is mostly because I feel that we are often not on the same page on finances and how to manage our money.

Support System

What support systems do you and your partner have?

We do have professional support in the form of our therapist and the support groups for NS wives. On the personal front, there are some friends who know about the diagnosis, and that's useful to have their support. We also have our church, my brother, and my sister-in-law.

Do you have friends individually and as a couple?

Yes, we have friends both as a couple and individually. We have friends as a couple, and they are mostly couples that we enjoy hanging out with and can talk about common interests with. Our individual friends, we hang out with on our own. He meets his friends, both women and men, by himself, and I meet my friends and family by myself. This really works for us, is so fun, and makes us both happy.

Do you have a spiritual practice? Does that impact your relationship?

Christian. I feel like having the same spiritual practice is very useful to get strength and encouragement to deal with the differences and challenges of a neurodiverse relationship.

Being in an ND Relationship

Do you feel that the challenges in ND relationships are unique?

I think so, because I have some neurotypical couples as friends, and I realize that they do not have the same troubles as us. But they cope with infidelity, loss of communication, and dishonesty.

Based on your experiences, how informed do you find people are about ASD and ND marriage/relationships?

There's not really a lot of information available, and people are not really aware about ASD.

What is your perspective on being in an ND relationship?

My perspective on being in a neurodiverse relationship is that opposites attract each other, so Oscar and I are like that. Our mantra is, "You have what I am missing, and I have what you are missing."

What are the positives of being in an ND relationship?

I would say that being in a neurodiverse relationship helps promote an inclusive and diverse world. We complement each other. We are also breaking stereotypes about this image of what the "perfect couple" or the "perfect relationship" looks like. It can be a successful relationship if both make the commitment to deal with the differences and challenges of being a neurodiverse couple.

What advice would you give to people who are in an ND relationship?

A neurodiverse relationship is a journey of lots of patience, deep love, and tolerance. It is worth the effort. Don't give up!

Couples Counseling

Have you pursued couples counseling? Was it useful?

Yes. After the diagnosis, we started to have couples therapy. It was so useful, and we are so blessed to have the best therapist in the world! My husband was comfortable and listened to her carefully. He is not as convinced about the benefit of therapy as I am, so now I continue counseling by myself. However, I share with him some of the issues that I discuss in my sessions, and he's open to hearing about it and still taking it to heart.

Concluding Thoughts

10-Point Marital Happiness Scale™

Now I can say 8. But before diagnosis, I felt very confused and frustrated, and, sometimes, I thought about getting a divorce.

Would you say that you're in love with Oscar?

Yes, I am in love.

Do you think your relationship will go the distance?

Now, yes! Because we are improving our marriage a lot and working on our differences.

CHAPTER 6

Leo & Roy

Aligned at Our Base Level
Together Three Years

INTRODUCING LEO AND ROY

*T*his story breaks multiple stereotypes all at once! It's a love story between two males, Leo and Roy, and Leo identifies as asexual. This is so unusual because it flies in the face of what is often assumed, that gay relationships are mostly about sex. Roy explains, "When we started our relationship, that was a little confusing to me. Not concerning, but just like, 'I don't know what this is, and how can I be in a relationship with someone who is asexual?' Learning about it was really cool and fascinating, so we are able to navigate and appreciate that." Indeed, Leo and Roy's relationship encompasses so much more than physical intimacy! Roy goes on to relate that, "I think there's an advantage to having this intersectionality of ASD, queer, and being in a neurodiverse relationship because I think it helps us with having empathy toward a broader human condition."

In some ways, Leo breaks the mold of typical ASD-related struggles. Even though he is the autistic one, he has the stronger financial skills of the two. Roy admits, "I would say that ASD influences our finances in a positive way. It is an area that Leo is more skilled in than I am, and he sees a place for him to help—which I appreciate!" Also, Leo is strong on empathy, another area that autistic people sometimes struggle with. Roy notices, "Leo, especially, is very empathic. That is one of his superpowers. I've learned from him in a number of ways in terms of empathy. It's super cool to hear him ask questions or interact with other people, including my friends."

Leo's honesty about his difficult diagnostic journey will resonate with readers. He admits, "Yeah, it was really hard and frustrating to get the diagnosis. I felt like I had this clear understanding of what was going on in the world for the first time ever and was being told over and over again that what I was seeing wasn't true. It felt like medical gaslighting." He had to go to three professionals before he finally met with me and received the ASD diagnosis that matched his internal experience.

Aside from their individual talents, you can see their complementary strengths coming into play when they help each other. Both partners focus on giving to the other in order to lift one another up, rather than leading authoritatively in the traditional manner. For example, Roy responds to Leo with, "I'm on this journey with you. How can I be a part of this? How can I help you?... What's my role in this? How can I support you?"

Many ND partners fear that they are doomed to disconnection or short-lived relationships. Leo offers much-needed assurance: "I think that there are people who hear the word 'autism' and they freak out. But it's not too hard to find someone who's reasonable and is willing to work together. I definitely think that neurodiverse partnerships are possible." According to Leo, success in an ND relationship is more dependent on the willingness to grow and learn, and less dependent on someone's neurological identification.

MEET LEO

Leo (he/him/his) is a 28-year-old, queer, asexual, white male. He has an official ASD diagnosis, and he works for a food company, as well as working on a master's degree in global food law. He lives in the northeastern part of the United States with his partner Roy and their dog, Golden Nugget.

Please describe any short- or long-term past romantic relationships

I had a couple of little relationships in high school with girls. I grew up in a pretty conservative area, and that was what was accepted. So I had a couple quick relationships there.

I think that we're just aligned at our base level. And I think that, as a pair, we make a good team, being creative and making things exciting and fun. I think both of us are "servant leaders..." So I think that, with the two of us together, we have the power to help build each other up.

In college, I started dating men. I had a relationship with a coworker at a summer job that lasted six months.

And then post-college, I dated some-one for seven months, and that was a challenging relationship. It was not healthy.

How did you meet?

We met online. I took a year off of dating after that harmful relation-ship. After that year, I kind of figured out that I was happy being alone. But I wanted to make some friends who were queer near where I was living. So I was looking on Grindr, the lo-cation-based queer space. When Roy and I met online, the two of us really hit it off. We had great conversations. I remember being excited to get off of work to talk with him.

I communicate best through text, so I always kind of put off that ini-tial meeting because it's scary for me. With Roy, I knew that I shouldn't and couldn't put it off for too long. So pretty soon after our online intro-duction, we decided to meet in per-son at a coffee shop right near my apartment.

When I showed up, he hadn't ar-rived yet. But a couple of my friends were there so I felt like, "Ah, this is a lot to handle." It was wintertime, and when he walked into the coffee shop, he had this huge white winter hat on that was just amazing! I don't know—it was a loud piece of clothing, but it was also perfectly right. I forget what the first thing he said was, but I re-member thinking that his voice was not what I was expecting at all. So it was a deep connection right away.

Diagnosis Journey

Did you receive any special education, support, or therapy while you were growing up?

No, I did not, as I was diagnosed late.

Do you or your partner have an official or self-diagnosis of ASD?

Yeah, shortly after the pandemic be-gan, I started to realize that I was on the spectrum and that I had ADHD. I started the process of trying to get diagnosed. I had a psych evaluation, and they told me that I wasn't on the spectrum. They couldn't even diag-nose me with ADHD. Then I did an-other evaluation for ADHD and was able to get that diagnosed. After that, I did another autism evaluation, and they told me that they wouldn't diag-nose me either. Then I went to Eva, and she was finally able to give me the official diagnosis for ASD.

How accepting do you feel you and your partner are about the diagnosis?

Oh, I am fully on board! Roy agrees too.

What advice would you give to someone who's just discovering either their own or their partner's ASD?

It can be overwhelming when just discovering ASD. Instead of look-ing at ASD as a problem, it's better to break down how to manage the relationship with the specific ASD traits your partner or you have. You can take a look at the various pieces—like sensory sensitivities—and what needs to be tweaked in order to deal with any challenges. That's a much easier approach that I think can benefit people. It's important to focus on the concrete things, such as making the accommodations needed for what they are, rather than on the emotional baggage that autism brings with it.

Anything else you'd like to say about the diagnosis?

Yeah, it was really hard and frustrating to get the diagnosis. I felt like I had this clear understanding of what was going on in the world for the first time ever and was being told over and over again that what I was seeing wasn't true. It felt like medical gaslighting. It was the strangest thing, and it affected me really deeply.

I've always been aware of autism stuff. Over the last couple of years, I realized that I would look at autistic peers and observe their behavior to learn how to mask. So it definitely was something that was always in my mind. I don't know what really brought me to it when the pandemic started, but it prompted me to start my diagnosis journey then.

Relationship Challenges

What are the main challenges in your relationship?

I'd say we struggle with communication. I think I struggle with communicating little things. It's hard for me to know what to share and when. I think that lack of information can kind of turn into frustration. Thankfully, I think both of us moderate our emotions pretty well and don't blame or dwell too much. I definitely struggle with showing affection. I guess you could lump that under communication, but I think that, specifically, I struggle with romantic gestures and that sort of thing. I guess maybe sex would be another challenge.

Do you struggle with executive functioning, sensory sensitivities, communication problems, and/or social challenges?

EXECUTIVE FUNCTIONING: Yeah, I struggle with planning and getting things together in time.

SENSORY SENSITIVITIES: I don't really like kissing. That's something that's always been really hard for me.

COMMUNICATION PROBLEMS: Yeah. For a little while, we had scheduled weekly meetings, which was really great. We probably should start doing that again. Sometimes we'll communicate via text, even if we're right next to each other. I guess I have started being more direct with questions that I have and stuff like that. Whereas in the past, I would've masked to pretend I knew what was going on, even if I really didn't. So now we're learning to communicate more about things that I might not really understand or things I might have questions about.

SOCIAL CHALLENGES: I feel like a strategy that I use is scheduling automated recurring meetings with people to talk. That way I'm not overwhelmed by constantly feeling like I should be reaching out to people or sending messages to plan a call or a get-together. That's the only conscious thing that I've done thus far to make these social challenges less stressful.

What have been some of the low points in your relationship?

The pandemic has been really hard. There was a move in the middle of the pandemic. I was not doing very well, and Roy had to do most of the heavy lifting. That was just a time with a lot of stress and tension.

If you had a magic wand and could wish away one of your marital challenges or a partner's trait, what would it be?

I don't know if there's anything that needs to be wished away. We definitely have communication trouble, but it feels possible to work on it with him. There's nothing that's distressing enough to want it wished away, I think.

Relationship Strengths

What are some of your relational strengths and highlights?

RELATIONAL STRENGTHS: I think that we're just aligned at our base level. And I think that, as a pair, we make a good team, being creative and making things exciting and fun. I think both of us are "servant leaders." I'm not sure if you're familiar with that term. It's leadership that's based on uplifting people, rather than leading in the traditional way. So I think that, with the two of us together, we have the power to help build each other up.

HIGHLIGHTS: Going to the island that Roy loves so much. Also, witnessing him holding services each morning in this beautiful chapel there. It was amazing to be there for him and see this beloved community gathering around him. It was a really lovely week. So that was definitely a highlight.

What do you love most about your relationship?

I love how playful our relationship is. Roy's always down to be goofy, which is great. He also has such an appreciation for the magic that children bring, which is just a lot of fun to witness.

Intimacy

Is empathy or emotional reciprocity an issue in your relationship?

EMPATHY: I don't think so, as both of us are very empathetic people. I'd say there are definitely difficulties with "theory of mind"—blind spots more than lack of empathy. There's a difference between missing something and accidentally stepping on somebody's toes, and not caring about them. I think there's a lot of empathy between us.

> Being asexual, I knew early on in the relationship that I would not be able meet Roy's or anyone else's sexual needs. I didn't want the expectation that I needed to meet his sexual needs, and so I made sure that he knew that.

EMOTIONAL RECIPROCITY: That's definitely something I struggle with. I struggle with knowing what to share and when. What's too much? What's appropriate? That's definitely a tricky thing for me.

Does ASD cause challenges in the area of sex/intimacy?

Being asexual, I knew early on in the relationship that I would not be able to meet Roy's or anyone else's sexual needs. I didn't want the expectation that I needed to meet his sexual needs, and so I made sure that he knew that. We had a chat about that early on in our relationship.

What makes you feel loved and cared for by your partner, and what makes your partner feel loved and cared for by you?

I think food is a big way that Roy likes to show love and appreciation. He often makes me breakfasts or nice little cozy meals. He's very thoughtful like that, which makes me feel loved.

I think the way that I like to show him love... I'm thinking about the love language of acts of service. I think that's where I try to show my appreciation for him. I've noticed that financial stuff is not his strong suit, and helping him with that I hope makes him feel loved.

Finances

Describe your economic situation. Does your financial situation impact your relationship in any way?

I work. Roy is a student, and he also has a student job. I'm sure the answer is that finances do affect our relationship, but I think that the way we approach money is collaborative. So that isn't a sticking point between us, at least right now. Any challenges that we face financially, we face them together. We don't use money to try to control or exert power over one another or anything like that. I also have trouble spending money, I guess. Roy has reminded me a couple of times that it's okay to spend money on yourself sometimes.

Student loans are definitely a stressful thing. I think in terms of money, for us it's just keeping ourselves organized. When I think of our relationship long term, I guess that's the stressful part. So we need to plan and organize, looking at the future.

Support System

What support systems do you and your partner have?

We each have friends that we go to for support. We have our families. My brother is a great support system for me. And, of course, we have each other.

Do you have friends individually and as a couple?

Yeah. For Roy, he is connected to this lovely island community off the coast of New Hampshire, so that's where most of his connections come from. My friends are people I've met at school or jobs.

Do you have a spiritual practice? Does that impact your relationship?

Yeah, one of the things that connected Roy and I was our church. We found out early on that we went to the same church, which definitely unified us, being that it's a small faith community.

Parenting

Tell us about yourselves as parents in this relationship

Roy and I are both dog people. When it became obvious during the pandemic that working from home was going to be a possibility for a long time, we decided to get a dog. We picked a little dog because we're in an apartment. Roy was not too keen on the idea of a smaller dog, but they've grown close now. The dog definitely looks to me as its primary caregiver but has also started looking to Roy a little more.

Being in an ND Relationship

Do you feel that the challenges in ND relationships are unique?

I think the answer is "yes," but I don't think it should be. I think that with a lot of the sticking points that I've had with people in the past, a different way of communicating could have helped for sure. Especially clearly communicating intentions and stuff like that.

Based on your experiences, how informed do you find people are about ASD and ND marriage/relationships?

Nobody has any idea what autism is at all. Even the people who claim to be experts!

What is your perspective on being in an ND relationship?

I'm thinking about the year that I took off, when I didn't date, and how I decided I was fine being alone. And meeting Roy was like, "Oh, this is a person I can partner with to do life." I think that there are people who hear the word "autism" and they freak out.

But it's not too hard to find someone who's reasonable and is willing to work together. I definitely think that neurodiverse partnerships are possible.

What are the positives of being in an ND relationship?

I guess post-diagnosis it's really nice to be able to be a little weird without it being a big deal. It seems like there's an understanding between Roy and I that we're not going to make a big deal of little things. So that brings a lot of freedom to both of us to just exist, which means more internal peace.

What advice would you give to people who are in an ND relationship?

I think that the advice I gave before is also helpful here, but I'd like to add one other thing that might be helpful. Sometimes I am a walking contradiction, so it can be confusing to people. If something is true at one point, it may not necessarily be true or apply at a different moment. Also, as far as communication goes, communication via text is usually best, but then all of a sudden that shifts. So I guess it's important to be understanding that people contain multitudes and that ASD can present in a lot of different ways at different moments. Accepting that is important when starting a relationship with a neurodiverse person.

Couples Counseling

Have you pursued couples counseling? Was it useful?

Not yet, but I could see that happening at some point. I'm feeling burnt out by the mental health field right now. I've been seeing therapists since I was in college. Even when I identified the autism myself, it still took me two years to get the help that I wanted. So I don't think Roy and I would be opposed to seeing a couples counselor at some point, but right now that's not where we are.

Concluding Thoughts

10-Point Marital Happiness Scale™

8 or 9. I'm pretty happy with Roy. Relationships—like anything in life—aren't perfect, but I feel really lucky to be on the journey of life with him.

Would you say you're in love with Roy?

Yeah, definitely. As kids, we're fed a lot of romantic information about what love is. But I think it's slightly different from the deep love I have for Roy, which continues to build over time. He's a great person to be around!

Do you think your relationship will go the distance?

Yeah, I think that we are going to be

partnered for a long time. We definitely have similar priorities and visions for the future. It's hard to envision what will happen in life, but I do think that no matter what, the two of us will be part of each other's lives. I'm a person that isn't opposed to polyamory. Not as much for me, but me being asexual, that's one way that I

could see our relationship evolving. So if Roy had sexual needs that he wanted to explore somewhere else, I could see partnerships and relationships happening there. But, regardless, Roy and I are going to be primarily connected as long as both of us are around.

MEET ROY

What I love most about our relationship is that it really is a partnership. There's a lot that we do together, because we enjoy doing things with each other. It's not like I have a separate life and he has a separate life and we just happen to live in the same apartment together. I think we truly share our lives together.

Roy (he/him/his) is a 37-year-old white/non-Hispanic, queer, gay male. He lives with his partner, Leo, and their dog. He is currently studying for his Master's of Divinity and is a full-time student. Leo and Roy have been together for three years. Roy does not identify as being on the spectrum.

Please describe any short- or long-term past romantic relationships

I've had two previous relationships that I would describe as committed relationships. These were more short term in nature. I guess most of my dating history has been using online dating apps and meeting people that way. That's how Leo and I met, as well—similar type of circumstances in terms of the start of the relationship.

How did you meet?

We met through an app—a queer, stereotypical, gay male app. We were both living in the same town, and those apps are generally distance-based. It was like two or three weeks of chatting back and forth on the app, and then we met in person at a little coffee shop. After that, we went on one or two more dates—the typical "go out to eat" sort of thing. Then there was a bit of an interlude when our schedules didn't align. After that, it just sort of picked back up again and has continued since.

Diagnosis Journey

Did you receive any special education, support, or therapy while you were growing up?

I had a tutor in math, but nothing else.

Do you or your partner have an official or self-diagnosis of ASD?

Leo does. I would say it was first a self-diagnosis, and then Eva diagnosed him recently. I didn't know that was a struggle for him and that he had gone through two or three previous professionals.

How accepting do you feel you and your partner are about the diagnosis?

I feel very accepting. As I stated before (I don't know if "skeptical" is the right word), but initially I definitely was like, "Oh, this seems to be a reaction to the world falling apart during the pandemic." Then, realizing it wasn't that, it was like, "I'm on this journey with you. How can I be a part of this? How can I help you?" I definitely took the stance of, "What's my role in this? How can I support you?" His response was, "Maybe you should just learn more about this." Since then, there's been lots of YouTube video sharing, lots of blog shar-

ing, lots of learning about how to be a supportive partner of someone with an ASD diagnosis.

I think he would say that he's very accepting of his diagnosis. He very intentionally sought out the diagnosis, and for him it is life-affirming to have it. So he feels very strongly about it.

What advice would you give to someone who's just discovering either their or their partner's ASD?

The best piece of advice I got from Leo when he was beginning his journey was for me to try to learn as much as I could about it. The nature of a spectrum is that the way people present as autistic isn't going to be the same for everyone. So there is a level of needing to learn the entirety of it in order to have a clear understanding. I would say reading and learning about ASD is key.

Anything else you'd like to say about the diagnosis?

I would say that Leo started his self-discovery journey just as the pandemic was starting. To me, it very much felt like a lot was happening at that point. There was a lot of uncertainty, and I thought, "Oh, this seems like potentially a reaction to this global pandemic where there is so much happening." But then as time progressed, I came to realize, "Oh no, this is definitely not a reaction to the pandemic. This is very real and very much something that he is feeling." I think in regards to the pandemic, time allowed us to digest and process life at a different level. I think that's sort of what sparked his movement to self-diagnose and try to seek a professional diagnosis.

Relationship Challenges

What are the main challenges in your relationship?

I would say communication is one. I think sometimes it's hard to communicate with each other. I think I am saying something; Leo thinks he's hearing something else. Then he will respond, and I'll be like, "That's not what I was saying." I'll try to rephrase it, and he'll be like, "Okay, this is what you're saying." I'll be like, "No, that's actually *also* not what I'm saying." So we can go back and forth like that. I feel like the same happens in reverse, as well. So that can be a challenge.

I think time management is also a challenge, in the sense that I consider myself to be punctual—I like to be on time. Especially when traveling, I like to know our schedule. I like that sort of detail. Leo's more laissez-faire with his approach to time. Early in our relationship, that was a bigger challenge than it is now. When we lived separately and he was coming over, I would prepare dinner. Then it would be hours later that he would show up, and I would've already eaten. So we would get into it, and that took a while to sort out. When

he was first learning about ASD (and I was learning about it too), I was like, "Oh my goodness, this makes so much sense and explains that."

I think another issue became very pronounced when we moved from Minnesota to Boston in the summer. We have our individual stress levels, and then there are things that overwhelm Leo. In the moment, I'm like, "Why is this overwhelming you? I don't understand." So my initial reaction used to be like, "Why aren't you helping?" And then only later, I was able to realize, "Oh okay, this is what's happening."

Do you struggle with executive functioning, sensory sensitivities, communication problems, and/or social challenges?

EXECUTIVE FUNCTIONING: Yeah, there are challenges for both of us. I think we've been balancing each other out for the most part, although recently, I've been slower to fold my clothes and put them away after doing laundry. Leo is not great at cleaning up after he cooks. There are definitely executive functioning things happening between us. Not sure we think of it intentionally, but I think we see that maybe this is a struggle for the other person. We try to pick it up if we can. I know that I sometimes am like, "Oh, the kitchen is messy! Leo used it to cook, and I have to go do something, so I'm not cleaning this up." And then at the same time, I'll come home, and he will have folded and put away my laundry.

Then I'm like, "Oh, you are so much better of a person than me!"

SENSORY SENSITIVITIES: There are sensory issues for both of us. For Leo, he definitely has a reaction to touch. When we're being intimate, there's only so much touch he can put up with, so I try to be mindful of that. There's a level of consent of checking in with him, "Is this okay? How does this feel?" And then he is always honest with where he is at, like, "This is too much" or "I need a break." Or "Just stop touching me." My sensory issues are more around sound. I do not like the sound of eating. We live in a studio apartment where we don't have a lot of space. Leo doesn't keep a normal eating schedule (or one that I would consider normal), so he's often eating in bed when it's 9 pm and we're watching something on TV. I try to cover my ears, and he bought me these ear plugs that I sometimes use.

COMMUNICATION PROBLEMS: Sometimes, we have difficulty understanding each other when we're communicating. I think it becomes stressful when I'm like, "I'm saying this." Then the other person is like, "This is what I'm hearing," and it is definitely not what is being said. We can end up in a spiral, where neither of us is understanding each other. But at the same time, we're each thinking, "I know what the other person is saying, but somehow I can't get there with words."

I think the strategy for this is, "Okay, we're just not going to talk about this for a bit and maybe come back to it." I wouldn't say it's systemized, where we say, "Okay, this is an issue right now; let's pause and meet back in 30 minutes." It's more of, "Okay, it seems like we're shutting down. I'm tuning this out for now. I have school work to do, so I'll talk to you in a little bit." That has always worked. It's not like we don't get into heated arguments, but we're able to come back and discuss things calmly. I think we're both better at communicating through writing, so sometimes even when we're in the same room, we'll text each other. Those are our best moments—the communication is very clear, as the texting makes everything a bit more concrete.

I think when we're in an actual stressful situation, we're very good at communicating to each other. And Leo is very good at checking in about emotion. For example, earlier this year we were flying to Minnesota to visit Leo's family. There was a misunderstanding about the time of the flight, so when we got to the airport, they were like, "Oh, you can't go on the airplane because you got the time wrong." That was a stressful situation because we missed the flight. I think at that moment, we were able to communicate that, "Okay, there was a mistake. Here's what we're going to do, and we will come back tomorrow."

SOCIAL CHALLENGES: I think probably the best example of that is in

ARMCHAIR CONVERSATIONS ON LOVE AND AUTISM

terms of spending time with friends. I don't know—the world is so strange right now, and I think that adds to the dynamic. I think Leo and I are both introverted in a way that makes going out, partying, or spending time with friends a very high-stimulus situation, which isn't what we're interested in. No matter whose friends we're spending time with, I think we're both attuned to wanting a quieter space that isn't obnoxious and super loud.

For Leo, he's very interested in who's going to be present and how much time we're going to be there. I'm also interested in those things, but I am more interested in how many people there will be. I try to have an escape plan in mind, like, "I promise myself I'm going to spend 90 minutes at this thing. Then I'm happy to leave—or maybe I'll be happy to stay. But I want to have a check in with myself at least and then decide from there."

What have been some of the low points in your relationship?

I would say the one that comes to mind is when we were moving this summer. I felt isolated, as if I was doing something by myself, even though it was both of us doing it. I think that would be acknowledged by him, as well. I think that would be a low point.

If you had a magic wand and could wish

away one of your marital challenges or a partner's trait, what would it be?

I think for me, the timeliness issues are the ones that, in the moment, feel the most critical. I think that's the biggest one, even though I think communication is the one that's most constant. I feel like we have a way, not of mitigating it, but of moving through those issues. I think with time-bound things, it's more like I don't have control of the trains or planes. We either have to be there at this time or not, and I feel like that causes unnecessary stress that I would be happy to leave behind.

Relationship Strengths

What are some of your relational strengths and highlights?

RELATIONAL STRENGTHS: I think, as I mentioned earlier, we do a great job with balancing each other out. Kitchen and laundry being an example of that. We each have a strength of recognizing when the other person is struggling a little or when the other person doesn't feel great about doing something.

For example, we both don't really like driving, but Leo feels even more strongly about not driving than I do. So I'll pick up the chore of driving if we need to do that. We currently don't own a car, so that makes it a lot easier. Leo, one of his strengths being financial, likes to not spend a bunch of money. So he does grocery shopping online for us and is really good about choosing the most affordable options. I am the beneficiary of receiving the groceries, and then I do the cooking. I think he appreciates that.

HIGHLIGHTS: For me, one of the things I have recently recognized is that Leo can prioritize me. That sounds very narcissistic, but, for example, last year he was like, "We're going for a month to spend time with your family." That was like, "Oh, that's so amazing that you are prioritizing this! You do not have to do that." He also recognized that I was feeling down about not being able to see my family, and so it was a way for him to help support me.

I think the other thing that I really appreciate about our relationship is Leo's ability to help me see things differently. I don't know if I do the same thing for him, as this is one of our struggles with communication. But later—even if it's later that day or later the next week—I'm like, "Oh, I see what he was thinking now." So I am able to change my perspective on things. That helps with being in school, where I can sit on things and then come back and view things differently—whether they're about our communication or something I'm reading for school. Sometimes my initial reaction is, "That's not what we're talking about, and this isn't really related to what we're discussing."

But then, after having some time, distance, and perspective, I can see how things connect a little more.

What do you love most about your relationship?

What I love most about our relationship is that it really is a partnership. There's a lot that we do together, because we enjoy doing things with each other. It's not like I have a separate life and he has a separate life and we just happen to live in the same apartment together. I think we truly share our lives together.

Intimacy

Is empathy or emotional reciprocity an issue in your relationship?

EMPATHY: Not in a negative way. Leo, especially, is very empathic. That is one of his superpowers. I've learned from him in a number of ways in terms of empathy. It's super cool to hear him ask questions or interact with other people, including my friends. I pick up on that and think, "Oh, I can use this in my work or with other friends, too."

EMOTIONAL RECIPROCITY: I would say we generally do well with that. I am probably the one who is more guarded sometimes. In contrast, when Leo feels like he is not understanding what my emotions are, he tries to ascertain, "What are you thinking or feeling?" So, yeah, I think that's part of growing up in my family situation, where we were not encouraged to be emotive, especially if we had negative emotions. So I'm definitely a little more guarded in that sense.

Does ASD cause challenges in the area of sex/intimacy?

As I mentioned earlier, because of the sensory issues, while there is a level of physical intimacy, there is also a boundary because of Leo's sensory sensitivities. So that exists, but I feel like we are able to communicate about that.

Also, Leo identifies as asexual or as being on the ace spectrum. When we started our relationship, that was a little confusing to me. Not concerning, but just like, "I don't know what this is, and how can I be in a relationship with someone who is asexual?" Learning about it was really cool and fascinating, so we are able to navigate and appreciate that. We can have separate experiences. We're not in a polyamorous or open relationship, but we can do things individually, where I think we both appreciate what the other person is doing.

What makes you feel loved and cared for by your partner, and what makes your partner feel loved and cared for by you?

FEELING CARED FOR: There are a number of things. One of the things I really appreciate about Leo is his ability to navigate complex things (or things that are complex to me) and help me with them. For example, he is really good at understanding financial things. That is not my forte, so something that he does from time to time is budgeting and helping me understand what we can afford. Having him give me those boundaries and not having to feel trapped within them is very helpful.

So he might say, "If you spend this much, then you need to think about this." He also demonstrates good listening skills. This manifests into little gifts from time to time that are based on things I might have said.

He's great at going along with my antics and hijinks. I feel like in improv, there's a lot of that. While I am not an improv actor, I know about it from reading. He basically goes along with things, as we create this little combined world in our heads that we both believe in. He also makes a lot of time for family events and is great at making sure that I get to see my family. When we lived in Minnesota last year, he organized a way for us to come back to New Hampshire for a month to spend time with my family.

CARING FOR LEO: I think time is an important thing for him. Having quality experiences together, even small things. It's not like, "Let's go on a cruise and spend all this money." It's like, "Let's do these really affordable things together." He also appreciates cuddling and low-energy sorts of experiences together. Also the way that we balance and support each other, like I mentioned earlier regarding the laundry and kitchen stuff.

Finances

Describe your economic situation. Does your financial situation impact your relationship in any way?

As a full-time student, I don't work. I have worked in the past, but now I'm on a full scholarship with a statement, so there's a level of security there. Leo works full-time. I was able to save during the early pandemic, and I have a safety net for myself in that way.

I definitely came from a low-income family and had a lot of personal stress around just being able to afford things. I have a lot of student debt. Leo comes from a background that's well-off. He has no student debt, and he has a safety net in that way. I think for me, there was a period of time where I was like, "Am I causing stress in the relationship? I have these financial issues. How is that going to be perceived?" I feel like I built up the stress around this, but Leo actually took this very well. He was very much like, "I can help you take care of this. I understand it." So I appreciated that a lot. For me, sometimes when interacting with Leo's family, there's a feeling of, "Oh, I don't fit in." In my family, we couldn't afford things, and his family may not always be able to relate to that. Not that it was directly asked or anything

like that, but there's a certain level of expectation, like, "Oh yeah, we can afford this. This is what we do." For me, it's hard to know what that feels like.

I would say that ASD influences our finances in a positive way. It is an area that Leo is more skilled in than I am, and he sees a place for him to help—which I appreciate! As I said, early on in the relationship, I think I may have viewed it as a negative (as in, *my* negative attribute). I was worried and concerned that it would impact our relationship, but I think it has only been positive in terms of our partnership.

It is one of the ways that Leo is supportive, and I think of it as being one of his attributes. I don't know if that's part of being on the spectrum, but it's definitely a benefit for me.

Support System

What support systems do you and your partner have?

We both have a network of family and friends, in terms of emotional-social support. Leo definitely has the family money safety net to fall back on. That's not my truth.

Do you have friends individually and as a couple?

We do, yeah. I would say there's a lot of mixing of friends. Being in Boston right now, my family and close friends are geographically closer to us. So when we go out to something, it's generally with my friends, but they are very much friends with Leo, as well. But primarily, they are people that I interact with individually. I know Leo has some friends back in Minnesota that he keeps in contact with on a regular basis, but I'm not part of those conversations.

Do you have a spiritual practice? Does that impact your relationship?

Yeah. I am a Unitarian Universalist. I am going to school to be a minister. I have spiritual practices. I would say that they are contemplative in the way that they allow me the ability to reflect on the relationship. And also to use the relationship as a means of understanding spiritual practices, as well. I feel like there's a nature of give-and-take there.

I think spiritual practices for me involve two types. There's the solitary type of spiritual practice, which is contemplative in nature. But there's also going to church or to a worship service, which is something that we do together. Being together that way is a great moment, and we get to reflect on, "What did you think of this? Or how did that feel for you?"

Parenting

Tell us about yourselves as parents in this relationship

Leo very much started wanting a dog during the pandemic. We live in an apartment, and he gravitated more

toward small dogs for that reason. So we went through the adoption process with a rescue and ended up with Golden Nugget. At that time, I was working full-time and going to school part-time. So as Leo was getting closer to adopting the dog, I took the stance, "I just want you to know that this is your dog. I'm happy to be there, but I don't feel like I have time to train the dog and care for him. I can't be the primary caregiver of this animal, as I don't have time." Also, I'm also not a small dog person, and so I didn't want to promise that I'd like this dog. But I was in full support of him getting one.

We both very much care about and love Golden Nugget, but he's still very much Leo's responsibility. I feel very connected to the dog and am very involved, but I also recognize that it is Leo's dog primarily. I don't interfere with how the dog is walked or the time he is fed or those sorts of things. We're madly in love with the dog and very much appreciate that he's a part of our lives, but he's much more attached to Leo. I feel like the dog knows that my role with him is secondary.

Being in an ND Relationship

Do you feel that the challenges in ND relationships are unique?

I don't know if they are unique, per se. There's a level of knowing that your partner is neurodivergent and then accepting that you're in a neurodiverse relationship, which can open up the NS partner to learn about the dynamic. I think in a purely neurotypical relationship, there can be instances where one person or the other might not feel like they need to learn about the other person because there isn't an appreciation for that sort of differentiation.

I think in our relationship, where we know about the diagnosis, it's an opportunity to expand our relationship. There's growth. I see ASD as an opportunity for growth on both of our parts.

Based on your experiences, how informed do you find people are about ASD and ND marriage/relationships?

There's definitely different levels, and there's stigma attached to it in broader communities. I found, being in school, that if I ever mentioned something about my partner and his autism journey, mostly everyone was like, "Tell me more about that" or "This is my experience with it." So, in my academic setting right now, it seems very normal.

What is your perspective on being in an ND relationship?

My perspective is that it involves learning—learning in a way that, "I am going to help you in this. Let me learn how we can be on this journey together." I think when Leo was first learning about ASD himself, I was like, "I also want to learn about this."

> There's a level of knowing that your partner is neurodivergent and then accepting that you're in a neurodiverse relationship, which can open up the NS partner to learn about the dynamic.

There were a number of articles I read that were like, "Don't be the parent. Don't try to solve things." So that was a clue to me to be like, "Oh, I'm here for this journey. But I'm not here to provide any solutions because there are no solutions. It's not a solution-oriented issue." So, yeah, my perspective is very much that I'm on the journey, too—let me learn what I can do!

What are the positives of being in an ND relationship?

I think one of the positives is that it's a way of approaching the world in a different way. We are able to have this almost radical worldview. Not that we're anarchists or anything, but, in a sense, we are able to see systems and structures that are negative or oppressive. I could say that this is true for a number of identities. But I think there's an advantage to having this intersectionality of ASD, queer, and being in a neurodiverse relationship because I think it helps us with having empathy toward a broader human condition.

What advice would you give to people who are in an ND relationship?

I think the same advice from earlier. It's an opportunity to learn; it's an opportunity for personal growth. It is not a chronic condition that needs solving; it is a human experience that is a journey.

Couples Counseling

Have you pursued couples counseling? Was it useful?

We have not pursued it. We're currently not planning on it, but it is something that I've thought about, as I see the value of individual therapy. As a couple, I think it will probably happen in the future, but it is not something we have discussed.

Concluding Thoughts

10-Point Marital Happiness Scale™

I would say, like, in the 9 to 10 range. I think from my perspective, there's always room for growth. I think keeping it at 10 lacks a level of perspective, and so a 9 seems more truthful to me.

Do you think your relationship will go the distance?

I think we're committed to letting ourselves grow. I think our relationship will go the distance. I think

our relationship could evolve in the sense that, even though we will always be together, we will need to give ourselves and each other space to grow. If, in the future, it ends up that we grow apart, I don't think that we will view that as a negative thing.

We're planning on being together, so I do think we will stay with each other for the long run. I think we are both supportive of each other and that we both allow each other the space for personal growth. But it's not like pressure, like, "I'm giving you space to grow—go grow, and that's going to benefit me!" It's more like, "Oh hey, we're both humans. We're both trying to be good humans. Let's do this, and let me share with you what I'm thinking and learning."

CHAPTER 7

Oliver & Camilla

Taken Care of Everyday
Together Four Years

INTRODUCING OLIVER AND CAMILLA

Oliver and Camilla's story feels like a modern-day, real-life fairy tale. Oliver was raised by two tender and devoted queer mothers; Camilla is a Mexican-American immigrant. Oliver has been diagnosed with ASD. Because of her trauma, Camilla deals with some of the same mental health issues, like anxiety and depression, that Oliver does.

Contrary to the myth that individuals with ASD don't have empathy, we see in this story that Oliver is deeply empathetic with Camilla. He is an emotional refuge for her. Camilla explains, "Oliver's very understanding. He knows the boundaries I have, and he listens to those a lot. He knows my upbringing, background, trauma, and abuse, so he's very aware of how much that affected me." This couple is committed to tuning in to each other's emotions.

You can also see that pets are a major part of their life. For Camilla, animals are a healing presence and an outlet for her nurturing instincts. Additionally, Oliver has a deep attachment to the pets that help with his anxiety, depression, and other issues related to his ASD.

Oliver and Camilla's strengths complement each other. Camilla explains, "I'm definitely the person that handles everything... That includes our financial status and what we do with the money. That includes driving, going out, making appointments, and picking something up." Oliver felt especially loved when Camilla thought to get him a pill organizer, which simplified his health-related memory tasks. Oliver reciprocates. He says, "But one thing that I've very much made my job is taking care of her. She's so busy taking care of the rest of us, but I make sure to take care of her. I try to make her the priority, try to watch out for what people can be doing to help her." Oliver reminds Camilla to take a break when she gets overly engrossed in her work and becomes stressed. He brings silliness and humor into their home. He also takes care of Camilla when she's feeling sick—something she didn't experience in her childhood.

Oliver and Camilla both express confidence that their relationship will go the distance. Oliver says, "Part of it is—I know it's cliché—but it gets better as time goes on." "Take it slow,"

Camilla advises, "Listen, I know this goes for a lot of relationships, but I think for ND relationships it's really, really important. A lot of things can be said or done and come off one way when they aren't meant to. So I think really knowing and getting the ASD partner's perspective is extremely important." This couple is a practical example of respect and active listening!

MEET OLIVER

Oliver (he/him/his) is a 25-year-old, heterosexual, Caucasian male. He identifies as having ASD, and he has a bachelor's degree in computer science and theater. He works as a software engineer. He lives in Massachusetts with his fiancé, Camilla, and their two dogs. He started dating Camilla in 2016.

Please describe any short- or long-term past romantic relationships

Not applicable, just Camilla.

How did you meet?

We met at college. I had taken a year off in the middle of my undergrad degree to focus on mental health. I did some neurofeedback and took some classes at a community college to keep myself doing something academic. When I got back for

I have someone who loves me and accepts me for who I am and is okay with the difficulties and stress that I cause. She still loves me, despite my difficulties with some things that are easier for other people. I'm very much in love with her. So many times, I look over at her, and I just start smiling.

my sophomore year, it turned out Camilla also had taken a gap year, so we were in the same place. We were in the same dorm, sort of across the hall from each other, and we both were computer science majors. I was computer science and theater, and she was computer science and art.

We had classes together and we had some of the same friends, so we started hanging out more. Then we decided to try dating. We broke up for a little bit. Then we tried to be friends, and eventually that turned into friends with benefits. Camilla never gave up on me. She was still interested and attracted to me, but I still very much didn't want to get into a relationship with her. I didn't want her to get hurt. Even when things got more real, I still wanted to wait. I wanted to be sure. Over time, I was just like, "Okay, let's try this again."

Diagnosis Journey

Did you receive any special education, support, or therapy while you were growing up?

A little bit. When I was young, I was diagnosed with ADHD. I think I was very close to a diagnosis for ASD at the time, but I guess it turns out that I didn't quite meet the standard. I think it might have been because I was young. At that point, a lot of the evaluation was based on parental feedback, as opposed to my feedback. So I think some of what I was feeling was misunderstood or misinterpreted. I remember doing some physical therapy on hand–eye coordination and stuff. I remember a little of that. I had a scribe for standardized tests because my handwriting was atrocious. Still is. Going through middle school, that's when my anxi-

ety started developing. It left me with a diagnosis of severe anxiety disorder.

Do you or your partner have an official or self-diagnosis of ASD?

Yes, I do. I don't remember off the top of my head, but I can definitely give you the year. I started college in the fall of 2013, and I took a break in the spring of 2014. So I think my diagnosis would've been in the fall of 2014.

Yes, I am on medicine for pretty much all of my diagnoses. I have been to see a therapist who specializes in CBT. I also did neurofeedback.

How accepting do you feel you and your partner are about the diagnosis?

I personally accept the diagnosis. I think it's very accurate. It's frustrating, though. There's a lot of personal frustration in dealing with why I have such difficulty with some things or why some things seem harder for me than for everyone else. My partner is very accepting of the fact that I go through these things, but I also think they can be frustrating for her as well. Having discussions over and over, having issues...so yeah, I think that part can get frustrating.

What advice would you give to someone who's just discovering either their or their partner's ASD?

Part of it is—I know it's cliché—but it gets better as time goes on. Take it slow. Try to find understanding, and just try to share things between the two of you. Remind yourselves what it is about each other that you're drawn to. Remember what works well between you two, and never let that go. Be aware that your difficulty doesn't have to be a bad thing. You just have to approach things from a different angle. I think for someone just finding out—you've made it this far in life! Now you have an awareness of what you've always dealt with. That part is not going to change.

Anything else you'd like to say about the diagnosis?

It definitely made a lot of things feel clearer. Like, "Okay, so this is not just me struggling with some things. This definitely makes sense." It allowed me to put more of a label on things. I realized that it wasn't just my personal feelings, but that my perceptions were due to more medical reasons and mental illness. So that aspect was definitely kind of helpful.

My diagnosis involved a psychiatric test of multiple different sections. It was almost like a bunch of activities. "Okay, try to solve this puzzle" or "Do this exercise." It was broken up over a bunch of exercises like that, and it was over a few different days. At the end, there was a list of individual things, like percentiles for different tests.

Probably the same thing you get from a lot of people—I wish I was normal.

Relationship Challenges

What are the main challenges in your relationship?

Probably me, me, and me...so, *me*. I think I have a harder time managing responsibilities, learning from mistakes, and rationalizing/not doing work that needs to be done. I know that can be frustrating.

I'm definitely very understanding and caring, but I have noticed that I am not good at seeing the big picture. Sometimes I see things in terms of black and white and have a hard time seeing things in context. I get frustrated or feel overwhelmed when I shouldn't. So that's a lot.

Also, my memory is not good these days. I'm planning to try to get some more testing done soon to try to see if that's something that has declined from before or if that's being affected by my medication. That can also lead to some frustrations when we talk about something, as I can completely forget that we talked about it.

I recently described another struggle as feeling that I have blinders on or feeling very tunnel-visioned on things. "Yes, we talked about trying to change this, but if I don't think before I act, there's no opportunity for that." That's kind of how my brain works a lot; I just instinctually act and think about it later. It's very hard to not do something if you didn't even think to do it, if that makes sense. What I'm reading is that this seems to be more typical in ASD. So that's difficult when I'm trying to work on things in terms of a relationship.

Do you struggle with executive functioning, sensory sensitivities, communication problems, and/or social challenges?

EXECUTIVE FUNCTIONING: Yes. Planning and time management—I'm definitely not good at that. Sometimes I feel like impulse control can be on that list. I think it was Eva who explained executive functioning to me and I was like, "Yeah, my executive has no idea what it's doing." It's disorganized up there sometimes.

Something I struggled a lot with in school was analytical writing. I'm not sure if this is the proper time to mention that. I did very well with creative writing, play writing, and writing stories. But writing something analytical... I have the hardest time putting thoughts into writing. I'm better at expressing myself vocally.

SENSORY SENSITIVITIES: No, I don't really have sensory sensitivities. I can definitely be really sensitive to loud noises, but that's it. I can get really terrified from loud noises, like fireworks. Fire alarms are always really difficult for me. I try to be aware so I can be out of the area for that. It can set off an anxiety attack for me, or I can get extremely anxious just anticipating it.

For example, our apartment buil-

ding is having fire drills on Monday, so we are traveling to my parents' house and staying there until Monday, after the drill is over. I remember I dealt with this in college too. They would give a vague announcement like, "Okay, it's happening *sometime* on this day." I would be like, "Oh god!"

COMMUNICATION PROBLEMS: I think communication problems come down to having a hard time seeing the big picture. I think my partner definitely holds a lot more responsibility for day-to-day operations than I do. What can get frustrating is when some smaller things will get passed on to me, and I will still get frustrated or overwhelmed.

We have something we call the "complain-inator," and right now mine's at zero. I have to pay attention to what it's indicating. Basically I try to think of the number of times that I've complained about doing a task without recognizing how much more Camilla is doing. It helps me keep in mind that when she asks me to do something, she's doing so much more.

SOCIAL CHALLENGES: I have had social challenges for a long time. Probably one of the biggest reasons is that I am terrible at reading social cues. Which I know is very typical of people with ASD. I'm actually not bad at reading them if I'm not involved. If I'm watching something scripted like a play, acting in a show, or even just in a real-life scenario that I'm not involved in, I can be pretty good at reading cues. But when I'm involved, I'm completely blind. I tell Camilla and most of my friends, "Please let me know when I'm doing something that's annoying or uncomfortable. I'm not necessarily going to pick up on it without you saying something."

I just want to mention that something I really struggle with is decisions. I don't know if that's due to ADHD or ASD or just me, but that's something I really struggle with. It's usually small things, but sometimes it's big things too. I can just get completely paralyzed and be like, "I don't know what I want. I don't know." I'm the kind of person who will default to asking the other person, "What do you want?"

What have been some of the low points in your relationship?

The times when I'm closed-minded and seeing things in black and white can lead to conflicts. Another low point is having the same arguments over and over. Sometimes I have a hard time learning from mistakes and executing a different behavior. I recognize that I have something to work on. But then it happens again because I sometimes don't have the capacity to notice in a moment that it's happening and change it.

If you had a magic wand and could wish away one of your marital challenges or a partner's trait, what would it be?

Can I wish myself neurotypical? I feel like it would be a lot easier. Our relationship would be a lot more helpful for her. I feel like there would be a lot less conflict and stress for her. I would pick up a lot more weight in the relationship. There wouldn't be so much difficulty. I wouldn't make her angry as much. It wouldn't make her so sad and frustrated. I want to be a better partner for her.

Relationship Strengths

What are some of your strengths and highlights?

I think I do a good job of taking care of Camilla. I make sure she's doing well and that she's taking care of herself. I always try to make her laugh and bring in some humor. I can be very silly. I definitely try to do what I can to help. I think there's definitely a lot of love, which is a strength. Caring and trust.

She keeps so many things in mind, and she keeps track of all these things. I have no idea how she does it. She's good at the budget, making appointments for us, and reminding me to take my medicine. Actually, something happened recently that was kind of nice. I was telling her that I was struggling. I mentioned my memory before. She went and got me a pill organizer that had those labels on it, a thing that actually had multiple days and morning, afternoon, and night. It's been really helpful. I haven't missed a dose yet!

What do you love most about your relationship?

The basic fact that I *have* a relationship! That I have someone who loves me and accepts me for who I am and is okay with the difficulties and stress that I cause. She still loves me, despite my difficulties with some things that are easier for other people. I'm very much in love with her. So many times, I look over at her, and I just start smiling.

Intimacy

Is empathy or emotional reciprocity an issue in your relationship?

EMPATHY: I think empathy is something I can struggle with sometimes. I sometimes have a hard time taking myself out of the moment or seeing something entirely from another person's perspective. It's something I very much try to do, and it's definitely something I'm aware of. I'm most empathetic with Camilla. I think the times we struggle are when she's trying to make me empathetic toward someone else.

EMOTIONAL RECIPROCITY: One thing I feel like I'm good at is picking up on when someone seems upset, but I can also be very bad at it. So usually I ask, "Is everything okay? You seem a little sad." Overall though, I do think the one thing I'm good at noticing is when something seems a little off with someone, and then we can have a little discussion about it.

Does ASD cause challenges in the area of sex/intimacy?

It can. I'm not good at knowing when is the right time. I'm usually either overly cautious or overly blunt. I ask bluntly because I never want to put her in a situation where she is not in control or doesn't feel like she has control.

I try to not ever assume things, especially because of the nature of the situation. I very much will try to ask if this is something she'd like, and I ask before doing anything. I would never want to put her in a position where she's uncomfortable. As much as I think it can be a little annoying, sometimes I still think I would rather do that than ever make her feel uncomfortable.

What makes you feel loved and cared for by your partner, and what makes your partner feel loved and cared for by you?

FEELING CARED FOR: A lot of things. When she'll say that she did something to try to help my anxiety, it means a lot. For example, when we saw that there was a fire alarm, she said immediately, "Okay, we can plan things around it. We can go visit your parents." It was just very nice. How sometimes she'll notice I am upset about something, and she'll be like, "Okay, what should we do? Let's do this—let's get some nice food or something."

CARING FOR CAMILLA: I try to always be taking care of her. I know

ARMCHAIR CONVERSATIONS ON LOVE AND AUTISM

that she puts in so much work taking care of the rest of us, me and both of our dogs. I know she has taken on so many responsibilities around the house and around our relationship. But one thing that I've very much made my job is taking care of her. She's so busy taking care of the rest of us, but I make sure to take care of her. Sometimes with work, she'll have a hard time stopping. I'll be like, "Wait! Let's do this fun thing!" I'll remind her to take time for herself, to try to relax. And then if she's stressed, I'll start giving her a massage.

Finances

Describe your economic situation. Does your financial situation impact your relationship in any way?

Yes. Not in any bad way. It's probably great for our relationship that we're both doing well. I mean, we're living in the Boston area, so it's relatively higher priced. We're trying to find a house, because Camilla wants to find a house so that we can have a yard for our dogs. In terms of money, I never really grew up thinking about how much things would cost. I think I am kind of sheltered. I was very much upper middle class growing up. I think, for Camilla, it's very liberating, being able to spend money. I think the stress comes from knowing that if one of us loses our job, we're going to have to make changes. I think we both try to not take it for granted.

In terms of finances, we don't keep it individual; we very much share. It leads to less strain that way. We have some separate spending money set aside for each month, but then sometimes we'll still dip into each other's.

I'm not always the best in terms of thinking about a budget. That's something that Camilla very much handles.

What are some of the stressors in your relationship?

It feels like Camilla does a lot more of the work. I think some of this comes from her being a workaholic and me being lazy. But also, her picking up more tasks can lead to her being frustrated about picking up so many tasks. I think sometimes she doesn't realize that this might be happening or that some of these could be picked up by me. But she knows I'm just not good at figuring out how to do things by myself. I know I can be annoying to teach sometimes, so I get that. I sometimes will be like, "I don't know how to start," and she'll be like, "Just Google it!" Just figuring out how to start is the solution. Once I figure out how to start, then I'm good to go. So I think that's a huge one—the uneven workload.

Temperature is another issue. I am someone who prefers cold, while she prefers hot. So there's some bickering about that. The temperature where I will be sweating and she will be shivering overlaps.

Support System

What support systems do you and your partner have?

My parents are a big support system for the both of us. They're very understanding, and they're always willing to help. It helps that one of my moms is a Director of Sports Medicine, so she has some medical background. It usually helps when we have things happen, and we're like, "What should we do about this? Is this the kind of thing we should get looked at, or do you want to take a look at it?" When we talk to them, they're always supportive. With love. They definitely think of Camilla as a daughter. Our best friends, too—we also consider them part of our support.

Do you have friends individually and as a couple?

Definitely, both. The two best friends I mentioned are friends of ours as a couple that we're both individually very close to as well. We all went to college together. We actually have a video call coming up with those two friends, my parents, and us soon. It's nice because they love my parents, and my parents love them. Before the pandemic, we've had them come and stay over at our apartment. Now we try to get in touch on video chats and stuff. We both have some individual friends as well, mostly from work.

Do you have a spiritual practice? Does that impact your relationship?

No, I am an atheist.

Parenting

Tell us about yourselves as parents in this relationship

We love our two dogs very much; they are very sweet. Nina and Lila are both girls.

Nina is six pounds, and she's three. She'll be four in May. Lila is a 13-pound Chihuahua mix. We give them lots of love. They have numerous different beds—six or seven beds in different rooms in this apartment so they can always be near us.

Camilla is a huge animal person; she always wants to have pets. Camilla's goal is to basically own a farm. One of the reasons she wants to own a house is so she can have a lot more pets of lots of different kinds. She wants to have a pet snake she can sleep with. I'm less keen on that one. She's very excited to have ferrets.

Being in an ND Relationship

Do you feel that the challenges in ND relationships are unique?

I think there are challenges in any relationship, no matter the type of relationship. There are going to be challenges just due to different personalities. I feel like some of the challenges probably are unique, due to the ASD. I think there might be different challenges for different relationships, but there are going to be challenges no matter what.

Based on your experiences, how informed do you find people are about ASD and ND marriage/relationships?

I don't know. I feel like there's not been a lot of discussion directly around that. I do feel like it's something we're becoming much more aware of in terms of pop culture. The perception seems to be more positive, in terms of characters being more developed and not being as one-sided. People are appreciating that more. They are recognizing that people with ASD are not necessarily defined by it. I think there's still probably a lot more awareness that needs to happen.

What is your perspective on being in an ND relationship?

As the ASD one in the relationship, I think it gives me a healthy dose of perspective on the things I struggle with. It reminds me that other people do not struggle with the things I do. It allows me to let Camilla handle things as she's better equipped to handle certain things.

What are the positives of being in an ND relationship?

A positive for me is seeing a perspec-tive that I don't have—the more neurotypical perspective. This perspective includes reading social cues, or things I'm not aware of within the social dimensions or what people mean or how some other people's minds work, and with seeing the big picture.

What advice would you give to people who are in an ND relationship?

Try to find a way to get on the same wavelength. Try to have open discussions about expectations, about feelings, about things that you're both going through. Figure out how you connect.

You can make it work, but sometimes things just don't work out. I think it's okay to be aware of that and to try to move on. That can mean that even if the romantic relationship doesn't work out, maybe a really great friendship can emerge. It's all the better to be honest with each other.

> Sometimes things just don't work out. I think it's okay to be aware of that and to try to move on. That can mean that even if the romantic relationship doesn't work out, maybe a really great friendship can emerge. It's all the better to be honest with each other.

Couples Counseling

Have you pursued couples counseling? Was it useful?

As part of my individual therapy, we often meet together, Camilla and I, so I think if we do more couples counseling, it will be helpful as well.

Concluding Thoughts

10-Point Marital Happiness Scale™

Yes, it's hard to rate, but probably 9 or 10.

Would you say you're in love with Camilla?

Yes. I am aware of a lot of these wonderful things about her.

Do you think your relationship will go the distance?

I mean, there's no way to know for certain. But I do, and I want to work at it to make sure it does. I think that's an important part of the relationship—you have to work at it. You have to feed it; you have to upkeep it. You have to be willing to put the work into it, and I feel like this is one that's worth it.

MEET CAMILLA

Camilla (she/her/hers) is a 26-year-old, pansexual, Hispanic/Mexican female. She lives with her fiancé, Oliver, and their two dogs. She has earned her bachelor's degree and is now working professionally as a software engineer. Camilla has been with her fiancé for four and a half years. She does not identify as being on the spectrum.

Please describe any short- or long-term past romantic relationships

I had a boyfriend in high school— from sophomore year until the first year of college. It was an on-and-off relationship.

He's very in tune with emotions, and he's very open about talking about those emotions. This has been great for me, dealing with that shift from my upbringing. We'll have conversations about how we feel. I think because he has all these mental health struggles, he can see me struggling and is able to help.

During the off period, I had another boyfriend for a few weeks, but mostly it was that five-year relationship. I also had a gap year between high school and college, so that was my longest relationship, give or take with the breaks.

How did you meet?

We met sophomore year of college. I met him at our building get-together. We quickly became friends. He kinda got added to my friend group, and we got to know each other. We were also both computer science majors, so we had quite a few classes together. I think we had like six out of our nine required classes together. It was a pretty small school, so there were only so many professors. But, yeah, I got to know him through our friend group and through the classes we shared. Then we dated for a little bit. I don't remember the exact amount of time—maybe a few weeks. Then we broke up because he was unsure between our relationship and his feelings for someone else. Then we became friends with benefits for a bit, and then we got back together. We've been together since then.

Diagnosis Journey

Did you receive any special education, support, or therapy while you were growing up?

No, not while I was growing up. I didn't really deal with any mental health issues until I came to college. I

did have moments of very high stress (as anyone does during school, growing up), but it wasn't until going to college that it was something that got talked about more freely. My family didn't really talk about it. Mexican culture isn't really big on opening up about mental health issues.

Do you or your partner have an official or self-diagnosis of ASD?

Oliver has an official ASD diagnosis. I know when he was growing up, he had a lot of difficulty with school. His parents talked to a therapist and doctors and he had different kinds of tests, like neurological stuff. He was then diagnosed with ASD. He also has ADHD, and he deals with anxiety and stress, as well.

How accepting do you feel you and your partner are about the diagnosis?

I feel very accepting. He was very open about it right from the get-go, so it's not like it came out three years into the relationship or anything. I remember specifically looking up more about ASD because I wasn't aware of what exactly that meant in terms of the diagnosis. It's a struggle in the relationship, as in any relationship where you do a lot of work to make it work. It's just that we have *different* work than what some couples may have.

I make sure I'm doing what I can to help him with some of the things he struggles with; for example, recently, he's had a bit of trouble taking his medication, so we got him a pill box.

I think he's accepting of the fact that he's ASD, but I know it weighs on him. I know that when we get into scenarios and he does something that's not the right thing to do, he feels terrible. There have been times when he's said, "I wish my brain was just normal." It's really disheartening to hear. I've even replied that there *is* no normal. Everybody is different; there's not a perfect version of normal. And he goes, "I know, but I wish it was different."

Relationship Challenges

What are the main challenges in your relationship?

I think one of them is that, with all of Oliver's diagnoses, it definitely stops him from doing things that come a lot easier for other people. I'm definitely the person that handles everything. He handles sort of what he can, but we also try to keep it lower in terms of amount. That includes our financial status and what we do with the money. That includes driving, going out, making appointments, and picking something up.

I think another big struggle is the fact that we see scenarios very differently. That's why we have those constant conversations about how I feel when he does something. I have to explain, "When you say *that*

I hear *this*." To him, it's like, "I never thought about it that way. This is what I meant." And I'm like, "Yes, you meant *that*. But then you say *this*, which isn't saying the same thing." So we've talked a lot about wording. My hope is that it stops him from hurting someone who doesn't know his situation or how his brain works.

I think the other struggle is more internal for him. In terms of our relationship, he's not very self-confident. It is a relationship struggle for us to help him feel confident at work or in what he does.

Do you struggle with executive functioning, sensory sensitivities, communication problems, and/or social challenges?

EXECUTIVE FUNCTIONING: Driving has always been a really anxiety-provoking thing for him. He got his license after graduating college, but he never drives. He had classes because his parents put him in driving school. He did fine, but he just never felt like he could drive. So he never went for the test.

I'm a very organized person and a very list-oriented person. That's one of the things I'm trying to get him to be better at. There's a reason he now has a planner, because that's something I do. It's been helpful for him to keep track of stuff.

SENSORY SENSITIVITIES: For him, I definitely think it's noise-related. Loud noises that he's not expecting freak him out. We have a really difficult time with fire alarms, specifically. It really, really messes him up. He's on edge for days because of it.

SOCIAL CHALLENGES: We used to go out every month on the fourth to celebrate our anniversary. At the very least—even if we were booked—we made sure we went out that day. In terms of going out to restaurants or movies, he doesn't really have any social issues there. I think that might be due to the fact that he's not having to do anything that's unexpected. The social issues come more from deep interactions, when he says something he doesn't mean to say.

What have been some of the low points in your relationship?

Definitely at the beginning, when we were dating and he still had feelings for other people. That was definitely a low point. Recently, I've gone through some depression. When I started my job at the end of 2019, I was going through a lot of anxiety. But he's always been really helpful there.

If you had a magic wand and could wish away one of your marital challenges or a partner's trait, what would it be?

I definitely think it would be when he says the wrong thing or says something without thinking it all the way through. Like, if there was a way to

be able to see how it comes off to other people who aren't him, I think that would solve a lot of issues.

Relationship Strengths

What are some of your relational strengths and highlights?

RELATIONAL STRENGTHS: I think a big one is that we're very in tune with how each of us is feeling. I think the fact that we both deal with mental health issues means that we can really understand the other person when they're having an issue. If I'm feeling depressed and I don't know why I suddenly feel kind of down, he can be like, "Okay, well, what can we do?" Then he comes up with some things that might be helpful. I think that's a really good strength in our relationship—being able to understand what each of us is feeling and come up with ideas of how we can help in the moment.

HIGHLIGHTS: We've gone to New York a few times, so that's always been fun. We're really big musical people. We've seen some musicals here as well. New York's very loud, so that can always be a little bit of a factor, but I think we always have a good time. The last time we went pre-Covid, we got to see two Broadway plays with the original casts, so that was really cool.

Trips I've taken with his parents and him—we've gone to Florida and

Disney World—have been highlights. Those have been really happy memories.

What do you love most about your relationship?

Also, just day-to-day stuff. There are times I'll look around our apartment and be like, "Did you ever think this is what our life would be like?" Where it's like, two tiny little dogs in an apartment and we're just like, "I can watch TV and you can play a game." Just those moments of realization that, in spite of how I grew up (and for him, in spite of thinking that he would always be alone), this gets to be our life.

How caring he is. How *extremely* caring he is. With me, growing up, I didn't get to feel certain things. Or I had to keep them inside myself. He says, "Well, if you're feeling bad, let's work on that." Or when I'm feeling physically ill, he's there to take care of me. That's something I haven't had before.

Intimacy

Is empathy or emotional reciprocity an issue in your relationship?

I think we both know what we struggle with. We've had a lot of conversations about that. He knows I struggle with anxiety and some depression and that I really stress myself out. I know all the things we struggle with.

So I think we're really empathetic with each other. We can tell when the other person is struggling, even when the other doesn't say anything.

Oliver's very understanding. He knows the boundaries I have, and he listens to those a lot. He knows my upbringing, background, trauma, and abuse, so he's very aware of how much that affected me.

Empathy and emotional reciprocity is not an issue. Like I said, we have long conversations about stuff. We're pretty open about how we're feeling. The only issues we have in that arena is with any mental health. It's hard to pinpoint it. If one of us goes, "I'm anxious" and the other person asks, "Okay, well, what are you anxious about?" it's not always clear. But that doesn't have to do with us not wanting to share. That's more about how we don't know why it's happening. So we're very open about sharing our emotions.

Does ASD cause challenges in the area of sex/intimacy?

Going back to when we first met, during the time we were friends with benefits, I think my sex drive was really high. Then we started dating, and there was a shift somewhere. His sex drive went really high, and mine went lower. That shift also probably coincided with when I really started dealing with the trauma from my childhood.

The sexual intimacy isn't there as

much now, and that's not necessarily because we don't want to. But we're both very aware of the fact that sex, for me, is very intertwined with bad feelings. One time I explained to him, "This is nothing against you, but every time there's a sexual element occurring, I have this nauseating feeling in my stomach." I know that's not what a healthy experience with sex should feel like. But that's just something I have not been able to control. So he's very understanding about that, and we have had conversations about it.

What makes you feel loved and cared for by your partner, and what makes your partner feel loved and cared for by you?

FEELING CARED FOR: I think one thing he does that really makes me feel loved is when I'm feeling down or sick, I know he'll take care of me. He brings me a blanket to make sure I'm warm. Or if I'm feeling nauseous, he'll bring me over a trash can or get me medicine. So I think that feeling that I get is amazing—even though I take care of so many things in terms of our life, I know that if something were to happen to me, he would always be there.

And, you know, if I'm feeling a bit depressed, he stops doing whatever he's doing and is like, "Well, what do you want to do? Like, we can just hang out, we can watch something, we can play a game together..." And sometimes I don't know what I want to do, so we'll just sit there and figure something out.

CARING FOR OLIVER: For him, I think a lot of it has to do with the fact that I do take care of a lot of details. This is not just because it takes a lot off his plate, but because he's just so overwhelmed. Doing some of the necessary day-to-day tasks would be a lot for him. So I do take the responsibility of doing a lot of things so he can have breathing room after work.

I know he also really appreciates the conversations we have where I explain how something can come off. He's a really nice person, and he doesn't want to hurt peoples' feelings. He's said to me, "Thank you for having these conversations. I really appreciate them, even though they can make me a little sad."

Finances

Describe your economic situation. Does your financial situation impact your relationship in any way?

Yes, we both work as software engineers. I don't think his diagnosis contributes to work struggles. I know he's stressed about work stability, but I think a lot of that stress is because he was laid off once. So he's just in constant fear that that's going to happen again. I think the diagnosis stresses him out, making him think that he can't do the job to the ability that he should be able to. It's more an emotional thing for him. But in terms of finances, we both make good amounts of money. We're financially stable, and we're starting to build up our savings.

Seeing things differently can cause some tension because one of us can mean something and the other can take it a different way. I think work stability is a bit of a stressor, because Oliver worries he will get fired from another job. And it stresses me out because that would affect a lot of things. So that is something that's in the back of my mind.

In terms of finances we're doing okay. I know it stresses me out in terms of future plans because we would like to get a house at some point. So those future plans are sort of on hold because we don't have that money to do the things that we would like to do. I would probably say those things are the top stressors.

Support System

What support systems do you and your partner have?

Definitely his parents. His moms are a huge support system. They know how much he struggled while growing up. I think they're really happy that we're together. I don't know if Oliver told you this, but he would have the same wish every single birthday—he wished he could have a girlfriend! He wanted a relationship, and he wanted not to be alone. His parents were always worried about that while watching him growing up, receiving these diagnoses, and struggling to socialize. So his parents say that one of the moments of pure joy in their life was when they found

out we were engaged. They were like, "He's not going to be alone anymore!"

They're fully aware of our relationship and some of the things we struggle with. I can ask them about how he was for certain issues regarding his diagnosis because they have that background. So they can be like, "Oh yeah, when he was in high school, he had the same issue. He had trouble doing this, this, and this."

Do you have friends individually and as a couple?

We also talk to those two close friends that we had in college about things we have issues with. We talk to them about things that we all start to deal with, like losses of loved ones, now that we're older.

Do you have a spiritual practice? Does that impact your relationship?

Not really. I try to meditate here and there, but nothing consistent.

Parenting

Tell us about yourselves as parents in this marriage.

Before we had the dogs, we actually had rats. The sad thing about small animals, especially rodents, is that they don't have a very long lifespan. I'm a very big animal person, so I told Oliver, "I cannot go without a pet." I can't. I think I struggle a lot more when I don't have one. He understood that it would really affect me if we didn't have one. So he was very open and said, "Okay, let's get a pet because I know you need one."

We wanted to adopt a dog. Nina was a one-year-old Yorkie mix. I remember we picked her up, and it was sort of like, "Yeah. I think she's the one." Then we were like, "You know what? She needs a friend!" So that's what led us to the journey of getting Lila, our second dog. They've been super close since.

In terms of responsibilities, I'm usually the one that makes the vet appointments. But in terms of day-to-day stuff, Oliver handles taking them out more than I do. We both share the responsibilities of food and water and making sure they have enough. I definitely think he's more the play-time person. I take care of it if they want cuddles.

Being in an ND Relationship

Do you feel that the challenges in ND relationships are unique?

Yes and no. I'm guessing most people don't have to deal with the noise thing. But I think in more of the day-to-day stuff, when we have those conversations of, "Did you mean this?" I think those are basic communication issues. He has communication issues because of the ASD, but it's still communication issues.

Based on your experiences, how in-formed do you find people are about ASD and ND marriage/relationships?

I haven't really had too many deep conversations about that. I mean, he's been very open about his ASD, and I've been very open about it, as well. I remember when he first told me he had ASD, I did some research about ND relationships. The struggles that came up were kind of disheartening to read because there were a lot of really negative things said about it.

I think the people that we're around understand where he comes from, and they understand that our relationship is unique in that way. But they also understand that we come from extremely different backgrounds. I don't think when people look at us they take into account too much of the ASD aspect of it. I think, if anything, people are more interested in the race element, us being a mixed-race couple. I've never had someone think that his ASD hurts our relationship or anything of that sort.

What is your perspective on being in an ND relationship?

It has its struggles, but, like I said, I think every relationship has its struggles. I had communication issues and mental health issues in my last relationship, too. Amazingly enough, I felt that in the past relationship, I had to do more taking care of the other person than I do with Oliver. While me and Oliver have struggles, I've never thought that maybe we shouldn't keep going.

> **I don't think when people look at us they take into account too much of the ASD aspect of it. I think, if anything, people are more interested in the race element, us being a mixed-race couple.**

What are the positives of being in an ND relationship?

He's very in tune with emotions, and he's very open about talking about those emotions. This has been great for me, dealing with that shift from my upbringing. We'll have conversations about how we feel. I think because he has all these mental health struggles, he can see me struggling and is able to help.

While he may have some trouble with doing specific things, he can also really hyper-focus on stuff. That can be helpful in a way because if he needs to get something done, he can get it done because he's hyper-focused on it. There are positives and negatives there—sometimes he can focus *too* much on something.

Also, we are very self-aware, so we can tell when we need a break. It helps him be fully aware on a whole different level than I've ever encountered with another person.

What advice would you give to people who are in an ND relationship?

Listen, I know this goes for a lot of relationships, but I think for ND relationships it's really, really important. A lot of things can be said or done and come off one way when they aren't meant to. So I think really knowing and getting the ASD partner's perspective is extremely important. I think if you don't try to see their perspective, the relationship is probably going to crumble really quickly.

I think another thing is also to be prepared to have those conversations. If you go into this relationship and you aren't prepared to have constant conversations about what, to you, might seem like the recurring issue, then you're really going to struggle. Because for someone with ASD, it may not seem like the same issue. To you, it may seem like, "Oh my god, we've had six conversations in the past year about this," but to them, it feels like this is the first time you've talked about this. If you don't tackle it every time it comes up, then you can't really see the growth. So really be prepared that you may need to have the conversation 20 times for it to start changing.

Couples Counseling

Have you pursued couples counseling? Was it useful?

Yes. What we're doing with Eva is sort

of couples counseling; it's more specific couples counseling to help us deal with the ASD aspect. We had discussed couples counseling for quite a while. We'll also probably do more couples counseling in the future, regarding my trauma.

Concluding Thoughts

10-Point Marital Happiness Scale™

I would rate it probably a 9 or a 10, just for the relationship's sake. I know there are some issues there, but the issues aren't due to any unhappiness in the relationship. It's other factors that we deal with. Overall, our relationship is an extremely happy one. We really love each other. Not saying that we don't struggle day to day—we do. But it's an ongoing process, with him having ASD and with both of us having mental health issues. But I don't think any of that affects how happy we are with each other.

Would you say that you're in love with Oliver?

Yes, definitely.

Do you think your relationship will go the distance?

Definitely. We do plan on getting married, and we do plan on getting a house at some point. I've told him, "As soon as we get a house, I'm prob-ably going to get a bunch more pets. Be prepared!" I definitely see us going the distance.

That was true even when I was doing therapy in college and I was talking about our relationship. I remember my therapist asking, "Have you ever thought about whether this is something you want to continue?" Even when she brought up that question, it was like, "Yeah, no, not really looking to end this. Just looking to work through whatever issues there might be." So, yeah, I definitely see us going the distance. It's unique that we were able to find each other at such a young age, and we don't really see it not lasting for any reason.

CHAPTER 8

Frankie & Autumn

Weathering Change

Married 11 Years

INTRODUCING FRANKIE AND AUTUMN

"We always celebrate the fact that we don't let society define who we are as individuals or as a couple. So I think that's a major strength," declares Frankie. Autumn is an NS trans woman married to an autistic, nonbinary individual. Their voices are crucial, because of the overlap between their queer identities, trauma, and autism. They also share the unique experience of both experiencing their transitions of gender identity post-marriage.

Frankie and Autumn's childhood experiences incline them to sensitivity and diverse perspectives. Frankie describes their growing-up experience: "Self-diagnosis was a revelation. I read a couple of articles from my favorite authors who described their experiences being autistic. I saw myself in those stories." Autumn experienced significant childhood trauma. She says, "You can hear from the trauma history that it can be hard for me to believe that anyone could love

me." Still, she discovers that Frankie's love is enduring. "I came out as trans eight years into our marriage. It was a big thing that we stayed together." Autumn tenderly recalls how Frankie regularly assures her, "You don't have to do anything. You don't have to earn my love."

Frankie explains, "One of the main challenges is the intersection of my ASD traits and Autumn's trauma history." Autumn agrees, "Am I having a sensory issue because I'm hypervigilant from PTSD, or is it an autistic trait?" Autumn's hypervigilance leads her to feel that any sign of discomfort in Frankie is her fault. Frankie shares their perspective on these scenarios: Autumn "is quick to jump in to fix whatever is bothering me, but, usually, all I need is a moment to feel my feelings, process them, and let them go."

Overall, this couple has learned how to skillfully support each other. Busy, crowded environments cause

Frankie stress. Because of this, Autumn does the grocery shopping, and they buy their clothes online. Frankie goes out of their way to express affection for Autumn through physical touch, which Autumn prefers. And clearly, they support Autumn's transition process.

"I love the queer nature of our relationship," Frankie shares. "Queer relationships require communication and co-creation of the relationship; there is no standard script...to fall back on." Frankie and Autumn have accepted the mission of working together to develop a life that fits their true selves. Autumn shares some wise words: "Being trans is an 'umbrella identity,' and so is being autistic. I mean, figuring out that you're trans or that you're autistic tells you something, but at the same time, it doesn't. I think both are a journey of self-discovery..." Welcome to the journey!

MEET FRANKIE

Yes, I think our relationship will go the distance. We have already weathered a lot of change in the last ten plus years. I can't imagine that we would face a challenge greater than Autumn coming out as trans and transitioning.

Frankie (they/them/their) is a 35-year-old, bisexual, Caucasian and Filipino, nonbinary/genderqueer/agender individual. They identify as having ASD. They have earned their PhD and work as an assistant director in a hospital. They live in Massachusetts with their wife and cat. They have had no previous marriages and have been married to their wife for 11 years, dating for two years prior.

Please describe any short- or long-term past romantic relationships

I had a high school boyfriend. That relationship lasted a few years and fizzled once we went to different colleges. I've had a handful of other shorter relationships with men. Besides Autumn, I've not had a relationship with a woman.

How did you meet?

Autumn and I met in grad school. We basically did the stereotypical lesbian U-Haul trope (despite passing as a straight couple at the time). We went on a few dates and moved in together within a month of meeting. We adopted a cat together and met each other's families that first holiday season. About a year later, we had a conversation that basically went, "So I guess we'll get married sometime soon." "Yeah, I think so, too. How about next fall?" "Sure."

Diagnosis Journey

Did you receive any special education, support, or therapy while you were growing up?

I've never been formally diagnosed, so I never had special support for autism as a child. I was self-diagnosed in March 2020.

How accepting do you feel you and your partner are about the diagnosis?

I am accepting. It just makes so much sense of my past experiences. Autumn agrees. She and I have been able to make sense of and move past many of the mistakes and missteps in our relationship by looking at those events and situations through an autistic lens. We lived in New York City for several years, and we were able to see that a lot of our problems with going out and getting chores done were because of my need to know the plan beforehand. We also noticed all the methods Autumn came up with to avoid my meltdowns and shutdowns while we were out.

What advice would you give to someone who's just discovering either their own or their partner's ASD?

My advice would be that there are some really great online communities for aspie people, which can help you see that you're not alone. Everybody's experiences are different, but there will probably be a lot of people who understand your experiences and don't think you're weird. Or they will celebrate your weirdness. I would also say that society is very non-consensual. It's important to unlearn those messages of non-consent and figure out what works for you.

Figure out what's best for you, what are the things that you can't live with, and what are the things that enhance your life—even if some would call them weird. It's better to live a weird life true to yourself than to live a repressed life that's acceptable to society. I would say to have an open mind about how aspie people see the world in a different way. That different perspective can be beneficial.

Anything else you'd like to say about the diagnosis?

Self-diagnosis was a revelation. I read a couple of articles from my favorite authors who described their experiences being autistic. I saw myself in those stories. But I didn't immediately connect that feeling of similarity to the idea that I had autism. It took me telling Autumn about those articles and her saying, "So do you think you might be autistic then?" Afterwards, I read more from autistic authors and kept connecting events and feelings from my childhood to autistic experiences. The more I thought about my life through the lens of autism, the more it made sense.

Relationship Challenges

What are the main challenges in your relationship?

One of the main challenges is the intersection of my ASD traits and Autumn's trauma history. Another would be my need for alone time conflicting with Autumn's need for social time. Our differing communication styles also present difficulties sometimes.

Do you struggle with executive functioning, sensory sensitivities, communication problems, and/or social challenges?

EXECUTIVE FUNCTIONING: Yes, I have executive functioning issues. I have difficulty initiating. This has been improved with knowledge of ASD and proactive planning on my part. It has also improved with knowledge and proactive prodding on Autumn's part. I have difficulty noticing that chores need to be done and/or remembering to do domestic tasks. Since my self-diagnosis, we've tried to be more explicit about who is responsible for what chores, including expectations around time frames. We hold regular household business meetings, and I've incorporated certain chores into my usual routines. I started bullet journaling in 2016, and it immediately slotted into my life, as if it were

a missing limb I had suddenly discovered. Turning my bullet journaling into a mindfulness practice has helped with my executive functioning issues. I use my journal to outline my plans for the day/week/month, and then reflect on how well I did. I also use it to keep notes during conversations with Autumn so that I can remember that she asked me to take out the trash or call the pharmacy or whatever.

> We hold regular household business meetings, and I've incorporated certain chores into my usual routines.

SENSORY SENSITIVITIES: Before my self-diagnosis, we had already negotiated going to events and doing tasks that affect my sensory issues. I dislike grocery stores (because they are crowded, noisy, and echoey), and so Autumn does all the grocery shopping. We do most of our clothes shopping online and limit in-person shopping because I loathe the mall (even more crowded, noisy, and echoey).

I've been able to notice and explicitly verbalize a lot of the sensory issues I'd been having, and we've been able to make tweaks that were relatively easy to implement. For example, we bought a white noise machine and a weighted blanket. Autumn tweaked a few recipes to accommodate my food texture issues. I sit with my back to the big window (and the TV) at the dining room table. Autumn cleared her perfume choices with me and is sparing in their application. It's been wonderful both to interrogate and to verbalize my sensory issues, as well as figure out easy accommodations. It makes me so annoyed that this is only possible in our home, where my wife is interested in making these accommodations for me. In other spaces, it's not possible—but only because no one is interested in how a space impacts those with sensory issues.

My last job was excellent. I enjoyed it immensely, until they moved us into a cube farm. I went from a nice office with a door that could close, to an open-plan space with almost 40 people all crammed in together. I could smell everyone's food and snacks, hear everyone clack on their keyboard, and hear all conversations (both work-related and not). Since I was more accessible, more people came around for a quick chat. It was hard to have a quiet one-on-one conversation with anyone. And the temperature control was not great.

I didn't realize how draining it was to work in a cube farm, or how unproductive I had become, until we had to all work from home. The natural light of the open space had been nice, but the massive room in which you could hear everyone and be derailed at any moment for a "quick chat" had been exhausting.

COMMUNICATION PROBLEMS: Com-munication is definitely an issue that Autumn and I are working on constantly. Each of us has a tendency to assume things about what the other did and did not say. We are working on being explicit with requests, delegation, and asking clarifying questions. Recently, Autumn mentioned to me that she often gets confused by my body language. Because of her trauma history, she is likely to attribute any indications of discomfort to be her fault, and she's working on addressing this impulse.

I also hate implication and ambiguity when it comes to task delegation and expected time frames. In the past, when it would be implied that I would do a task, I would intend to do it, but then Autumn would do it before I got around to it. Also, we would try to put off difficult conversations until both of us were in a good frame of mind to have the conversation, but then it would never happen. These days, we try to be explicit about who will have a task done and by what time (or when a check-in will be done to see if the task has been completed). Or we set aside a specific time for when we will have the conversation.

SOCIAL CHALLENGES: The social challenges are hard, especially since we're making these realizations about autism during the pandemic. Just the week before lockdown, we were discussing how it would be okay for Autumn to go to social events without me (and in a lot of cases, it would be preferable). But now that we're in lockdown, going out to social events is basically impossible, given our low-risk tolerances. Since Autumn's primary source of socialization is me, it's been very hard. We've tried to create other socialization opportunities for her. She video chats with a particular friend every week, and she's part of an online community. But she needs more socialization, and most of the time, especially with my last job, I'm over-socialized. It doesn't help that Autumn's trauma history predisposes her to episodes of self-isolation because she thinks everyone would be better off without her.

We do set aside time for the two of us to socialize and connect, but we're still working on the right balance. Watching TV together (with a few exceptions) is not connecting enough. Conversation can sometimes tire me out, and it has the added disadvantage that it can devolve into Autumn monologuing and reliving trauma, especially if I'm not in a state to redirect her.

What have been some of the low points in your relationship?

One of the lowest points in our relationship was 2017. That was a year of uncertainty for me at a time when I could not handle uncertainty at all. There was uncertainty about my work and our living situation. Autumn was grappling with gender issues, and she disclosed to me that she was trans that Christmas. We

were both dealing with the fear about what her being trans meant for our relationship. It was a very stressful time, and neither of us dealt with that stress well. Our connection was basically nonexistent.

Another low point was right before my self-diagnosis. Even with transition going relatively smoothly, Autumn felt disconnected, isolated, and despairing. She felt I was withdrawing from her. I was almost constantly in shutdown, due to work stress and sensory overwhelm (because of working in a cube farm). She was suicidal, and I took off work in order to reconnect. I am grateful that we were able to connect at that time and come to the realization that autism was a thing for me.

If you had a magic wand and could wish away one of your marital challenges or a partner's trait, what would it be?

I would wish away Autumn's self-confidence issues and her tendency to think the worst of herself. I wish I could remove her traumas, but I know that they, in part, shaped her into who she is today.

Relationship Strengths

What are some of your strengths and highlights?

I think one of the strengths in our relationship is that we have always dismissed the societal norms for relationships. Before we had language for transgender or anything queer, I think we celebrated the fact that we did not follow gender norms and stereotypical heterosexual roles. I was always the breadwinner, the aggressive one, the one in front. And she was always the one hiding behind me. This is just funny, because it's an individual who's 5'10" trying to hide behind a person who's 5'0". We always celebrate the fact that we don't let society define who we are as individuals or as a couple. So I think that's a major strength.

The highlights are the ways that we encourage each other and support each other. Autumn supports me in my creative endeavors, my weirdness, and my ways of expression. And she helps me think things through. When I was deciding about work and deciding to change jobs, she was there to encourage me and talk to me about that. And I think that I can do the same with her. I can help encourage her to be the person that she wants to be, that she's meant to be, that she deserves to be. And I feel like we help prop each other up. We help encourage each other to be the best version of ourselves.

What do you love most about your relationship?

I love the queer nature of our relationship. Queer relationships require communication and co-creation of the relationship; there is no standard script (such as the relationship elevator of het monogamy) to fall back on.

The individuals in the relationship are forced to discuss the shape and bounds of the relationship, and they do not have to follow what society says relationships should look like.

What I love most is that she accepts me for me. Even before I could really articulate what that was, she was always accepting of me. My quirks and my weirdness and my strengths.

Intimacy

Is empathy or emotional reciprocity an issue in your relationship?

EMPATHY: Yes, empathy can be an issue in our relationship. Empathy is so hard. I've received some feedback that says I have no empathetic skills whatsoever, and other feedback that says I am very empathetic. It confuses me. In one sense, I try not to assume I know how another person is feeling, since everyone is different. My emotional responses to a situation may not be the same as another person's responses. In another sense, I try to be compassionate and allow for other people to have emotions that impact their behavior.

As for Autumn, empathy is problematic because her emotional experience is vastly different from my own. And sometimes, she interprets intellectual understanding (instead of empathy) as an indication that her emotional experience is wrong and not valid. This doesn't always happen, but it is very difficult for me to handle when it does. Since my emotional reciprocity is low, this can compound her feelings of not being seen. The flipside is also problematic. Autumn can sometimes feel it is her responsibility to manage the emotions of everyone around her, and her empathy is highly attuned, especially to me. She is quick to jump in to fix whatever is bothering me, but, usually, all I need is a moment to feel my feelings, process them, and let them go.

EMOTIONAL RECIPROCITY: Yes, this is an issue. Sometimes, when I am unexpectedly confronted with someone overflowing with emotion, I immediately shut down. With certain types of expected emotion, I can reciprocate. For example, if someone is grieving, I can offer condolences. Or if someone is ill, I can offer words of healing or good health. But when I am confronted by another person's anxiety and worry, especially if it seems out of proportion to the situation at hand, I find it difficult to respond in the face of emotion I don't understand.

Does ASD cause challenges in the area of sex/intimacy?

Executive dysfunction means that I rarely initiate sex. This can be problematic for Autumn because it can trigger her fear of being seen as a man and acting in stereotypically "manly" ways (such as the view that only men initiate sex). She has some-

times attributed my lack of initiating sex as an indication that I do not find her attractive.

Sensory things enter into sex, as well. Especially touch—soft touch versus firm touch—in the context of autism. It's definitely been positive to talk about our sex life through the lens of autism. There have definitely been times when there has been some sensory stimulus that has been too much for me, and we've had to talk about it.

What makes you feel loved and cared for by your partner, and what makes your partner feel loved and cared for by you?

Autumn shows love through cooking. She makes really delicious things that take into account my preferences and textural sensory issues.

I also feel loved and cared for when I can do weird things (like sprawling out on the floor or singing random song lyrics), and Autumn appreciates it as me doing "me things." What makes me feel loved by Autumn is the encouragement to do the weird, quirky things that make me feel good. So when I break out into song or dance, she smiles and makes room for me. I feel loved when she encourages me to do things like knit and buy yarn that's acceptable to me from a sensory perspective. She notices when I tell her things that bother me from a sensory perspective. She helps me think, "Well, can you do something different? You don't have to use that yarn if you don't like it." She encourages my creative outlets.

Autumn is comforted by hugs and physical closeness. She often tells me she feels loved and cared for by physical touch, so we have to make sure that we have time to cuddle. I think it's also the physical things that I do. I try to make sure that when she says something, I write it down so I don't forget it. I try to accommodate her communication needs, even though they are very different from my communication needs.

What makes her feel loved? That one's hard. I mean, I try to make sure that she gets to live the life that she deserves, so I make sure she knows that her transition costs are essential. They're not optional. I reiterate to her that she doesn't cost too much, because that was something that she had been made to believe all throughout her childhood. I try to tell her in little and big ways that she's important to me.

Finances

Describe your economic situation. Does your financial situation impact your relationship in any way?

I work, but Autumn doesn't. This financial situation means that I have more power in the relationship than Autumn. I do try to exercise that power in consensual ways, but the power dynamic itself is unavoidable in our situation. My ASD traits have helped me obtain a postgraduate degree, learn new skills quickly, and maintain a high-paying career.

I think that I have been lucky because I have been able to leverage my creativity and turn it into a very lucrative career. Autumn and I trained as scientists, and that's how we met in grad school. While neither of us pursued science as a career, I have used that experience and knowledge because I deal with scientists. I work with scientists in creating educational offerings. Having those three letters after my name helps them see me as a peer, and it also helps me approach them in ways they understand. It helps me communicate with them with their lingo.

Support System

What support systems do you and your partner have?

We have good insurance, and we are connected with good medical providers. We have very good local friends. These local friends are not physically able to provide individual, personal support sometimes, depending on what it is, because of various physical disabilities. But they are able to provide emotional support, as well as suggestions for other avenues of physical support. I guess we have access to my employer's assistance program, which we have used occasionally in the past. Support systems...we don't have a lot, I guess. That's all that I can think of right now. One of the things that

Autumn talks about is getting more involved in the community. She feels like we are pretty isolated, which I won't disagree with. That is one thing that I'm trying to do—get involved in the community. I think that is something that would benefit Autumn, too. But I think she might need a little bit of mental help first, just to make sure that she doesn't again get involved in a situation where she gets taken advantage of.

Do you have friends individually and as a couple?

We have friends both individually and as a couple. I encourage her to find and cultivate more individual friendships. Our best friends are Eloise and Lars. Autumn and Eloise went to high school together, and she is basically part of our found family. While Autumn and Eloise have a history of a close relationship that spans decades, Eloise and I also have a lot in common, and so we have a close relationship, too. Lars is Eloise's spouse and is a more recent addition to our group.

Do you have a spiritual practice? Does that impact your relationship?

I was raised Southern Baptist, but I deconverted to atheism in my twenties. I have an interest in Eastern spiritual practices, particularly Buddhism, and I have attempted to start up a meditation practice several times in my adult life. During the pandemic, I succeeded in starting and maintaining a meditation practice. This has helped me tremendously in connecting with Autumn, managing conflict, and dealing with Autumn's panic attacks. I am able to ground myself in the moment and not let my worry run away with me. I am able to be present to support and connect with Autumn. The practice also helps me manage my sensory difficulties. If I am feeling overwhelmed, I can take a few moments to center myself by focusing on internal sensations while letting external sensations come and go.

Being in an ND Relationship

Do you feel that the challenges in ND relationships are unique?

I don't know that they are unique. I think that one of the benefits we have is that we don't have to follow society's script about what a relationship looks like. I think that our challenges are about navigating those waters, without giving in to society saying, "You have to go this way." But I don't know if they are necessarily unique. If we discarded the societal script and slowed down to think, "How do we want to shape our relationship?" I think most people would have the same questions. People are different, and people want different things. Without the burden that society places on us and without what we "should be," we can fully explore those questions individually.

Based on your experiences, how informed do you find people are about ASD and ND marriage/relationships?

I have no idea. I guess I don't really talk about ASD with a lot of people. I talk about it with one of our friends. So I feel like I don't have a good sample size of what an average person thinks. I don't have an average group of friends. With the various identities of aspie, queer, and kinky, the group of people I'm most comfortable with are nonconformist. I've always felt more at home with people who throw aside society's expectations or purposely subvert them. I've always been drawn to people like that.

What is your perspective on being in an ND relationship?

I mean, I think it's great! Well, I'm neurodiverse, so any relationship I have is going to be neurodiverse. But I also think it's great for some of the reasons I mentioned before. You have to throw aside society's expectations of what relationships look like and co-define for yourself and your partner what your relationship will be.

What advice would you give to people who are in an ND relationship?

Communication—that's the thing! Try to figure out ways that the two of you can communicate. Work on it, and be open to the idea that the

other person can see the world in a different way. And that being able to see the world through their lens can benefit you.

Couples Counseling

Have you pursued couples counseling? Was it useful?

Yes, we've pursued couples counseling. Yes, it's been useful. It helped me connect my meditation practice and the skills I was learning in that practice to my relationship with Autumn. It provided a safe space for us to discuss the difficulties that either of us might not have raised on our own.

Concluding Thoughts

10-Point Marital Happiness Scale™

I would rate my happiness in our relationship to be a 9.

Would you say you're in love with Autumn?

Yes, I am definitely in love with Autumn.

Love is so hard to define and pin down, and as a scientist, I know there is limerence—the scientific state of falling in love. This is the kind of obsessive love that occurs at the beginning of a relationship. I've been with her for, gosh, it's been over a decade. It's probably close to 12 years now since we first met. Every day is a new adventure, and I always tell her that she's special to me.

I dislike society's idea that you have to have one person to fill all your social and love needs. She and I have talked about polyamory before, and that's something that we are open to discussing, though it's hard to find people. And one of the things that I think about with polyamory is that it's not about pre-defining what a relationship will be when you first meet someone. When you first meet a stranger, they could be a good friend, just an acquaintance, or the life partner you never knew you wanted or needed! So I am open to the fact that there are lots of people out there who could add value to our lives as individuals or as a couple. I feel like if—or when—that ever happened, it wouldn't detract from my relationship with Autumn. To me, that's what love is about. It's about holding people with open-handedness, like the Buddhist idea of open-handedness. You hold something precious to you with an open hand so it's there and you can appreciate it. Because if you close your hand, you cannot see it, and if it's gold, you might deform it. That's kind of what I think about with love—you hold people gently, with open hands.

Do you think your relationship will go the distance?

Yes, I think our relationship will go the distance. We have already weathered a lot of change in the last ten plus years. I can't imagine that we would face a challenge greater than Autumn coming out as trans and transitioning.

MEET AUTUMN

Autumn (she/her/hers) is a 37-year-old, lesbian, white trans woman. She has a master's degree and is a homemaker. She lives in Massachusetts with her spouse, Frankie, and their cat. She has no previous marriages, and she has been married for 11 years and been in the relationship for a total of 13 years.

Please describe any short- or long-term past romantic relationships

I didn't really have that many long-term relationships. Most of mine were short-term. I tended to end up involved with couples who were together. Usually, my relationship with the female partner would develop into much more than friendship, in terms of emotional intimacy. So I tended to be the one they went to for emotions, and then usually they would have a boyfriend that was for physical stuff.

How did you meet?

We met at graduate school. I guess we kind of just started spending time together. It's kind of funny because we playfully argue about when our relationship really became romantic. I thought it was when we went out to dinner at some point, but Frankie was like, "Well, we went grocery shopping together this one time, and it was nice." We didn't do much formal dating. We weren't really like, "Oh, this is a date." I guess at some point, we went back to my apartment. We were watching *The Princess Bride*, and I kissed Frankie. I guess that was when it was obvious that it was serious. That whole weekend we were inseparable. We definitely did the U-Haul thing. We moved in together, probably a couple weeks after that first kiss. We pretty much have been together ever since.

Diagnosis Journey

Did you receive any special education, support, or therapy while you were growing up?

No, not really. I was considered sort of gifted and talented. When I was very young, there was an enrichment course, where they taught me Spanish when I was like five. But most of the schools I was at didn't really support special needs children or gifted children. So I kind of just floated along.

Do you or your partner have an official or self-diagnosis of Asperger's/ASD?

My partner is self-diagnosed. I am currently waiting to get tested to see if I have either ADHD or am on the spectrum.

> I think our relationship has gone through a lot of things that probably many people would consider deal-breakers. We've been through a lot together, both the positive and the negative. It builds a certain bond. We both want to stay together for the rest of our lives because we've been through so much, and we still feel so safe around each other. When we live in a world that's quite hostile to both of us for a lot of reasons, we're not masking it.

How accepting do you feel you and your partner are about the diagnosis?

I think I'm pretty accepting. Even before there was a diagnosis, I knew there were things that were a little unusual. I always knew this was a quirky individual. I also viewed myself that way, before I understood that I had PTSD and gender dysphoria and stuff. I feel like I already understood, "Oh, there are these needs, and these are things that I can do to help." I guess it was kind of a relief when we realized, "Oh this is autism!" It became much clearer what would help those needs. We understood now why a specific behavior was happening—because of executive functioning around initiation.

I think it was sort of a shock for Frankie when they first talked about it. I remember clearly that, for a while, they had been telling me that they had being reading this nonbinary author on Medium, who also had been diagnosed autistic. They said to me at one point, "Oh, I really get these articles that this person is writing about being autistic!" In my head I was thinking, "So maybe you're thinking about whether or not you're autistic." A few months went by, and I'm like, "Well, you know you mentioned that you resonated very much with this person? Have you looked into that more?" And Autumn just looked at me with this cluelessness, and then I could see the lights pop on from the dots I had just connected. They were like, "Ohhh!" So I think they were sort of in shock for a little while. But then they read a lot and did a lot, and I think really embraced who they are.

What advice would you give to someone who's just discovering either their or their partner's ASD?

Be patient and go slow. I think that would be the best for any kind of transition.

Being trans is an "umbrella identity," and so is being autistic. I mean, figuring out that you're trans or that you're autistic tells you something, but at the same time, it doesn't. I think both are a journey of self-discovery, realizing, "Well, what is it that bothers me? What is it that I need to do? What is, 'Okay that is just me,' and what is stuff that I've just forced myself to do because I need to be safe in society?" That's why I say, "Go slow." You need some time to think about things. But at the same time, don't be afraid to embrace things once you do figure them out. Imposter syndrome is a real thing, both for individuals and for communities.

Anything else you'd like to say about the diagnosis?

My therapist probably thinks I may be on the spectrum because I am trans, and there is a higher prevalence of neurodivergence among trans individuals. Part of it is also that I have PTSD from a lot of childhood trauma, and so it's kind of hard to tell these apart. Am I having a sensory issue because I'm hypervigilant from PTSD, or is it an autistic trait? The way to treat that is different, depending on which source is correct. Or maybe both are correct! So I guess I sort of view myself as being in a nonbinary situation. I've seen this from other things I've read, where a lot of autistic people feel similar to people who've experienced trauma growing up. They might be sort of neurotypical, but they definitely understand a lot of neurodivergence. Sometimes their behaviors wouldn't be seen as neurotypical. There are definitely things that I do that I know a neurotypical person would not view as normal.

Relationship Challenges

What are the main challenges in your relationship?

Well, I guess the first one would be my own insecurities from PTSD. You can hear from the trauma history that it can be hard for me to believe that anyone could love me. Even if it's independent of what anyone is doing. I know, like right now, "Yes, I know Frankie loves me." But when I'm in crisis, that all goes out the window.

The second challenge is that I think sometimes Frankie can have trouble sensing what I might need, or how the things they say might impact me. That's definitely a theme.

I guess the third big challenge would be, because we both have mental health stuff and I have some physical stuff, so it can be hard to manage domestic chores. There was a time when my physical health was better, and I would do all of it. But that's not really sustainable. Sometimes, when I'm not doing so great, Frankie will have trouble picking up the slack because of their executive function stuff. It's a lot easier when I have the energy to direct them, and I can be like, "Hey, don't forget to start this thing." And then that gives them the push they need, but when I'm not doing well, that doesn't happen.

Do you struggle with executive functioning, sensory sensitivities, communication problems, and/or social challenges?

EXECUTIVE FUNCTIONING: There are some definite executive functioning issues. I've talked about initiation. Moderating is also a hard one for Frankie. Those are the two big ones I see routinely. Frankie has even worked into their daily routine before bed a time to check for bruises. They run into everything because they don't moderate, like "Oh, there's inanimate objects. Oh, whatever."

SENSORY SENSITIVITIES: Frankie definitely has a lot of sensory issues and gets worn down really fast if it's a high-input sort of environment. It sort of works out because I have a lot of hypervigilance, so I can also not handle large crowds and noise. But I also have more tolerance than Frankie does. We've worked it out. They definitely take a lot of time to meditate to help stay even. We talk about what events Frankie can go to. "What's going to be an okay environment? What is our escape plan if it ends up being a bad idea?" Things like that.

I know smells sometimes can be an issue, but especially when we were living in New York, it was me dragging Frankie around. They were in constant sensory overload, and we had no idea. I didn't know about my PTSD, so I was in high-anxiety mode. I was trying to just make everything work, so it sort of worked. But it's not what you really want in a relationship.

The only sensory issue I think I have is from hypervigilance, which is a little different. Like if there's a sudden loud noise, I might break down and cry because it's too much. But that's not so much sensory—for me, a sudden loud noise means panic.

COMMUNICATION PROBLEMS: I think things have gotten a lot better as Frankie has read up on things. They recognized that maybe they missed a lot of cues from me. Sometimes it can still be hard when I'm in crisis or when I'm not feeling well. That one can still be hard. Some of it comes from me just trying to remind myself that Frankie will do things if I just tell them what to do. I have to be really explicit, you know. But I think also from Frankie's point, they have also tried to develop, "What is the simple algorithm when Autumn is not doing well?" Like, "What things can I try to say or do or offer that might work?"

SOCIAL CHALLENGES: It's hard not having neurodiverse friends because I worry about people being accepting. They might not understand that something might come out sounding not very tactful, but that they don't have to be freaked out by that. I want

them to understand that if there's too much sensory stuff going on, somebody might bow out, and that's okay. It doesn't mean that there's anything wrong that's happened.

I also tend to have my own issues around feeling safe with people. Frankie is one of the few people I feel safe with. So it can be difficult because if I want to go out and meet friends, it's much easier to have somebody with me that I already feel safe with. But that can be hard for Frankie. So that's sort of a work in progress.

What have been some of the low points in your relationship?

Oh god, definitely living in New York was a very low time. I was dealing with gender dysphoria and PTSD but didn't know it at all. Frankie was still autistic then and didn't know it. It was very difficult because we were both in such overwhelm for different reasons all the time. My lab in particular was a really bad place to work. I was getting a lot of workplace abuse—getting taken advantage of and exploited. I'm pretty sure I ended up where I did just to re-victimize. A lot of similarities between my home and my workplace unfortunately.

If you had a magic wand and could wish away one of your marital challenges or a partner's trait, what would it be?

Probably their difficulty with discerning what is needed when I'm in crisis or sick. That's probably one of the hardest ones. For example, when Frankie's sick, I check in, "Oh, do you want soup? Do you have enough water? Should I bring you meds? Do you need more tissue? Would you like to watch something on Netflix? Let me find something." I'm doing all these things because I can sense that these are the sorts of things a sick person would probably like to have happen because they have no energy whatsoever.

But when I get sick, I have to figure out these things and tell Frankie. There's not as much natural sensing of my needs. It's been getting better—especially since them recognizing their autism—but that's always been hard for me to understand. Like, "I'm sick! Can you maybe guess a few things?" It also gets into my trauma history because I have experience of neglect. It can be doubly triggering for me.

What are some of your relational strengths and highlights?

I think we're very accepting of each other and of all of our differences. We've always had our core focused on loving each other. I came out as trans eight years into our marriage. It was a big thing that we stayed together. Frankie told me that I've helped them understand themself better. I think it was maybe a year or so after I came out that Frankie really started to embrace being nonbinary. Coming out actually helped them, which I know is not always or often the way it goes. I consider my-

self really lucky to have a partner that accepts that. I think part of it comes from the neurodivergence because there's not as many assumptions on how something should be.

What do you love most about your relationship?

I love the quirky playfulness of our relationship. When we're alone together, we don't really have to put on a show for each other or anything. Spontaneously, we'll be silly around each other. That's something I appreciate, and it partly comes from some of my mental health stuff and Frankie's neurology.

Intimacy

Is empathy or emotional reciprocity an issue in your relationship?

EMPATHY: I don't think empathy is as much an issue; I know Frankie is very empathetic. It's more like what I alluded to earlier. They sometimes don't know how to act on it. That's where I see a big disconnect. It's very obvious to me that Frankie feels for people that are in bad situations; they get upset when I'm in crisis and hurting. It's that they struggle with the ability to bridge that empathy into effective actions they can take now.

EMOTIONAL RECIPROCITY: Actually, we can both struggle with this. Sometimes it's like, "Does Frankie have the energy for emotions?" If Frankie has the energy to emote, then that reciprocity comes. On my end, PTSD and trauma lead to numbing out. I struggle with the experience of, like, "Oh, my emotions are numb. I feel nothing." It's hard to reciprocate; it's like someone put a screen in front of me.

> **Frankie's very cuddly. They really like to give hugs and to curl up with me. Frankie's gotten a lot better at expressing appreciation. So when I cook, they're very appreciative.**

Does ASD cause challenges in the area of sex/intimacy?

I think the biggest area that ASD causes challenges in is initiation. Frankie struggles with initiation, so that has always meant that I have to be the one to initiate. Prior to the ASD diagnosis, that was always uncomfortable for me on a number of levels. One, because it was hard to tell, like, "Okay, are you really interested in sex? Or are you just going along with it because something has been initiated." That's not the same as consent, and so that was often a thing I worried about. Some of this gets to gender. Initiation is commonly what men are expected to do. Before I came out and transitioned, that

didn't feel great for me. So now that continues, but even more so. With Frankie, I name the problem and ask, "Can you initiate some? I want to not feel like I have to be the guy all the time." So I think a lot of what has helped is talking openly about sex—about what we need and how we feel about things. I think more couples should do this, instead of just assuming roles.

What makes you feel loved and cared for by your partner, and what makes your partner feel loved and cared for by you?

There are a lot of things. Frankie's very cuddly. They really like to give hugs and to curl up with me. Frankie's gotten a lot better at expressing appreciation. So when I cook, they're very appreciative. In general, Frankie has become very affirming, especially in the past year. They even validate me when I'm just a mess and not doing well. They clearly say, "You don't have to do anything. You don't have to earn my love." This is a big deal because that's not how much of my life has worked.

I think definitely the cuddling. They like being cuddled, as well. I try to do little things that they like and that they forget to do for themselves. I try to be like, "Would you like some tea in the afternoon?" Or the cooking. I try to remind them about things that they say they want to do that got sidelined or that they didn't initiate because it's easier for me to remember these things.

Finances

Describe your economic situation. Does your financial situation impact your relationship in any way?

We're recently well-off. I think that ASD is a benefit in this case because Frankie has a job that involves a lot of information organization. It involves lots of spreadsheets, lists, and this sort of thing. It's perfect—right up their alley. So I don't think there are any major stressors, usually.

Frankie has a pretty good salary, which, you know, sometimes can work out with autism. They are high-performing and can read a lot, and so they're very desirable. Frankie has a good salary, which is good because I can't really help much right now. At least not with a full-time job. Frankie does our finances and is on top of it. They still manage some of the transition care for me because some stuff is out-of-pocket. They don't cover certain things. We want to look for a better place to live (that's one of our longer-term goals), but Massachusetts housing is expensive.

Support System

What support systems do you and your partner have?

Let's see...we both have our cat, Ben, obviously. He's a great support system. I have the one friend that I mentioned. We have some mutual friends. I have an individual therapist. Frankie now has an individual therapist, who is focused on gender identity stuff, which I think is good. We have Eva for couples therapy. I have a psychiatrist and a primary care doctor, who have both been pretty awesome to me. This is also a new thing in my life—that medical care doesn't have to involve horror stories.

Do you have friends individually and as a couple?

We definitely have friends as a couple, and I've been trying to branch out. It's just hard. I do have one friend who's basically my individual friend. There are a lot of things he can relate to because the rest of his family is autistic. His wife and kid are autistic, so he's kind of like, "We can both share these experiences." There have been a number of times when I've said something and he's like, "Oh God, that's happened to me! Exactly what you said!" For example, Frankie wanted to praise me because I can cook with two or three pans at once and thought this was amazing. I told him this, and he just laughed. He said, "I've had that exact situation! My wife thought it was so amazing that I could do that." So that's been a good relationship.

Do you have a spiritual practice? Does that impact your relationship?

I don't really have a spiritual practice.

I came out as an atheist when I was 13. I guess I try to think more about how I can incorporate things like nature and things. I've always enjoyed being in the woods and things like that.

Being in an ND Relationship

Do you feel that the challenges in ND relationships are unique?

I think they can be. I think there are some things like executive dysfunction that you have to learn about. That's not a thing that you're going to necessarily know how to approach until you've been in a situation with somebody who has those sorts of issues. I also think that a lot of things are not that different. I think the solution a lot of times is finding out how communication works between you two.

Based on your experiences, how informed do you find people are about ASD and ND marriage/relationships?

I guess my experience is that people aren't too aware of it. I don't have a huge social circle, and most people I'm around are autistic or know autistic people. A lot of times, people seem to not really understand what it means. They don't understand the degree of diversity that it means. To say somebody is autistic doesn't really tell you much about the person.

What is your perspective on being in an ND relationship?

I think that it works well for me because I have a lot going on with me that people would see as not normal. Having someone that doesn't really respond to the idea of societal norms takes a lot of pressure off of me. I don't feel like I have to perform a certain way so that I won't embarrass my partner.

What are the positives of being in an ND relationship?

The lack of needing to perform to some social standard. I think it's made us more receptive to what works best for us, instead of insisting, "*This* is the way it has to work because society says so."

What advice would you give to people who are in an ND relationship?

Figure out what communication works for you because it can look like a lot of different things. Don't let people judge you for it. People have told me that some of the things Frankie and I do are bizarre, and that they would hate it if they were in the relationship. Well, it's not your relationship.

Couples Counseling

Have you pursued couples counseling? Was it useful?

Yes, obviously. I find it helpful for us, especially as a check-in. It helps to set aside some time on a reasonable basis to see if there are any issues. Sometimes surprises happen, and usually when they come out is in therapy.

Concluding Thoughts

10-Point Marital Happiness Scale™

I think we'd be at a 10.

Would you say that you're in love with Frankie?

Yes. I think our relationship has gone through a lot of things that probably many people would consider deal-breakers. We've been through a lot together, both the positive and the negative. It builds a certain bond. We both want to stay together for the rest of our lives because we've been through so much, and we still feel so safe around each other. When we live in a world that's quite hostile to both of us for a lot of reasons, we're not masking it.

Do you think your relationship will go the distance?

We've overcome a lot of things together. We've been through a lot of big things that are hard societally, hard personally, hard on a lot of different levels. Our relationship has only grown more loving as those things have happened. At this point, I have trouble imagining what kind of a scenario could somehow break that.

CHAPTER 9

Amalia & Rajeev

A Belief System That Unites Us
Married Six Years

INTRODUCING AMALIA AND RAJEEV

*A*malia and Rajeev's story offers an influential narrative on many levels. Voices from the South Asian community are traditionally underrepresented, especially in the autistic and mental health space. Also, Amalia is the one with ASD, while her husband has his own rather significant executive functioning challenges. This makes them another double ND couple offering valuable perspectives. Additionally, many of our couples are non-religious or Christian. This couple, however, talk about how they implement Buddhist philosophy into an ND relationship. They also seem to have a spiritual village that promotes their continued growth.

Rajeev and Amalia show us how to take personal responsibility for breaking unhealthy family and personal patterns. They are able to view their relationship in the context of their past and avoid making the same mistakes. They also each see the strengths that the other brings and are committed to working on themselves and view it as an integral part of marriage. For example, Amalia is not always able to meet Rajeev at an emotional level, but she's aware of this and says, "I try to make up for it with physical affection and lots of hugs and kisses for him." On the other hand, Rajeev has difficulty sharing his emotions with Amalia. He explains, "I do not usually like to share my feelings with her because it makes me feel less of a man." He typically expresses his feelings through facial expressions or body language; however, because of her ASD, Amalia often misses these cues. He is learning to intentionally demonstrate his affection through hugs or saying, "thank you." He has also taken time in couples counseling to work on communicating his feelings verbally. Rajeev accommodates Amalia's ADHD when talking with her by keeping his sentences short and direct. Amalia makes a conscious effort to not over-talk and—after Rajeev pointed it out—to not cut him off in conversation.

Amalia and Rajeev function as a team. Amalia shares, Rajeev "is more emotionally intelligent than me, so I find comfort in the fact that I can go to him when I'm confused or need support interpreting people's feelings." Rajeev adds, "We work together on many aspects of our marriage, from cooking, to parenting, to maintenance of our house. We do not follow traditional gender roles, so are able to be more supportive of each other." Rajeev spends more time with the children, while Amalia focuses more on the practical planning and leading. Amalia admits, "Rajeev and I both struggle with executive functioning, but his challenges are more severe." Rajeev used to forget upcoming events, but now the couple has worked out a family calendar system that works for them.

This couple simply delights in each other. Rajeev puts it this way, "Ultimately, in spite of my many flaws, she treasures me as a person." He adds, "I think both our desire to improve our marriage, our awareness of our respective traits and the fact that we love each other trumps any challenge that our neurodiverse relationship brings." What a privilege to get a glimpse into their love story!

MEET AMALIA

Amalia (she/her/hers) is a 44-year-old, straight, Sri Lankan-American female. She identifies as having ASD and has a formal diagnosis. She has earned her MBA and works as a consultant. She lives in California with her husband Rajeev and sons, Adhyaan and Ravi. She has one previous marriage that lasted two years. She has been with her current husband for six years. They married after less than a year of dating.

Please describe any short- or long-term past romantic relationships

My first marriage and three serious relationships prior to this marriage

What has been great for us is that we both share a belief system that unites us.

were traumatic *and* life-changing. Having unsuccessful relationships made me realize that having a lot of narcissistic and ASD traits in the family and gene pool makes me a difficult partner in many ways. My relationships ended at least in part due to my tendency to have meltdowns, and say mean things in the heat of the moment, so I had to learn from all that heartbreak that something was different about me. It was a wakeup call for me and I had to commit to working on myself. Without the honest feedback I received from previous partners, I don't think I would have realized what my issues were, as I had huge blind spots. I've had to work on myself over the years.

Also, as an ASD woman and having special needs, these relationships also helped me realize what I didn't want in a partner. So for example, I learnt that I couldn't be with someone who was an extrovert, wasn't loyal, emotionally strong, or didn't have a stable family because that meant that the guy would need much more emotional support, repair, and validation from me...also someone who was on the same page philosophically and values-wise.

In a way, I'm glad I didn't meet my current husband earlier as I don't think I could have made this relationship work then.

How did you meet?

I met my current partner at our Buddhist center, we're Soka Gakkai Nichiren Buddhists. When I first saw him, he was just fresh off the boat from India—here to study as a foreign student—but I noticed how cute he was and he had an air of confidence about him. However, nothing happened at the time as he wasn't keen on dating because he was very focused on his master's program, so I moved on and met other guys.

Before my Buddhist practice, I used to get attached very quickly to men I didn't even like and were terrible fits. Then I'd get depressed and it would take me a while to heal. After my practice, I became more grounded, no longer got completely overwhelmed by my emotions or infatuation. When I did, I was able to get out of it faster.

After a couple of years, our friends found out about our mutual attraction and encouraged my husband to ask me out. It was an easy courtship and we were married in less than a year.

Diagnosis Journey

Did you receive any special education, support, or therapy while you were growing up?

No, maybe some ADHD meds would have helped, but I grew up in Sri Lanka and they don't really have such awareness there. Typically schools don't understand learning differences or mental health issues.

Do you or your partner have an official or self-diagnosis of ASD?

I was diagnosed with depression and anxiety after a breakup. That's when I first went on anti-depressants; they probably saved my life. I got an ADHD diagnosis because they told me at work that I was spacing out in meetings. I thought I was borderline personality for a while...Eventually, I self-diagnosed with ASD after reading some articles and books. This was in the midst of another painful, intense relationship. Everything became clear, finally.

How accepting do you feel you and your partner are about the diagnosis?

I like that I'm ASD! ASD makes me earnest, scientific, a deep thinker, and concerned about the state of the world. Although, in my early years, my intelligence didn't translate into success in the workplace, so there's that. I was underemployed in the first decade and a half of my adult life.

However there are days when I don't particularly identify with ASD, especially if I'm around people who are even more low emotional quotient (EQ) than me... I think my partner believes that I'm on the spectrum even more than I do. It helps him to better deal with all of my nonsense, you know? Without the ASD diagnosis, he might have just thought I was heartless. He has ASD in his family too, so maybe he married me because it felt familiar. But I think my husband has a few traits too; he's definitely ADD. He has major executive function issues and knowing that about him helps me be more patient and accepting of him. So it works both ways.

What advice would you give to someone who's just discovering either their own or their partner's ASD?

Read a lot about your ASD traits and own them. Don't dismiss your partner when they speak about ASD. Understand how hard it is for your partner. Say sorry often. Pay attention!

Read Eva's book, *Marriage and Lasting Relationships with Asperger's Syndrome*. Eva's book was eye-opening in how I view myself in the context of relationships.

Anything else you'd like to say about the diagnosis?

I wish I had an official diagnosis in my teens versus my late thirties, but the knowledge just wasn't available for someone like me to have received the appropriate evaluation. Eventually, I spoke to Eva and she wrote me a formal diagnosis letter, so I keep that around to remind me that it's official.

I've known for a long time that there is a significant amount of ASD in my family, but my traits are far less pronounced. I've read some books and forums about this. In comparison, my ASD presentation is subtle and other than my husband, I don't think anyone would have an inkling that I'm on the spectrum. I often say I'm ADHD versus ASD, depending on the group I'm in. I'm exhausted explaining myself to people who are not as informed, which is the majority of people, especially in South Asia.

Relationship Challenges

What are the main challenges in your relationship?

Right now, I would say having two young children makes it hard for us to spend time as a couple. His executive functioning issues are challenging. I want him to get some ADD meds. We've been seeing a couples counselor for a year now. The pandemic sort of made it necessary to focus on some things. My lack of emotional awareness might be challenging for him. You'll have to ask him.

Do you struggle with executive functioning, sensory sensitivities, communication problems, and/or social challenges?

EXECUTIVE FUNCTIONING: Rajeev and I both struggle with executive functioning, but his challenges are more severe. I use a lot of strategies for this, and now thanks to some couples therapy, he's been using the "bullet journal method" and working on lists, timelines, reminders, calendars, and other strategies. He has improved a lot, so I hope that we'll do even better as time goes on.

SENSORY SENSITIVITIES: I have chemical sensitivities, so he's had to change some of his bath products from the early days of our relationship. But now our house is mostly chemical free. We only buy cruelty-free, non-toxic when possible. I'm sensitive to the sun, but using polarized sunglasses helps. I like deep pressure hugs and my husband is great at those without my having to ask. I also love rocking chairs and swings and we have some of those in the house!

COMMUNICATION PROBLEMS: My husband would say that I overtalk, but he's supposed to let me know

when I'm doing that. I've also deliberately tried to work on this, it's a work in progress.

Also, I try to not excessively talk about work to him, and try to just speak to colleagues when I need to. I also have one or two girlfriends that I can rely on for support on a regular basis. Having ASD traits, he too struggles with expressing himself, but working with a couple's therapist has been useful for us to voice our thoughts and feelings. I do wish we had more time to talk in general or spend leisure time, but it's been hard with children and work pressures. Hopefully that'll get better in time.

SOCIAL CHALLENGES: I defer to him on how to handle certain social situations that arise, because I tend to get anxious and overthink how people might misunderstand me. He is more emotionally intelligent than me, so I find comfort in the fact that I can go to him when I'm confused or need support interpreting people's feelings. We have different strengths with the kids so we talk a lot about them and how to be more present to them.

What have been some of the low points in your relationship?

Sick kids, housework, job pressures, home repairs...it's a pile-on of stuff that causes frustrations. Our competing needs for alone time and time to connect can be hard to juggle.

When I have my meltdowns, those are low points that really suck for Rajeev. I remember when we were in Spain for our honeymoon. We were late getting on a train, and I really let him have it. That was really horrible for him. My meltdowns are rough and can erode the relationship. My past relationships didn't survive my outbursts, so I think it says a lot about Rajeev and how solid he is.

I need to cut him more slack on his absent-mindedness and such. I'm working on it. I've started keeping track of my meltdowns in terms of when they happen and what triggers them. That's helped reduce them.

If you had a magic wand and could wish away one of your marital challenges or a partner's trait, what would it be?

His executive functioning issues. It really raises my anxiety sometimes, especially if I haven't chanted, you know—as part of my Buddhist practice. I'm sure he could say the same about my emotional blindness. I hope it doesn't frustrate him too much. And my meltdowns.

Relationship Strengths

What are some of your strengths and highlights?

We love each other very much and have a natural chemistry. We like being together even when we're just watching a favorite show or sitting on our deck at night just relaxing. We're a good team. I rely a lot on him. He tends to ground me and helps me settle down. We make decisions to-

gether. He's a good person. Loyal, emotionally tough. I'm grateful.

What has been great for us is that we both share a belief system that unites us. I would say having children has been the absolute highlight of our relationship. Our travels together, which I hope we will have a lot more of.

> We're a good team. I rely a lot on him. He tends to ground me and helps me settle down. We make decisions together. He's a good person. Loyal, emotionally tough. I'm grateful.

What do you love most about your relationship?

I like that we have a happy family. We co-parent well together. Our sons are so gorgeous and there are days, when I just take it all in...and I have to pinch myself. My beautiful husband, my sons, our puppy, and our lovely home.

Intimacy

Is empathy or emotional reciprocity an issue in your relationship?

Yes, my husband thinks I lack empathy. Sometimes I'm too logical and not always able to see the emotional side of things, especially when it comes to him. So if he's not feeling well or whatever, I don't always recognize it unless he tells me and even when he does, it takes me a while to be present to him.

I try to make up for it with physical affection and lots of hugs and kisses for him. If I'm in work mode or whatever, it can be hard for me to slow down or be present. I overwork which is another problem. Sharing feelings is hard for us both, but I make sure to check in with him. I have a blind spot here, so I'll be curious to see what he thinks.

Does ASD cause challenges in the area of sex/intimacy?

We have a good sex life, although I wish my husband would initiate more. I think that's more of an absent-minded thing with him and also he grew up in a household where conversations and knowledge about sex were repressed, which I think makes him more inhibited. We could also do with having sex more often, it happens more on holidays. We have great sex when we do get around to it. We could probably be more adventurous, but with children, time and energy are at a premium. And we have good chemistry even outside the bedroom; there's a lot of physical affection and attention.

What makes you feel loved and cared for by your partner, and what makes your partner feel loved and cared for by you?

I love spending time with him, cuddling and making love. All of that

helps me feel loved and connected. When he goes out of his way to celebrate my birthday or does something special for me like remembering my favorite chocolate or clothing brand, that really helps me feel special. I also feel cared for when he preemptively stays on top of all his tasks, the household chores, and takes care of the baby.

I think he likes it when we sit and watch a movie together that he's picked for us. I probably should ask him this question to be honest. I suspect he likes it when we cuddle and lay in bed just being and not talking too much. He also prefers more spontaneous connections that we can have here and there, which I have to make sure I'm present for.

Finances

Describe your economic situation. Does your financial situation impact your relationship in any way?

We both work and make a decent living as skilled professionals. I think my ASD helps with our finances as I believe I owe my career to my ASD traits. We also work with an accountant and financial advisor to help keep us on track about finances as neither of us have a big strength in this area.

Support System

What support systems do you and your partner have?

Our families to various degrees,

mainly his—his parents are kind and always available to listen and be there. We have some good friends in our community who live close by and some far away. I've a close friend in Germany, and another in Florida who I also talk to weekly. Rajeev has his own set of friends and I do as well. And we're resourceful in terms of finding support when we need it... even if it's professional.

Do you have friends individually and as a couple?

Both! A lot of our friends are from our Buddhist community, college, work, and neighbors. I also think that we're happy by ourselves too given that we're both introverts. I once had a boyfriend who was an extreme extrovert and being with him was exhausting. Rajeev and I are more compatible.

Do you have a spiritual practice? Does that impact your relationship?

Both of us found SGI Nichiren Buddhism a few years before we met. We chant this mantra "nam-myoho-renge-kyo" and this has been a great tool to manage my anxiety, frustrations, and negative emotions, but recently I also got on anti-depressants, and ADD meds. All baby doses—and I use marijuana on occasion as well, but the Buddhist practice helps a lot.

Parenting

Tell us about yourselves as parents in this marriage.

I think we parent well together. A lot of communication about the kids. Some days an almost play-by-play unfolding of how the day is going and how the kids are doing and what needs doing with them and the house. My husband is very hands-on and loves playing with our boys, while I'm more the practical planner and leader. I think it's a good mix.

Being in an ND Relationship

Do you feel that the challenges in ND relationships are unique?

The executive functioning issues related to my husband and my lack of emotional presence in the relationship can cause problems for us. So that must be unique to us.

Based on your experiences, how informed do you find people are about ASD and ND marriage/relationships?

Not at all. A lot of misconceptions and people generally think it's something that only children have or very socially awkward adults. Women like me are invisible even to the medical community. We live in the shadows. There's still a lot of stigma.

What are the positives of being in an ND relationship?

The positives are probably that we don't adhere to gender stereotypes. We do try to communicate honestly about things. We're trying to be aware of our issues and are working on them.

What advice would you give to people who are in an ND relationship?

Admit to your faults, even when it's painful. Address your weaknesses and baggage and don't blame the other person. If you want to change your partner completely, then perhaps you're with the wrong person. I've been there with other autistic partners. They had no interest in working on their issues. It was downright depressing, just too stressful. So commit to working on your issues.

Couples Counseling

Have you pursued couples counseling? Was it useful?

Yes, we started couples counseling with Eva last year and it helped resolve a lot of things. We meet less regularly now, but it's helpful. It's important to have that time to air out grievances. Counseling helped my husband get over the shame over his disorganization, which has enabled him to create solutions around that. Yeah, couples counseling is great.

Concluding Thoughts

10-Point Marital Happiness Scale™

I would say we're at 9 or 10 most days. Occasionally when we have a big blow out, I think we are probably at a 7 maybe. I'm curious to hear what my husband would say about this.

Would you say you're in love with Rajeev?

Yes, he's very cute. In the past though, I've had a hangup over an ex. Thankfully, I've moved on and can say that I'm in love with my husband. I just wish we had more time to spend together. We got married when I was older, so we then had to focus on making babies right away, but I hope we can make more time for each other and fall even deeper in love.

Do you think your relationship will go the distance?

Yes, I think our relationship will go the distance. We also enjoy each other, and have enough excitement checking off things on the bucket list for me to envision us being together well into our golden years.

MEET RAJEEV

Rajeev (he/him/his) is a 35-year-old Indian male. He lives with his wife and child in Southern California. He has a master's degree and works as a software engineer. Rajeev and Amalia were together for a few months before getting married. They have been married for six years. Rajeev suspects he has ASD traits too.

Please describe any short- or long-term past romantic relationships

None. Of course, I had crushes on a few girls growing up and before meeting Amalia, but none of them grew into any sort of relationship. I was always, and still am, a shy and introverted person. Talking to girls, let alone communicating a romantic interest in them, was a task too hard to imagine. However, over time, my Buddhist practice enabled me to develop a stronger sense of self, which helped a lot in navigating through such insecurity and nervousness.

How did you meet?

I had known her through our Buddhist community for at least a couple of years before we started dating. My impression of her was that of a smart, attractive, and wise person. However, I was a foreign student working on a demanding master's degree, and I was more concerned about whether I would get a job after my graduation or not. I had no idea at that time she was romantically interested in me—I learned that through common friends.

It was while she was on a trip to see her family that I found the courage to message her on Facebook. We continued with some back and forth text messages, then one evening she

called me and bluntly told me that we should go out on a date. She caught me off guard, but we finally went out on a date.

> *If I were to marry someone who is more docile or tolerant, I might be more in control, but ultimately, it would not help either one of us. I believe an effective relationship needs to have partners who complement each other, so that each can improve. I would rather have this than a "fantasy romance."*

Diagnosis Journey

Did you receive any special education, support, or therapy while you were growing up?

No, I didn't.

My father was very well-accomplished in his engineering career. He had graduated from a very prestigious institution. My brother was also much better in studies than I was. The generally accepted solution was that I just needed to concentrate more on my studies and work harder.

Do you or your partner have an official or self-diagnosis of ASD?

I do not have any official diagnosis of anything yet, but my wife believes strongly that I have ADHD and executive functioning issues. I might have some ASD traits too. She wants me to get officially diagnosed as she believes it will help me understand how my brain functions, and get treatment.

How accepting do you feel you and your partner are about the diagnosis?

Amalia had told me that she had ADHD. When we were dating, I had seen her working with a coach to help her achieve her personal and professional goals. I kind of admired her for that because if it were me, I would resist that. She has difficulty following me in conversations if I take too much time trying to describe something. So when I talk to her I have to keep my sentences brief and to the point.

She has some strong ASD traits. Sometimes, she kind of reminds me of my father—very logical and practical over empathy or emotion. Like my father she is driven by practicality and almost never by emotion. It's hard to have "fun" conversations with her. Most of the time when we are alone, our conversation revolves around future plans and finances, or how her family treated her. Not that I am great at initiating fun conversations, but sometimes I wish we could just behave like cute couples. The only exception is when she is drunk and acts funny, or if she smokes weed.

As for myself, it's complicated. On the one hand, I do see certain traits in my behavior—both ADHD and ASD. On the other hand I feel I can "solve" them by brute force—work harder, pay more attention, and there's an unwillingness to seek professional help. I know I am wrong, because my "strategy" has not really worked out so far. It has to do with how I was brought up. I was never diagnosed during my childhood. As a family, we were totally ignorant of such things. I grew up with low self-confidence and I was introverted. So, seeking help always felt like a weakness, and I did not want to feel that I was weaker than I already was. That's why I have been avoiding getting an official diagnosis, because then I have to admit that there's some limitation or disability in me. But I need to get it.

What advice would you give to someone who's just discovering either their or their partner's ASD?

Apart from educating themselves on ASD, I would suggest doing things together on a regular basis that both of them enjoy. It is also important to give each other space. But the bottom line is that it is important to get educated about ASD, especially in relationships. If you know about it and know how to work with your partner, then you can overcome many relationship challenges and live a more fulfilling life.

Relationship Challenges

What are the main challenges in your relationship?

Initiation—I struggle with initiating tasks and affection or love making. Displays of affection are hard as growing up adults in my life never showed affection or love toward each other, so it's hard for me to keep in mind that I need to show love and affection toward my wife. But I try to take some action like hugging her or giving her a kiss, or even forcing myself to say thank you in response to a nice gesture (I feel very awkward saying thank you's by the way).

Amalia usually is not empathetic toward my feelings or my condition during certain moments, even though it might be apparent. She expects me to communicate my feelings, but I struggle with it since I feel it's "un-manly" to do so.

Our marriage counselor advised me to challenge my tendency to repress my feelings because it's not healthy, regardless of whether what I feel is positive or negative, or whether I am at the right end of the argument or not. So, over time, I find myself expressing more. In fact by communicating like this, I understand my error if I am in the wrong. And regardless of the outcome I feel better about myself for voicing my feelings.

Also, many times in the past, our individual activities or plans would clash with each other, or I would forget about an upcoming event. Nowadays, we keep a common calendar which we update with our individual events. It prevents us from stepping on each other, and reminds us of important schedules.

Do you struggle with executive functioning, sensory sensitivities, communication problems, and/or social challenges?

EXECUTIVE FUNCTIONING: I do not think she has any issues with executive functioning, but she says she has. She is the planner in our family. She plans for both short and long term and gets the steps done. Does not forget things like I often do. She has a pretty good memory—especially the names of people and places, of events that took place when and where, etc. I remember things based on imagery in my head. It's hard for me to remember names of places, people, etc. Not her.

SENSORY SENSITIVITIES: Like I suggested above, I am a very visual person. My wife likes to talk a lot but if she does not describe visually what she is saying, then I quickly lose interest. In fact, I am realizing it for the first time because I am posed with this question. Apart from that, my wife is sensitive to smell. She smells the trash sometimes from far away and forces me to clear out the trash even if the bag is not full, or at odd hours when I want to rest. She is also very sensitive to smells and fragrances used in toiletries and insists on using fragrance-free products as much as possible. One the plus side, she is a physical person. She needs physical touch and affection to feel loved and connected.

COMMUNICATION PROBLEMS: She has a bad habit of interrupting me when I am speaking to someone. If I am trying to explain something to someone, she interrupts me and tries to "fill in for me." Often what she says is not what I intend. So, you can imagine how annoying it can be for me. She also has difficulty understanding how I feel based on my non-verbal cues, even if they might be quite apparent. Since I struggle to express my feelings, I expect others to read my body language. Some people can do it to various degrees, but Amalia has a really hard time. This frustrates me, especially when I am unwell, in pain, or tired and she talks to me like everything is okay.

Another thing is that she expects me to get into a sexy mood instantly in order to have sex with her, without giving me time to transition. It's hard for me to have sex with her when just minutes ago I was engaged in something else.

SOCIAL CHALLENGES: I am an introvert, so I find it difficult connecting with people I do not know. At such times, I tend to depend on her to engage with people till I'm comfortable. She's more social than me. Some-times she would advise me on how to connect with others. However, I've noticed that she has difficulty empathizing with people or reading people's state of mind. This leads her to say things she did not intend to.

What have been some of the low points in your relationship?

There are at least two that I can think of—our communication and meaningful time spent with each other needs some big improvement. It usually translates to not going on date nights as much as we would like to and not spending romantic moments with each other. We're seeing a couples counselor to address these things.

However, I do not know whether we have had a "low point" really. I mean, we do sometimes argue, and I tend to lose my temper and shout at her because sometimes I think she is in control and it pisses me off, and also because sometimes she does not listen to my side of the argument. More often than not, I realize she is right, so I end up getting frustrated and angry with myself. For example—there have been a few times when we were on a long drive, and she thought that was the best time to confront me. I couldn't avoid her, so she would push me about certain things I wasn't comfortable discussing. Like, she would ask me why I wasn't looking for a better-paying job. So we ended up arguing, she strongly communicated her feelings and thoughts, and

I ended up sulking the rest of the way. I felt angry that she wanted me to challenge my comfort zone, and frustrated at myself that I was not doing anything about it. It made me feel sort of powerless—as opposed to being "the man"—and that is a terrible feeling to have.

Another example was when I had failed to give her a gift or a card on our wedding anniversary. She did her part, which made me think that I was this selfish guy. A couple days later, we drove a few hundred miles to visit my family. While we were on our way and I was driving, she asked me why I had forgotten about our anniversary, and I had absolutely nothing to say. It was the worst drive of my life. I still remember vividly how I felt. It's been a good lesson I guess.

So yeah, I do have complaints about her. I guess that's how relationships are—you cannot get everything the way you want, there's always some compromise, but that's how you learn together and get the opportunity to become better people.

If you had a magic wand and could wish away one of your marital challenges or a partner's trait, what would it be?

Her lack of empathy. To her credit, she does try to empathize, but her natural tendency keeps her from noticing how I feel, and I have to point it out. She is a very kind-hearted person when she realizes what the situation is. And I wish I could improve myself with a magic wand so that I feel equal—but that's not the answer to this question.

Relationship Strengths

What are some of your relational strengths and highlights?

In terms of highlights, I think of when we had our babies. To conceive our second son, we sought out professional help. It was stressful in a way because Amalia was doing so many check-ups and visits, was taking fertility medicines, that I had to inject her with. And we were not guaranteed a favorable outcome, in fact the odds were stacked up against us. We were unsuccessful once, so the second time the process was more intense and stressful. But we made it. Even during childbirth, there were complications, but we were a solid team. She showed amazing courage. I was able to take care of her even though things happened fast and I was unprepared. And when she finally gave birth, it was so amazing. It was a shared magical and intimate experience—amid all the months of stress and hard work. It showed us how united we were.

What do you love most about your relationship?

We complement each other—my wife keeps a check on the practical and financial side of things, whereas I lend the emotional support. We have a common spiritual practice, which acts as the backbone of our relationship. We work together on many aspects of our marriage, from cooking, to parenting, to maintenance of our house. We do not follow traditional gender roles, so are able to be more supportive of each other.

She likes and values me as a person, and involves me in all decisions.

> *During childbirth, there were complications, but we were a solid team. She showed amazing courage. I was able to take care of her even though things happened fast and I was unprepared. And when she finally gave birth, it was so amazing.*

What are some coping strategies you use in your relationship?

Having a spiritual practice helps a lot. We do our daily prayers together, we make some common goals, ask each other about what we want for our family. We watch movies and TV, taking turns to choose something. Certain programs we would like to watch together, and sometimes, we introduce each other to something new. She's made me watch some films that I would not have otherwise, and I have ended up enjoying them. Another strong coping strat-

egy is vacation—she insists on going on a vacation for a change of pace and environment. Although I also enjoy traveling, I think she benefits more from it because for her it's a huge stress relief and grounds her in our relationship.

For me, I tend to prioritize some time to myself alone doing things that I enjoy. I think it's because I am an introverted person. Activities like reading, watching movies, doing some artistic stuff, playing video games, in general having some time for myself alone, helps me get refreshed.

Intimacy

Is empathy or emotional reciprocity an issue in your relationship?

I feel that my wife struggles with empathy. She is unaware of my emotional state, and forgets things of an emotional nature. However, once she becomes aware of it, she tries to make up for it. I do not usually like to share my feelings with her because it makes me feel less of a man; however, she does reciprocate well when I share positive emotions like love, affection, or praise.

Does ASD cause challenges in the area of sex/intimacy?

I think my biggest gripe is that for her, it's a scheduled activity. She tells me beforehand that she wants to have sex, which is a turn-off for me because it's something I feel like she tries to fit in amid a busy schedule. She thinks that it's because I am not initiating, I'm not thinking about it, but it's not always true. I do sometimes initiate, and it happens naturally. I think, instead of scheduling sex, she should focus on spontaneity.

I have to do my part in showing my affection for her frequently. I've got to work on going up to her and giving her a hug or kissing her, or thanking her when she does something nice for me.

What makes you feel loved and cared for by your partner, and what makes your partner feel loved and cared for by you?

She knows a lot about me and my family, and tries to buy me thoughtful gifts on special occasions. She also initiates activities to spend time together. She cares about my health as well as looks. Ultimately, in spite of my many flaws, she treasures me as a person. This point is apparent in her many subtle behaviors. She remembers many things about me, gleaned from whatever I have shared with her about my life since I met her...she remembers the details. If I mention to her that there is something that I like, then when she does something nice for me—for example on my birthday—she buys it for me. I feel it's the little things she remembers that's really awesome. I wish I could say the same for me.

However, when I make the effort and buy her thoughtful gifts and make plans for her special occasions, cuddle with her at night and when we have sex, that's when she feels connected to me. I also try to do as many household chores as I can. I love choosing outfits and dresses for her...she feels that I have good taste. One more thing—spending time together, just talking and holding each other—she kind of likes that very much. For example, just the previous night I sat down beside her while she was working. We did not talk much because she was busy, but I am sure she appreciated my presence.

Finances

Describe your economic situation. Does your financial situation impact your relationship in any way?

We both work. So financially we are doing pretty well. We were able to buy a house in the neighborhood that we like, and have met some financial goals together. It definitely makes us feel secure.

Early last year I got laid off from my previous company. Although my unemployment did not cause a financial impact that was as bad as I had feared, Amalia felt the financial strain. I could see that she was overworking, and was stressed and exhausted, while I was anxious about getting employed. In spite of that, however, it united us in my struggle to find a new job. And we did not let the challenging period get the better of us, thanks to our spiritual practice. Eventually, after a few months, I began working for a company I liked.

Support System

What support systems do you and your partner have?

Our spiritual community and practice are probably the biggest support system. She has a few friends that she relies on for emotional support. I have a set of friends of my own who I enjoy. We enjoy traveling together which gives us time to reconnect and allows a change of pace. Our sons, they are really funny and help me relieve stress and anxiety. On top of that we have our puppy and he's an important emotional support.

Do you have friends individually and as a couple?

Yes, we do. I have been introduced to many new wonderful people through Amalia, and together we have them over on a regular basis for lunch or dinner. It makes us happy. I have a group of college friends whom I have maintained communication with over the years, but they live out of state, or country, so it has been challenging. I have friends in our Buddhist community. Those are the ones that I am more in touch with, just because we live closer. Having a family makes it hard to stay connected, but when I spend time with friends it takes away the stress from

married life. Amalia likes to hang out with her friends too and I watch the kids when she does. I feel like such interactions strengthen our relationship as a couple.

Do you have a spiritual practice? Does that impact your relationship?

Yes. Amalia and I are Nichiren Buddhists, and we practice with an organization consisting of people from all walks of life. It helps us in many ways. First, it helps us to decide and work toward our common goals, i.e. it unites us. Secondly, it enables each of us to self-reflect on our shortcomings and helps us face and overcome them. For example, I am able to understand myself and have become more self-aware thanks to my practice, which in turn helps me to reflect on my behavior toward Amalia.

Parenting

Tell us about yourselves as parents in this marriage.

We love our boys very much. Amalia is a very practical person, and very grounded. She takes care of many practical things—books, toys, etc. for them, planning for schools and education, their growth and development. I am more involved with the emotional and behavioral stuff—interpreting their needs, communication, spending time and playing with them, feeding them, etc. Amalia is good at teaching them to become independent, and getting them to help us around the house sometimes.

Being in an ND Relationship

Do you feel that the challenges in ND relationships are unique?

I would imagine typical relationships are somewhat easier, but I know things are always much more complex than that. I feel some degree of neurodiversity is essential because then both partners can complement each other and cancel out at least some of their individual weaknesses. I think if I were to marry a non-ASD person, I would not grow as much, or become aware of myself (or my limitations) to the degree that I currently am. Again, saying this is probably oversimplifying things, as I have never known a "typical relationship" given my family history. Amalia is my first romantic partner. But I can say for sure that I am currently happy in my relationship. Of course, both of us have traits we do not like about each other, but that doesn't make me concerned about our future.

Based on your experiences, how informed do you find people are about ASD and ND marriage/relationships?

I grew up watching behavioral patterns in my family, but because there wasn't violence or classical addictions, I assumed my family was normal. Back then I did not even know of a term called ASD. I was aware of

autism but only the severe kind. Now that I am better informed, I realize that various people from both sides of the family display ASD traits to varying degrees.

At present, I do find more and more people are aware of these traits, but there is some stigma around the topic. I think people, even I, see ASD traits as a defect, rather than an explanation of how their brain functions. Nobody wants to be labeled as having a defect or be perceived that way.

What is your perspective on being in an ND relationship?

We do have some issues in our relationship regarding communication and intimacy, but we are working together to improve on those fronts. I think both our desire to improve our marriage, our awareness of our respective traits, and the fact that we love each other trump any challenge that our neurodiverse relationship brings. Rather than seeing it as an issue, I see it as an opportunity for my personal growth as a human being. Also it helps me in other ways because the skills she brings to our relationship are the ones I lack, and vice versa. So we end up complementing each other.

If I were to marry someone who is more docile or tolerant, I might be more in control, but ultimately, it would not help either one of us. I believe an effective relationship needs to have partners who complement each other, so that each can improve. I find such dynamics to be the case with us. I would rather have this than a "fantasy romance."

What advice would you give to people who are in an ND relationship?

I think the most important thing is to learn about yourself and your partner, and to educate yourself about ASD and how to cope with it. I and my partner regularly see a couples counselor which helps us a lot, so that is one suggestion. Lastly, you have to decide how happy and secure you are in the relationship. You have to realize that you need to take responsibility in the relationship too—you cannot blame your partner. When you are self-empowered through educating yourself, learning about yourself and your partner, and taking responsibility in the relationship, you will find that you are happier and more fulfilled than you could have imagined, or you will find that you are in a much better position to decide whether you want to leave the relationship.

Couples Counseling

Have you pursued couples counseling? Was it useful?

I was initially quite reluctant when Amalia suggested we see one. But I gave in finally and yes, now we see one regularly. I find it quite useful because it allows me to voice my opin-

ions without the feeling that I will be judged. I also have someone who can listen to my point of view and give me suggestions on how I can improve my behavior or communication with my partner. And it also lets me vent off steam.

Concluding Thoughts

10-Point Marital Happiness Scale™

I am quite happy with my marriage with Amalia—a 10. We get along quite well. I love her. And she is very wise and gives great suggestions. I admire that. Most of the time (like 95 percent) when she suggests something, I do not question her because I know she is right. She is very pragmatic. These things are very important for a happy marriage because then you know you can rely on you partner long term. It takes away a lot of uncertainty and stress when you have a partner like that. Now, I just need to improve myself and do a better job in being a husband.

Would you say that you're in love with Amalia?

Yes, I am in love with her. I enjoy our romantic moments and our intimacy. I think aside from being pretty, she is very much grounded in reality and has a lot of wisdom and courage. This is a combination that is very hard to come by. But I think most importantly she really loves me too. She accepts my shortcomings. I have never felt that I needed to pretend to be someone else when I am with her. Sometimes when I think about it, I am thankful that she loves me for who I am. Yeah, in short, I think it would be quite hard imagining living with someone else.

Do you think your relationship will go the distance?

I think it will go on forever. We sometimes joke that in our next life we will swap places—she will be the husband and I the wife! Anyways, I think that we have a very strong and secure base of trust, financial security, and mutual love. We know that our relationship has some issues, and we are actively working on improving ourselves. I think this is a reflection of our commitment toward each other.

CHAPTER 10

Robbie & Viola

How Much of Myself I Can Be
Together Three Years

INTRODUCING ROBBIE AND VIOLA

*T*his story is of the youngest couple in the book, and, therefore, it's like looking into the future! Viola is bisexual, black, and an engineer. Robbie is white, Italian-American, and an engineer with ASD. They play video games together. They geek out on the same things. Viola explains, "We sometimes do projects together, like programming. We speak the same language for that, so we'll both program in the same way. We'll talk to each other like we're talking to a computer." Their support for each other is deep and unwavering.

Even their painful experiences have united them further. Viola and her family members have had many traumatic experiences of racism, and she helps Robbie to understand this marginalized perspective. Robbie's loyalty and support during an abortion early on the relationship brought them closer. Even their family members' rigid and orthodox views drive them nearer to each other. It's what

every relationship should be, ND or otherwise.

Viola and Robbie have put in significant effort to overcome unhealthy patterns from their families of origin. They learned in couples counseling how to be explicit with each other in their communication, clearly requesting what they need or expect from each other. They've also developed the habit of clearing the air before bedtime—making sure they end the day united and at peace with each other.

Not everything is sunshine and rainbows, though. Until he met Viola, Robbie had not developed regular habits of personal hygiene. Robbie admits, "I was ashamed that I didn't have the habits already. I need to get better at the very basics of brushing my teeth and taking showers." Viola helped push him to mature in this area.

It doesn't take long to see that the love in this relationship is absolutely sincere. Viola shares, "He's said, 'I love you,' so many times, but I think that was the first time he said, 'I'll never leave you.' Autistics are the most honest people in the world, and when I looked into his eyes, I knew that it was true." In Robbie's words, "Mostly, she's sort of perfect. I kind of love her."

These two are convinced that they want to get married and raise a family together. Based on the hard work and personal growth they've already experienced, it's not hard to see them creating a lasting life together.

MEET ROBBIE

I think the thing I like most about our relationship is how open I can be with Viola and how much of myself I can be around her. She doesn't judge me, and if she does, it's in a playful manner. There's no mystery, and there's no fear of being myself around her.

Robbie (he/him/his) is a 24-year-old, cishet, Italian-American male. He identifies as having ASD. He has earned his bachelor's in computer science, and he works as a software engineer. He lives in Massachusetts with his girlfriend and a roommate, as well as a cat and several fish. He has been dating his girlfriend for three and a half years.

Please describe any short- or long-term past romantic relationships

None. I hadn't really been in a relationship before I met Viola. I did not

have any prior sexual experience. I did not know how to approach relationships. I did not know how to talk to girls. Even in my teens and twenties, I didn't really talk to them. There was also another challenge—I did not really know how to talk to *people*.

How did you meet?

I remember first seeing Viola in a shared class that we had in college, and I was infatuated with her. I wanted to talk to her. I found out she was into *Dungeons and Dragons*, so I messaged her on Facebook a *Dungeons and Dragons* role-playing thing, and she played along with it. That's how we started talking, and then we went out on a date.

Diagnosis Journey

Did you receive any special education, support, or therapy while you were growing up?

Yeah. I was diagnosed in elementary school with ADHD. I was in a special education program, and then I had accommodations in that program where I could take longer on a test. But toward my senior year (maybe it was my junior year) when I started getting rebellious, I convinced my parents that I did not want to be in special education anymore.

Do you or your partner have an official or self-diagnosis of ASD?

I don't remember where it was, but I remember just being in a test room. They did all these tests, and they came out with an official diagnosis that I have ADHD.

When I was in college and I was depressed, they took me to a psychiatrist because they could not figure out why I was depressed. It seemed like I did not have any reason to be depressed. They had this little app where you could see the doctor's notes, and one of my doctor's notes for the last session I did with them said "potential ASD." I think the next session they were going to have me do an ASD diagnosis test, and I stopped going because I did not want to find out that I had ASD. I sort of regret not going because it would have been nice to know. Recently, I have been looking into it a lot, and I think I do probably have it. I want to get an official diagnosis.

How accepting do you feel you and your partner are about the diagnosis?

I rejected it completely when I was 21 or 22. I don't know why I rejected it.

I think it was mostly because I didn't understand how I could have ASD when I was younger because I was officially diagnosed with ADHD.

When Viola started talking to me a lot about it last year, I accepted it. I realized, "I do have this diagnosis, and I have to deal with it." Not "deal with it" in a bad way, but just *confront* it. It is something that I can't just sweep under the rug.

Yeah, Viola's super accepting of it. I think maybe that was one of my fears of getting diagnosed—I wasn't sure how a relationship would work if I had ASD. But Viola's super accepting of it. She's even helped me find and get better at things that I didn't know I had trouble with.

What advice would you give to someone who's just discovering either their own or their partner's ASD?

I would say, be very understanding and do research. I think that helped Viola a lot. And be very understanding that a lot of the things that they do, it's not just them. It's how their brain works. Once you understand what's going on in their brain and once you communicate with them, you get to know the problems that they're having. Then you can have a very fruitful and a very loving relationship.

Relationship Challenges

What are the main challenges in your relationship?

I think the first one that came to mind was my hygiene. I don't have good habits of hygiene. It's gotten a lot better since we started dating, but when we first started dating, Viola did not like my lack of good habits. We had a lot of arguments about it. Not fights, but she would say, "You know, Robbie, you need to do this." And I was ashamed that I didn't have the habits already. I need to get better at the very basics of brushing my teeth and taking showers. I've gotten a lot better, though, and I thank Viola for that—for really pushing me to do that.

I take things very literally. When I do say things sarcastically, people don't think I'm using sarcasm. So I don't say things sarcastically; I say almost everything literally. But before Viola found out I had ASD, she didn't realize that I was saying and taking everything literally. I think that is still a struggle we have, but we're a lot better at it now.

I think the third thing would probably be my lack of romance. I really want to get better at that. There was a time when Viola would say, "I know you love me, but I don't feel loved." That really hurt me because I didn't know how to show her that I love her besides saying that I loved her. She wanted *romance*. She wanted to be shown love.

Last year, that was a big struggle for me. I've been looking up online how to be romantic—I sort of feel like a teenager when I do it. But I search, "How do I send flirt messages over text?" I have been using more emo-tion in my messages, rather than being so literal. I've also been watching this guy on YouTube, who has ASD. He explains certain things in really good ways.

Do you struggle with executive functioning, sensory sensitivities, communication problems, and/or social challenges?

EXECUTIVE FUNCTIONING: One struggle would be related to my short-term memory—it will sometimes empty out. Occasionally, if I have a list of things in my head that I just got like two minutes ago, I'll all of a sudden forget what I was supposed to do. We've started writing things down more. Then it's not lost in my mind; it's written down somewhere so I can look at it again. We do this for almost everything.

SENSORY SENSITIVITIES: For sensory things, I know when I was getting into the habit of brushing my teeth, there were certain toothpastes that were too minty. I hated the "minty fresh" that some of the toothpastes had. I don't know how to describe it—I couldn't handle the toothpaste. If I use deodorant instead of just an antiperspirant, then I get rashes underneath my arms and down my sides. Same with shampoos—some shampoos burn my scalp when I use them.

COMMUNICATION PROBLEMS: One thing I've noticed is that I sometimes mis-hear what Viola says. Like yesterday, she wanted me to get a chocolate snack for her while I was at CVS. I swear I thought she said, "Maybe two, please." So I went to the store, got the milk, and got two of the chocolate things. When I came out, she was like, "Why did you get two?"

SOCIAL CHALLENGES: I guess the social problem I had was that I wasn't really social at all. I learned that my friends' first impression of me was that they thought I hated them. That is not what I wanted at all. I have been making it a point in the last year or so to be more social. My friend gave me this book of slang that isn't in the dictionary, phrases like "I'm down." I have to practice things like this, and that's just something I do by socializing.

That's something that Viola's been helping me with. She makes sure I go to my friends' houses and makes sure I'm hanging out with them. She would be like, "Do you want to go to your friend's house tonight? You can do something; I can stay home." I need to build that skill of being social and having friends. She wanted to make sure I was being social.

What have been some of the low points in your relationship?

The lowest point was probably when Viola moved in with me at my parents' house. We didn't have our own space. Our own space was my bedroom, which was very small. We lived there for about a year.

We were alone in our bedroom, surrounded by my family, and we didn't have anywhere to go. I think that's what led us to move out and live on our own. We realized that we were great as a couple but that we can't stay there for very long. I think a lot of our problems came out at that time, too, because we were stuck in one bedroom together. We noticed all of the flaws in each other. We noticed things like me being forgetful and messy and her being cranky and mean when she was in a bad mood. Mostly, she's sort of perfect. I kind of love her. But you know, when you're in a small room with someone for a year, you kind of learn all of the flaws of each other.

If you had a magic wand and could wish away one of your marital challenges or a partner's trait, what would it be?

I wish I just knew how to be more romantic, I guess. It wouldn't solve all of our problems, but I feel like it would make Viola a lot happier. I want her to feel more loved.

Relationship Strengths

What are some of your relational strengths and highlights?

Me and Viola are amazing as a team. When we're working on something, like when we were moving from my parents' house to the apartment, we had a game plan going in. Viola wants to plan everything out and be organized. I am task-oriented and want to do everything on a list. So that makes us a great team.

Viola likes design, and she likes colors. Now this apartment is kind of like our pseudo-house. The furniture we have here, we'll most likely bring into the house that we'll buy. Now, I want to have a living room and a porch and a sunroom and things like that. I think that I would never have explored those possibilities if it wasn't for Viola showing me pictures of things on Pinterest. She'd say, "Doesn't that look really cool?" and I'd be like, "Oh yeah, that does look really cool." I think that was probably the highlight. Us building our lives together and me realizing that there's more than just the things that you need. There's also the things that you want.

What do you love most about your relationship?

I'm sorry, there are a lot of things. I'm trying to pick just one of those things. I think the thing I like most about our relationship is how open I can be with Viola and how much of myself I can be around her. She doesn't judge me, and if she does, it's in a playful manner. There's no mystery, and there's no fear of being myself around her. I can be on the computer for the entire day, and she won't judge me for that. I don't do that often, but when I do, I know that I'm not hurting her. She just knows that's how I am.

Intimacy

Is empathy or emotional reciprocity an issue in your relationship?

EMPATHY: I feel emotional when Viola's sad. I feel sad when Viola's sad, even when it's not me that caused the problem. I feel what she feels, I think.

EMOTIONAL RECIPROCITY: I think emotional reciprocity is probably more of a problem. I have a hard time expressing my emotions. I sometimes get scared that how I'm feeling might make her mad, even though it's irrational. I think it extends from trauma growing up. I think the other problem is that when I am excited about things, I don't outwardly show excitement. Viola has a hard time with that.

Does ASD cause challenges in the area of sex/intimacy?

I think our sex life is really fun. I think the main problem is my inability to be romantic. So starting out, it's either her initiating it, or we both agree that we want to do it, so we just start. But I think she would like it if I was more romantic about it and surprised her in some way. Starting sex out that way has always been a struggle for me. I was trying to figure out what the best way to do that is. And that's something that I haven't looked online yet for. I've been tempted to, but I sort of want to figure this one out with experimentation. I know that Viola's very open to that, and I think that's always a good thing.

What makes you feel loved and cared for by your partner, and what makes your partner feel loved and cared for by you?

She does a lot for me. Viola's just amazing. I remember I was telling her today that I was nervous about this interview. She asked if it would help if she was here. I said, "No, I don't want you to be here while I'm doing it." But ten minutes before I started, she made me food and brought me water. She asked if I needed anything, and I said, "No thank you, though I really like the food you made. It was really good!" She cares for me.

I try to do the same thing for her. I try to make sure that Viola's cared for, that she's spoiled. I try to make it as obvious as possible that I love her by writing her love letters over text, or by tucking her in every night. I make her coffee every morning.

Finances

Describe your economic situation. Does your financial situation impact your relationship in any way?

We both work. Finances don't really affect our relationship, beyond the debt that we have. The work that I do very much works for me. I think being very attentive to my work has always been really helpful for me career-wise. I think the only downside was when I was working in the

office, I had a very hard time concentrating because I wasn't in my own quiet space. There was a lot going on—people walking by or people having conversations outside while I was trying to think. I finally had to get headphones.

My student loan debt is a stressor. We actually just talked about that last night. Viola thinks that I am going to have this debt forever. I don't believe that we're going to have it forever, but we're going to have it for a long time.

Support System

What support systems do you and your partner have?

We have each other. Viola has her whole family behind her, so if something bad were to happen, she could always ask her family for help. For me, I always have my family, but more from a financial perspective. I think the way our families help each other is very different. Her family is mostly emotional support.

Besides that, I know Viola has her friends. I have my friend group. There was one night when Viola's sister had to stay over at the apartment, and Viola wanted her to stay in the bedroom. That meant I had to either sleep on the couch or go to my friends' house. My friends were like, "Oh yeah, definitely! Yeah, hang out with us! Stay the night!" That was awesome. I think that was the first time I had asked my friends for help, even though it was something that wasn't a big deal. I had that support system that day.

Do you have friends individually and as a couple?

Yeah, we have friends, I have friends, I have a group of friends I made in college. They're a really, really cool group of friends. Me and Viola have Mackenzie as friends, and I think we met someone pre-Covid as a couple, but we never stayed in touch because of Covid.

Do you have a spiritual practice? Does that impact your relationship?

Umm, so I know Viola's family is Christian. My family is Catholic. When I was growing up, I identified as an atheist. But then when I reached my twenties, I decided to be agnostic because I was not sure what faith I believed in, really. I think me being atheist was just more about being rebellious. I believe in reincarnation, but I don't know if I am Buddhist, or what other religions also believe in that. I haven't really looked into this as much. That's why I say I am agnostic, because I think this is something I want to figure out later, I guess.

Parenting

Tell us about yourselves as parents in this marriage.

The fish tank is very much another

hobby of mine. I enjoy it because whatever I do to the tank is going to affect the ecosystem within the tank, so I have to take very good care of it. I make sure everything is in order and that everything is healthy. That gives me peace, in the sense that I can control this little tank and it's my own tank. The temperature is very particular. It's something I can focus on...I don't know how to describe this. I have to check the PH and the ammonia and the nitrates. It's an arbitrary system that I have to keep tabs on every day, but it's also a good distraction from the stressors that I have.

Being in an ND Relationship

Do you feel that the challenges in ND relationships are unique?

I don't really know what a typical relationship is. If I were to base it off of the things that I hear from my friends and the things I see on Netflix, I think the difference is that the problems that other people have are more social problems. I think in a relationship like mine and Viola's, the problems are more things that you wouldn't normally think are problems. Things like me having sensory issues with the shampoo.

Neurotypicals might wonder why that's a relationship problem. They might wonder why Viola has to buy me three shampoos. It's the communication that I think makes the difference. There are no communication problems in an ND relationship; their problems stem from social stuff.

Based on your experiences, how informed do you find people are about ASD and ND marriage/relationships?

It's not a big stigma, but there's still some stigma toward it. But an ND relationship is not impossible. There are methods that work, as long as you're attuned to what's going on. It's a lot easier to be in a relationship like that. A lot of the stuff I read online is from people who didn't know their partner was ND, and so they had different expectations. I feel like, if you know ahead of time, then you can work together on those problems.

> I think in a relationship like mine and Viola's, the problems are more things that you wouldn't normally think are problems. Things like me having sensory issues with the shampoo.

What is your perspective on being in an ND relationship?

My perspective is that I'm always going to be in a neurodiverse relationship, since I'm neurodiverse. I'm sort of like a normal person. I just have different quirks. When we communicate, we can work together on those quirks.

What are the positives of being in an ND relationship?

Like in any relationship, when you can communicate with each other really well, then every other aspect of the relationship is going to be amazing.

What advice would you give to people who are in an ND relationship?

I would recommend going to marriage counseling or premarital counseling. Us talking to Eva was extremely helpful to us. Even though we already had a good set of things, going to premarital counseling only helped us.

Couples Counseling

Have you pursued couples counseling? Was it useful?

Yes it is. It helped us learn even more communication tools and skills. It also showed us problems that neither of us knew were problems beforehand.

Concluding Thoughts

10-Point Marital Happiness Scale™

I would say probably a 10. I do plan on proposing to Viola this year, so I would say a 10.

Would you say you're in love with Viola?

Yes. If I could be with her forever and have life as it is, or if I could live life without her (and without any remorse or any heartbreak or anything), I would always pick living my life with Viola. Because I don't think I could live my life without Viola. I mean, I guess I could, but I think it would just be a quiet, "whatever" kind of thing. I would rather have her every time.

Do you think your relationship will go the distance?

I think it will. I think we will go the distance. And I think it's because we have been through a lot together, and there's nothing that life could throw at us that could break us apart. I think that we've learned so much this year, and I think as long as we remain open and honest with each other, then we will go the distance.

MEET VIOLA

Viola (she/her/hers) is a 24-year-old, bisexual, multiracial female. She lives with her boyfriend, best friend, a cat, and some fish in Massachusetts. She is currently a student working to get her bachelor's degree in computer science. She works as a software engineer. She has been with her boyfriend for almost four years. Viola does not identify as being on the spectrum.

Please describe any short- or long-term past romantic relationships

All my relationships before Robbie ended in less than a year. My best friend's mom gave me really good dating advice. She said, "If you don't see a future with them or if they're a jerk, just dump them." And I dated a lot. Robbie is the first person I see myself growing old and becoming a cranky old lady with.

I know we don't handle stressful situations in the best way. But at the end of the day, we're going to talk about it, and we're going to tell each other that we love each other. And we're going to go to bed happy. I don't think a lot of relationships can say that. That's something I'm so proud of and that I'm so happy I can have.

How did you meet?

We met in school. We had Java class together, but I didn't know he was around. He was really white, and it was all guys in the class, so he blended in. Then he messaged me on Facebook one day. He sent me a really nerdy *Dungeons and Dragons* reference, and that's how we started talking.

Diagnosis Journey

Did you receive any special education, support, or therapy while you were growing up?

When I first entered public school, they put me in a special education program because I didn't know how to socialize. I was homeschooled, and I didn't know how to talk to people. I am pretty shy. Then I got diagnosed with ADHD. In high school, I got diagnosed with PTSD.

Do you or your partner have an official or self-diagnosis of ASD?

I think during his sophomore year of college, he started the process of being diagnosed. But I think the realization that he was autistic was so surreal for him that he didn't want to pursue it. It was too overwhelming. So I think he's going to get officially diagnosed later this year.

How accepting do you feel you and your partner are about the diagnosis?

To me, it's like an "ah-ha" moment. Everything makes sense! I think that it helps me better understand our relationship. When he has meltdowns, now I know that it's not something he can control. It's not something that I

did wrong. It's just him having a meltdown. It's helped me so much.

I used to think, "Wow, he's kind of harsh!" Sometimes I ask, "Does this look good on me?" He'll just say, "No." It makes sense. He is really honest, really loyal, and I wouldn't want to date someone else. I like how logical he is, and I like his passion about things. Everything just clicks. I think coming to terms with his autism solidified our relationship. I don't think we would've lasted if I didn't know.

What advice would you give to someone who's just discovering either their or their partner's ASD?

Don't feel like you have to tiptoe. Be explicit. Seek help because it's hard feeling alone. I know what that's like. When you realize that there are so many resources and when you realize the power of explicitness, it will change your love life.

Anything else you'd like to say about the diagnosis?

I think there's a stigma behind it. I hate that he's seen getting a diagnosis as a burden because it's real now. I think that he doesn't want that label. He approaches it with such intimidation that it does make me sad. He thinks that I'm going to leave him because he has a diagnosis, which makes me feel like crap. I love Robbie more than anything in the entire world, and a diagnosis wouldn't change that. Even if it's a neurological difference, it's not that big of a deal. It's fine.

Relationship Challenges

What are the main challenges in your relationship?

I feel like, with premarital counseling, we've addressed so many of our issues. So, right now, I feel like we're good. The small things, I guess, are the biggest issues. Like him not putting the toilet seat down or forgetting to do things. I think it's just learning how to function as a unit, now that we live together.

Also matching each other can be an issue. We talked about this yesterday, though our communication has improved so much with premarital counseling that I wouldn't even call it an issue. I was so frustrated when I was in a meeting, and Robbie came down and just started eating, even though we had groceries that had been sitting out for like 40 minutes. I was like, "Robbie, you need to put away the groceries." He was like, "I need to eat first. I have a meeting in ten minutes." And I was like, "Well, babe, I'm *in* a meeting." He was like, "Fine." He matched my frustration. When we talked about it later, we discussed how there was no need to match my frustration. I calm him down often, and he calms me down when I'm really hormonal. We need to do that more.

Do you struggle with executive function-ing, sensory sensitivities, communication problems, and/or social challenges?

EXECUTIVE FUNCTIONING: Yes, but I feel like he's learning how to cope with it. I am, too. In the mornings, if I need something done as soon as possible, I might text him a "good morning" message. Something like, "Good morning, my love. I hope you have a great work day. During your break, can you do X, Y, and Z?" Or I'll leave a little post-it note next to his toothbrush, because he has certain routines that I try to not disrupt. I try to make sure that he sees what I need. I know I can't tell him, "Robbie, unload the dishwasher" because he's probably going to forget. But if I text it to him, write it down, or put it next to his computer, he's going to remember.

COMMUNICATION PROBLEMS: I'm so used to play-fighting that sometimes I'll say, "Robbie, you're so mean to me." He'll take that literally, and he'll say, "What am I doing wrong?" The diagnosis was so helpful because it helped me learn how to be more explicit. It helped me learn that sarcasm doesn't go far when talking to Robbie.

SOCIAL CHALLENGES: Before knowing his neurological differences, social challenges caused a lot of frustration. For example, if we were in a mall for holiday shopping, he would be very flustered and shut down. I would get so upset because we were in the middle of the mall around a bunch of people. He would break down, and I had to be in charge. I hated it. But now, knowing what I know, I understand that he's over-stimulated. I say, "Let's get out of here and take a breather. Before we come back next time, we can plan around busy times."

Also, it makes things kind of funny. When he met my extended family, my uncle was like, "So, Robert, have you ever had dinner with black people before?" And he was so uncomfortable with that question that he couldn't tell if it was genuine curiosity or a test. It was so funny to see him try to figure that out and process it. Our friends tend to be more technological people. They work in medical fields, or they are engineers, too. I feel like it's so common that I wouldn't be surprised if a quarter of his friends had a neurological difference.

What have been some of the low points in your relationship?

Oh boy. I got pregnant two years ago. That was really, really tough because I didn't have a job. I was looking for work, and we couldn't afford an abortion. It was really scary. I remember taking the pregnancy test, seeing the positive, and thinking my life was over. I don't even know how Robbie processed it, but he didn't leave me. He just said, "What are we going to do?" I said I wanted to terminate

the pregnancy, and he drove me to an abortion clinic. We ended up getting aid to have the termination. He waited with me in the waiting room. He wasn't there when I had the procedure, but he was there afterward. I didn't tell anybody. I haven't told anybody. He stood by my side. He didn't tell his family. It was something that we did together.

Now I donate to that clinic from every paycheck. He stood by my side, even when I had to wait two weeks before I could get the abortion. He was just there. He said, "You know, you made the right decision. I'm really proud of you. I'll never leave you." He's said, "I love you," so many times, but I think that was the first time he said, "I'll never leave you." Autistics are the most honest people in the world, and when I looked into his eyes, I knew that it was true. I knew, in that moment, that I was looking at my husband, and that was surreal. That was really cool.

I can think of one other thing—he failed a biology class in college, and that was tough. But I think me being pregnant trumps that.

If you had a magic wand and could wish away one of your marital challenges or a partner's trait, what would it be?

That's tough. I feel like my first thought was the meltdowns. They don't happen that often, but they're so frustrating because I know I can't do anything to help. I don't want to say anything, because I love Robbie for exactly who he is. I love everything about him, including his fascinations and his quirks. I wouldn't change a thing about him. I feel like his Asperger's complements his personality in a way that I find absolutely infectious. I wouldn't change a thing.

Relationship Strengths

What are some of your relational strengths and highlights?

One highlight was him graduating college. He had to take a community college class because he failed biology. It was really hard for him to manage work, biology, me, the fish, and family (because he lived at his house then). But we did it! Being able to watch him walk up and pick up his diploma was so cool.

Last year, we went to New York together for our first vacation. That was really cool because we got some wood from New York to put in our aquarium.

I feel like every day is a victory. Just looking back and seeing the progress we've made—that's the biggest highlight.

What do you love most about your relationship?

We are a unit. Before I knew resources like this, we would tell each other, "United front! Let's do this!"

We would make a game plan. No matter what it was, if we decided we were going to be a united front in something, then we would remain a united front. Nothing would faze us. No matter what Robbie does or says or smells like (because his farts are really bad), I will love him. I know Robbie feels the same way about me. I know that we don't always communicate in the best way. I know we don't handle stressful situations in the best way. But at the end of the day, we're going to talk about it, and we're going to tell each other that we love each other. And we're going to go to bed happy. I don't think a lot of relationships can say that. That's something I'm so proud of and that I'm so happy I can have.

I love how explicit we are now. I love how logical we are. I love how we work together well. We sometimes do projects together, like programming. We speak the same language for that, so we'll both program in the same way. We'll talk to each other like we're talking to a computer. We're very good at communication when it's something that we're both experts in.

> We are a unit. Before I knew resources like this, we would tell each other, "United front! Let's do this!" We would make a game plan.

Intimacy

Is empathy or emotional reciprocity an issue in your relationship?

EMPATHY: I think because we're so explicit with how we feel, it's easier for Robbie to be empathetic toward my issues or needs. I think that Robbie doesn't really struggle with this. He has to process emotions in a logical way in order for him to empathize. He knows how I'm feeling based on my facial expressions. I know he cares for me, but sometimes I feel like he's not in love with me. But I feel like that's just when he's hyper-focused on programming or something.

EMOTIONAL RECIPROCITY: Being explicit in communication totally changed our relationship. Now I can say, "Robbie, when you did X, Y, and Z, it made me feel like *this*. Going forward, can you do A, B, and C?" He'll listen, take the advice, and correct himself from the feedback. We take turns talking when we have issues, and I love our dialogue. My little sister heard Robbie and I talking, and she asked, "How often do you and Robbie clear the air? Can you give me advice on doing that?" She's 16, and she just got a boyfriend. It was so cool to be able to tell her, "Yeah, this is what we do."

Does ASD cause challenges in the area of sex/intimacy?

At first, I had a really hard time with touch and sex. I feel embarrassed to talk about this, but he doesn't like it when I touch his shoulders. It's a sensory thing. But now when I touch his shoulders, I know when he wants it and when he gets overstimulated. His shoulders, his stomach, and his whole front are problem areas. At first, before we had a diagnosis, he would always finish before I could. That was really frustrating. But learning that he was just really sensitive there was really helpful. Like, he can't directly put water on his penis or else it will hurt. So learning different sex positions has been really helpful in order to keep me fulfilled. So that might mean—oh my gosh, I don't know if this is helpful—but that might mean that he might masturbate before we have sex to help him last longer.

Because he doesn't know the social rules, and even though I'm his first girlfriend, it's kind of awkward to start sexy time. But sometimes, when we're going over our plans for the day, we'll say, "Oh, what do you want to do?" We'll say, "Oh, you know, I'd like to have sexy time." That sets the expectation that, when I'm lying down, he knows that it's okay to have sex. It also helps to communicate about whether something feels good or not. Like with oral stimulation, it helps to ask if it feels okay or if he's comfortable with it. It's truly helpful just texting and being explicit over text messaging. That way, there's no room for miscommunication. If I was being really suggestive with Robbie, I don't think he would pick up on the signal. But having that explicit conversation in the morning has been so helpful for us. Then I can just watch TV because sexy time wasn't on the agenda for today.

That's what I would say if anyone asked me for sex advice. There's no room for guesswork. I feel so fulfilled. It's—I'm not going to send my parents this book—it's like the best sex ever!

What makes you feel loved and cared for by your partner, and what makes your partner feel loved and cared for by you?

Every morning, he'll make me coffee. I'll kick his feet (not in a mean way) and tell him, "Coffee maker." Then he'll go make me coffee. He'll say, "It's made with love," and he'll kiss the cup. I know he loves me, just by that alone. But when he just randomly looks at me and says, "Viola, I love you," it's like, "Ugh, he means it!" That's so cool. I know he doesn't share his emotions with everybody, so that is such an honor.

Just being around him, I feel loved. I think that when you go to different people's homes, you get a vibe. Sometimes it's kind of cold. But I feel that, when I'm in his presence, there's such a warmth. My little sister just loves coming over because she feels the love that we have. That is probably the coolest thing about our relationship. She aspires to have a relationship like we do, and that's so, so cool.

I think me just being there for him is love. And telling him that I love him in a way that he understands.

And never giving up on him. I'll make him lunch. I'll make him dinner. I'm just there for him, and I think it's like air. You know, it's there even though you can't see it.

Finances

Describe your economic situation. Does your financial situation impact your relationship in any way?

Robbie is very logical about finances. At the beginning, I was making more, and that was fine. Robbie didn't see a problem with it. When I was unemployed, Robbie was like, "Well, we're together, so my money is your money. But you can't take all of it." And I was like, "Well, I'm not going to, so that's fine." Now that we're almost financially equal, it feels like autism doesn't play a role in it. I think it's more about our dynamic together and how we view things. We see that we're in it for the long run. We're going to be together forever, so if you need money, that's fine because next week I might need money. We don't really keep track of who gave who what or what we owe each other.

I think his student loan debt is really, really high. He's paid off about 10 percent of it, but I think at its peak it was at $30,000–40,000. Mine was more like $20,000. That stresses me out. Being kicked out at a young age, not having anything, and having to find a job immediately—his debt does scare me.

I think some people in Robbie's

life perceive me to be a gold digger, which is really frustrating and annoying. I think people's perceptions of us do affect me. I don't think Robbie's really aware of them, but they are hurtful. There are months that I take home more than Robbie, and there are months that he takes home more than me. People's perceptions of me and worrying about financial security are the two biggest worries that I have.

Support System

What support systems do you and your partner have?

You. And our friends. I remember when Robbie told them about premarital counseling, they were like, "What? You need that?" It was weird that they thought that people only go to therapy when there's an issue. Then, I viewed it as a preventative measure. Now, I realize that we wouldn't have made it if he didn't have the right tools to communicate things. Our friends are really supportive of us. They are really supportive of our relationship. My sister and my dad are big supports, as well.

Do you have friends individually and as a couple?

Our friend groups used to be separate. But now that we moved in together and act as such a unit, we share a lot of friends. I think he does have his respective friends. I know his friends are also my friends. But I

know if we were to break up or something, they probably wouldn't talk to me ever again. We're independent, but we're also together.

Parenting

Tell us about yourselves as parents in this marriage.

Robbie is really into his pet fish. He got started when his nephew got tired of his betta fish. Robbie took the fish, and then it died. He was like, "Well, I can do better!" So he got a five-gallon tank, and he filled that up. It lasted like six months, and then he got a ten-gallon tank... and then a 20-gallon tank... and then a 50-gallon tank! It's really calming. We used to sleep with it right next to our bed. He's just so passionate about his fish.

We have talked about children sometimes. I know he really wants kids. He watches *Bob's Burgers* a lot, and he thinks that we would be those parents, which I think is the sweetest thing. That family just loves each other!

I know when we have kids, discipline will be a thing. But I know when we're ready for that, we'll talk to somebody who has experience with children. We'll definitely reach out for help, now that we know how important it is. I know that when we have kids, we're going to be incredible parents. I hope that we'll give them the love that every child needs. That means love that's unconditional no matter what their orientation is, or what their hopes and dreams are.

Being in an ND Relationship

Do you feel that the challenges in ND relationships are unique?

I think they have the same group of problems. I feel like, in all of my relationships prior to this, there's always been a communication issue. I feel like that was me trying to be subtle and cute. I was just young and stupid. When I talk to my friends about their relationship issues, the issues are very similar. They just present themselves in a different way.

I think a lot of my relationship issues with Robbie just get solved with communication and being explicit. I feel like if they were explicit with their partners, most of their relationship problems would be solved. In past relationships, I didn't want to tell them I didn't like their gift because I didn't want them to get upset. But with Robbie, if his gift stinks, I can say, "Robbie, that gift really stunk." He won't get upset; he'll ask how he can do better. I think it's an advantage, but I don't want to sound like an elitist or something.

Based on your experiences, how informed do you find people are about ASD and ND marriage/relationships?

I know I wasn't informed, because I didn't recognize the signs in the beginning, even though now they're so blatantly obvious. A lot of our friends are engineers, and I suspect a lot of them are on the spectrum. It's really frustrating to see how many relation-

ships aren't successful for them. They could just tell their partner straight away, "I do have this difference, so if you could just be really explicit that would be super helpful." I feel like people just don't understand what autism is.

People don't think that people with autism can have relationships, which is really weird and strange. I know one of Robbie's friends who hasn't had a partner ever. He thinks that he can't because of his autism, and that's heartbreaking.

What is your perspective on being in an ND relationship?

I love it. I wouldn't want anything else, but I don't know if that makes me sound bad. I love being explicit. Now that I can say, "I don't like this gift" or "I don't like what you're cooking," I don't want to go back to tiptoeing around an issue. No, I'm happy where I am.

What are the positives of being in an ND relationship?

Explicitness is my favorite thing. I also like how Robbie's special interests and my hobbies are very similar; we're both into computers and programming. It can be kind of frustrating when he gets really interested in something that I'm just discovering, and then two days later he's an expert. But if you're interested in the same things, it's really cool. I understand if you don't share those interests, it might be hard trying to get along with your partner. I can't imagine every girl wanting to go to a computer store every Saturday for the first year of their relationship, but for me it was really cool.

What advice would you give to people who are in an ND relationship?

Don't take offense at what your partner says because they are still learning.

Couples Counseling

Have you pursued couples counseling? Was it useful?

So useful. Yes. I'm so glad my dad told us to do it. It's been so helpful. We use every tool that you give us in our daily life. Like clearing the air—we do that like every other day. When I do say something a little harsh while trying to be explicit, he never takes it the wrong way. He'll just say, "Viola, can we clear the air on something? What did you mean by that?" This is so helpful because I didn't realize how he sometimes receives my tone.

Concluding Thoughts

10-Point Marital Happiness Scale™

I know I'm supposed to say that nothing's perfect...but I'm sorry, I have the best. My relationship is like the best in the world, and no one can tell me otherwise. That sounds really pompous, but I'm so confident in that.

I didn't realize what love was until I met Robbie, which is so sad and mussy and gussy. But it's such a cool feeling when you love someone relentlessly. I have no idea how to describe it. You just love everything about them. Not that many 24-year-olds talk about, "Oh when we have kids, can we do this?" But I know he's serious about it. He says, "Oh Viola, do you think our kids are going to sleep in our beds when they have nightmares?" It's like, "Ugh, I love you! Yes, I think so."

Would you say that you're in love with Robbie?

Oh my god, yeah. I love him more than anything in the entire world. I get lost in his eyes. He's my best friend, and it's so cool to be in love with my best friend.

Do you think your relationship will go the distance?

I think so. I think without counseling, it wouldn't have worked. I felt like such a bad partner because I would get so frustrated. But I feel validated every time I go. It affirms that Robbie's not toxic, I'm not toxic, there's just a communication difference. It's sad to think we're going to die one day and that's how we're going to end it—death. That's kind of gloomy, but I know he's my partner forever.

CHAPTER 11

Ten Secrets of Happy Neurodiverse Couples

And How to Use Them in Your Relationship

Over the last decade, working with numerous ND couples has given me an insider's view on what makes these relationships tick. And now, I'm so happy to able to take you inside the relationships of some of these amazing couples so that you too can see and experience the unique hardships and joys of ND relationships. My hope is that in getting the inside scoop on these well-kept secrets and strategies of these couples who so generously shared their experiences, numerous couples like you all over the world will read them and be inspired to try them for yourselves! In addition to all of the wisdom and resources that the couples revealed in their sto-

ries, I'm also including some shared themes, best practices, and must-do actions that I have distilled as I absorbed their perspectives. While I have come up with ten best-kept secrets and techniques that these couples put into practice to help their relationships last, of course there are hundreds more hidden within all of the stories in this book, so try to learn from these couples and keep adding to your relationship toolkit. In the next chapter, I've also included a worksheet with some discussion questions and relationship exercises/challenges to help you get a strong start in applying these concepts to your own relationships.

1. ACCEPT YOUR DIAGNOSIS AND TALK ABOUT IT OFTEN!

I got a formal diagnosis from Eva. I was diagnosed a year after getting married with ASD. We saw Eva pretty consistently for a few years then, on and off, after

that. Mostly together, but some one-on-one sessions.—Siddharth

Next year, it will be three years since I

received my diagnosis. Once I was diagnosed with ASD, it made all the sense in the world. It explained to me why my brain works like this. I was always aware of my thinking differently, but then it all made sense. Especially to my wife, it was like, "Oh that's why you did this, and that's why you behave this way and that." It was liberating in many ways.—Oscar

All of the ASD partners in each of the ten couples either self-identified or sought out an official diagnosis on their own initiative or with the support of their partners. Additionally, the NS partners who had ADHD or depression and anxiety or other health issues also acknowledged and accepted their struggles and actively worked to address them. Therefore, the number one trait that these successful ND couples have is identifying, accepting, and working on their issues regardless of what they are or how difficult it is.

Another important point to mention is that *both* partners accept the diagnosis and seem to discuss it often. I've often seen that when one person is in denial regarding the true cause of their relationship problems, they can often go around in a circle getting no traction as neither is able to address the issues at the root. Acknowledging ASD traits and deepening understanding around them truly helps both partners forgive each other's weaknesses as they're able to realize that their partner isn't hurting them intentionally and that the difficulties they're experiencing are due to bona fide neurological differences. Such discussions can often dissolve defensiveness, blaming, and resentment and couples can then work together to create the appropriate solutions for their unique situations.

2. LEAN ON YOUR SUPPORT SYSTEM

If there are some things you can't get from each other, try to find them outside of the relationship—and I don't mean sex or anything like that. I mean like, "Oh, I want to learn how to roller skate." Go do it with your girlfriend, and then come back home and love your husband. He doesn't have to do everything with you. Find people who will support you.—Mona

That's something that Viola's been helping me with. She makes sure I go to my

friends' houses and makes sure I'm hanging out with them. She would be like, "Do you want to go to your friend's house tonight? You can do something; I can stay home." I need to build that skill of being social and having friends. She wanted to make sure I was being social.—Robbie

His parents are kind and always available to listen and be there. We have some good friends in our community who live close by and some far away. I've a close friend in Germany, and another in Flor-

ida who I also talk to weekly. Rajeev has his own set of friends and I do as well. And we're resourceful in terms of finding support when we need it...even if it's professional.—Amalia

In an intimate relationship, it can be tempting to expect one's partner to fulfill every need and desire. The reality, however, is that no partner—ASD or otherwise—can manage to fulfill all of our expectations. Healthy relationships require security in both proximity and distance. It's not a slight to the relationship to enjoy doing some things separately, it is in fact necessary.

Almost *every* couple in these stories had support from friends and family and a community they could rely on. And almost *every* partner took time for themselves to do things that rejuvenated and refreshed them. A relationship cannot be satisfying if either of the individuals is running on empty. So, create, select, and lean on your community, a special-interest buddy, an arts class, or an exercise club as every relationship, ND or not, thrives in an ecosystem of support and interdependence!

Healthy friendships and support systems benefit the marriage. There is no shame in seeking additional input from wise sources. Reach out—select and build your support system. There are so many people who both love and care about you and often we don't know this because we don't want to reach out to them so as not to be a bother. And often, as we confide in others, we may find that it helps to not only deepen our friendships, but also allows the other person to be there for us. Feeling useful and supportive of others is deeply meaningful to most humans, if not all. It all evens out in the end, as support systems are often reciprocal and leaning on someone can often mean that they will trust you to support them in times of need—it's this mutual support that makes the world go round.

3. EMBRACE YOUR DIFFERENCES

I think the other thing that I really appreciate about our relationship is Leo's ability to help me see things differently. I don't know if I do the same thing for him, as this is one of our struggles with communication. But later—even if it's later that day or later the next week—I'm like, "Oh, I see what he was thinking now." So I am able to change my perspective on things.—Roy

We can just be silly together, and we can recognize our differences. Sometimes we hate the differences, but I think knowing our differences, and at the same time being silly together and having some fun moments has been good.—Siddharth

In all of the ten couples, both partners ASD and NS deeply appreciated what the other person brought to the table. They acknowledged that they had complementary strengths and weaknesses. Much of the discouraging literature about the failure rate of ND marriages focuses on the irreconcilable differences. You can see how the couples in this book use these differences to their advantage. They have open discussions about their challenges so that the negative qualities don't become a death sentence to the relationship through ignorance, silence, and inaction.

Again, I am suggesting that you work hard to see your partner's perspective. Focus on respectful communication; work on style, tone, or speed. Patient, repeated dialogue more often than not helps bridge differences. Appreciate the fact that neurodiversity much like biodiversity helps create a much more diverse and beautiful world or like in a painting, all of the hues work together to create a picture rich with emotion and visual interest. Similarly, in a relationship, neurological differences can be "hues" to be celebrated and enjoyed rather than erased so long as both partners also make efforts to minimize the negative impact of these differences.

4. HAVE A BEGINNER'S MINDSET

It's never boring. We're always dealing with new stuff, and I'm always discovering new things to obsess with. My wife, she's interested in more things too because of that. We're always learning from each other, and it's been fun.—Oscar

I feel some degree of neurodiversity is essential because then both partners can complement each other and cancel out at least some of their individual weaknesses. I think if I were to marry a non-ASD person, I would not grow as much, or become aware of myself (or my limitations) to the degree that I currently am.—Rajeev

I think there are some things like executive dysfunction that you have to learn about. That's not a thing that you're go-ing to necessarily know how to approach until you've been in a situation with somebody who has those sorts of issues. I also think that a lot of things are not that different. I think the solution a lot of times is finding out how communication works between you two.—Autumn

One of the keys that leads to success in an ND relationship is maintaining the lifelong willingness to grow and learn for both the ASD and NS partners. Often, we unconsciously set out to achieve a state in life where growth is no longer required. We want to settle into a home we won't have to move from, a job where we know the ropes, and a marriage where we feel comfortable. But what we've seen from all ten of our trailblazer couples is that greater satisfaction is to be found by remaining a perpetual learner.

Resetting ourselves to a beginner's mindset leaves the possibility for change within ourselves. By continually being in learning mode, a greater realization of our own limitations and abilities will unfold. This type of mindset helps us take responsibility for our own growth versus focusing on ways in which our partner isn't growing. And while it takes courage to allow our spouse to stretch us to greater levels of maturity and wisdom, the reward is pride and confidence in our own ability to facilitate change in our relationship by changing ourselves. Additionally, a growth mindset by both partners makes for lasting intimacy and an ever evolving connection.

5. FINE-TUNE YOUR PERSPECTIVE-TAKING SKILLS

But one thing that I've very much made my job is taking care of her. She's so busy taking care of the rest of us, but I make sure to take care of her. I try to make her the priority, try to watch out for what people can be doing to help her.—Oliver

Autumn is comforted by hugs and physical closeness. She often tells me she feels loved and cared for by physical touch, so we have to make sure that we have time to cuddle. I think it's also the physical things that I do. I try to make sure that when she says something, I write it down so I don't forget it. I try to accommodate her communication needs, even though they are very different from my communication needs.—Frankie

I think the other thing is the fact that she says that I should observe other couples and how they pay attention to each other even when they are independently socializing with other people in the same event. I guess I don't do that as well. I *don't know how, but I try—I try to be more aware of it.—Siddharth*

Chronic self-focus drains the life out of any relationship. This proclivity may be especially prominent in ND relationships, since the thinking patterns of individuals with ASD tend to revolve intensely around themselves. However, I've seen many an NS spouse having a difficult time detaching from their own interpretations of the relationship and validating their partner's autistic perspective.

The magic happens when both partners are willing to view the world through the eyes of their spouse. The result resembles a tranquil garden waterfall, which flows and flows but is never empty because it is also being filled at the same time. After all, who doesn't want to be heard and understood and have that reflected back to us. Even though developing perspective-taking and theory of mind can be challenging, with motivation and practice, it is possible to make small improvements over time. Mutual selflessness ultimately leads to mutual satisfaction. It is much more important for each partner to feel honored simply for who they are and what they need. So, fine-tune your perspective-taking skills, and this way of living will serve you well not only in your marriage or relationship, but in every relationship! Trust me.

6. STAY HUMBLE AND CURIOUS

Listen, I know this goes for a lot of relationships, but I think for ND relationships it's really, really important. A lot of things can be said or done and come off one way when they aren't meant to. So I think really knowing and getting the ASD partner's perspective is extremely important.—Camilla

One thing I feel like I'm good at is picking up on when someone seems upset, but I can also be very bad at it. So usually I ask, "Is everything okay? You seem a little sad." Overall though, I do think the one thing I'm good at noticing is when something seems a little off with someone, and then we can have a little discussion about it.—Oliver

Lack of curiosity can keep us from truly listening to our partner. If we assume we already know what they want or what they're about to say, we are neither curious nor humble. Instead, if we are interested in hearing our partner as they communicate their thought process and inner world, we will not only learn about them, but we might also learn more about the relationship as well. Understanding the relationship requires understanding each other.

Humble curiosity can be demonstrated during conversation. Slow down. Put your phone away. Assume an open body posture as you listen—relax, take a few deep breathes, uncross your arms, have a pleasant facial expression, and even lean forward a bit. These actions communicate your interest. As you listen, focus on what your spouse is saying, not on what you will say next. Respond with clarifying questions and validating comments: "So what I hear you saying is... Am I understanding? You're right about this. I hear your point. I never thought of it like that before." Learn to have constructive discussions. Learn to negotiate what you need from each other.

Remember, you're in a relationship with your partner because you find (or found) them attractive and intriguing. Continue to unveil the mystery and intrigue...who knows what you will discover as you listen with humble curiosity? It is not so much about who is "right," it's about who your partner is. And remember to incorporate points four and five into this one as well.

7. RELY ON TOOLS AND STRATEGIES THAT WORK

During the pandemic, I succeeded in starting and maintaining a meditation practice. This has helped me tremendously in connecting with Autumn, managing conflict, and dealing with Autumn's panic attacks. I am able to ground myself in the moment and not let my worry run away with me. I am able to be present to support and connect with Autumn. The practice also helps me manage my sensory difficulties. If I am feeling overwhelmed, I can take a few moments to center myself by focusing on internal sensations while letting external sensations come and go.—Frankie

Do the work. Do the reading. Read the books. Go to therapy, couples therapy if that works for you. If not, do it on your own, but do it. Forget about your expectations... That is something I have learned. Be brave.—Oscar

We chant this mantra "nam-myoho-renge-kyo" and this has been a great tool to manage my anxiety, frustrations, and negative emotions, but recently I also got on anti-depressants, and ADD meds. All baby doses—and I use marijuana on occasion as well, but the Buddhist practice helps a lot.—Amalia

As you can see from so many of these stories, these couples are willing to engage in ASD-informed cooperative problem-solving, and they often arrive at solutions that are satisfactory to both individuals. It may not look normal, but it meets the needs of both parties. This probably depends on whether a person's priority is to stay stuck in their own ways versus learning to be flexible and do whatever it takes to maintain a healthy relational connection.

Resolving your ND differences is crucial to the success of your relationship, so seek out the tools and strategies that work for you. Experiment with the best practices in this book. Learn from other successful couples. Things like reading ASD books and learning coping strategies, meditation practices, looking into medications if needed, negotiating the best solutions for both of you when problems arise—these are all the hallmarks of couples in happy ND relationships. Take notes in couples therapy and implement the tools and strategies you come up with in those sessions.

8. SCHEDULE FUN AND DO IT OFTEN!

We've been to places I never thought I'd be able to go, being a poor kid from Montana. She always wears these fancy glasses, and she does that because that's

her personality. It's always an adventure with her... She's such a breath of fresh air. I don't think we've done the same thing twice in a row, ever.—Tom

I love that we can have companionable silence together, or have long conversations about theology, or sing in the car for hours. I love nerding out with her about our favorite fictional characters, learning new things together, praying together, cuddling on the couch and watching Star Trek.—*Ellie*

All too often, long-term relationships (ND or otherwise) turn into drudgery, but the couples in this book demonstrate that scheduling fun is necessary in order to thrive in any relationship. Fortunately, the only aspect that needs to change is our attitude! Instead of viewing differences as obstacles to be overcome, accept them as adventures to explore together. We've all heard that "opposites attract." I believe that the opposite aspects of each person are actually the invitations to adventure. Let your partner's interests influence you and you might just discover new aspects of both of you.

And pick new activities to do together and do them often. Take turns picking out something to do that's on your bucket list and do it. I often find that the couples who are most in trouble are the ones not spending any time with each other and certainly those who don't schedule fun. There's a reason why couples bond and fall in love so easily on TV dating shows, it's because they are busy going on adventures over the course of filming which is the fastest way to help people bond and fall in love!

So, make sure you schedule time to have fun together. These experiences can be hobbies, movies, board games, or day trips. Fun can be easily accessible adventures such as a picnic lunch on a grassy patch or even a simple walk around the block. Don't get going so fast on the treadmill of life, compulsively fixating on chores and doing tasks, that you forget to rest in the quiet places that exist and are already beautiful.

9. SEEK OUT ASD-SPECIFIC COUPLES COUNSELING

I think without counseling, it wouldn't have worked. I felt like such a bad partner because I would get so frustrated. But I feel validated every time I go. It affirms that Robbie's not toxic, I'm not toxic, there's just a communication difference.—*Viola*

I was initially quite reluctant when Amalia suggested we see one. But I gave in finally and yes, now we see one regularly.

I find it quite useful because it allows me to voice my opinions without the feeling that I will be judged. I also have someone who can listen to my point of view and give me suggestions on how I can improve my behavior or communication with my partner. And it also lets me vent off steam.—*Rajeev*

Yes, we've pursued couples counseling. Yes, it's been useful. It helped me connect my meditation practice and the skills I was learning in that practice to my relationship with Autumn. It provided a safe space for us to discuss the difficulties that either of us might not have raised on our own.—Frankie

Nine out of ten couples have been to or are currently in couples counseling, getting a diagnosis and pursuing marital counseling within the first few years of the relationship or marriage. If there are repeated, seemingly unresolvable disconnects that are causing pain in your relationship, a counselor can be an irreplaceable asset in teasing out what the crux of the problem is and then working out possible solutions. Often, just having a couples counselor in the room helps a couple to have the dedicated time to focus and work on the relationship which otherwise may not happen, much like getting out of the house and going to an exercise class, working with a personal trainer, and signing up for a gym membership are sure-fire ways to add physical activity to our lives as they give us the accountability to actually show up!

Most importantly, be sure to find a couples counselor who is ASD informed, as we've learnt from our couples that this is the type of counsel that has proven to be the most constructive to them and working with someone who doesn't understand ASD can even be harmful. Additionally, and this may sound controversial to some, I've found that when people try to use individual counseling to problem-solve or even vent about marital issues, it's a recipe for disaster. Often the autistic partner may not have the perspective-taking skills to fully inform the individual counselor regarding what's truly going on in the ND relationship, so expecting them to work on the marriage through the process of individual counseling can be rather challenging. Stick to couples counseling instead.

To sum up, when you need help, don't go at it alone. Find an ASD-specific couples counselor. It may just transform your whole relationship, as I've seen happen over and over again!

10. EMPHASIZE A CULTURE OF ADMIRATION AND GRATITUDE

We're a good team. I rely a lot on him. He tends to ground me and helps me settle down. We make decisions together. He's a good person. Loyal, emotionally tough. I'm grateful.—Amalia

The final relationship-saving secret may be the most powerful of them all. If you want to be a part of this group of successful and happy ND couples, make sure you demonstrate

38

your appreciation for your partner and practice gratitude on a daily basis. Identifying what you love and admire about your partner can breathe fresh life into your marriage! You are in this relationship because you were drawn to this person naturally and freely. What is it about them that inspired you, brought you joy, made you roar with laughter? It's easy and natural to nitpick and focus on our partner's flaws. It's human nature even or why would the divorce rate be 50 percent?

So what do all of these successful couples have in common? They realize that they can't take their partner for granted, and they focus and magnify their partner's positive qualities. They ignore their partner's limitations or focus on concrete strategies to create solutions. With a focus on the positive and by cultivating gratitude for their partners, their relationships truly exude a culture of mutual admiration. This way, each partner in the couple feels like they lucked out with the other! Over time, this kind of a mindset and daily practice fosters genuine trust and mutual support. With that kind of united bond, a couple can go far and create a beautiful relationship and push through long periods of discontent and disconnect.

So don't be discouraged by statistics that refer to any external characteristic—whether that be autism, race, family background, sexual orientation, gender identity, or financial status—as the determining factor in relational success. As you can see from our star ND couples, the quality of emphasizing the positive and having a self-growth mindset is what makes the ultimate difference.

Have you found a gem of a person with a heart of gold, who happens to be on the spectrum? Congratulations! Let your love story begin...after all, a relationship can reset and flourish at any point as long as the people in it are able to embrace fresh perspectives and modes of interaction thereby forging a path anew.

CHAPTER 12

The Neurodiverse Love Worksheet

Exercises for How to Use the Ten Secrets of Happy Neurodiverse Couples in Your Own Relationship

*G*rab a pen and paper before you get started on any of these exercises.

Keep a dedicated notebook to document all of the exercises so that you're able to keep track of your efforts and progress. If I haven't specified which partner needs to do the exercise, then it might mean that you both should do it. Start on these exercises by yourself if you can, and make them a habit.

EXERCISE 1. ACCEPT YOUR DIAGNOSIS AND TALK ABOUT IT OFTEN!

For the ASD partner, do you understand what your ASD traits are? Are you willing to read a book, listen to a podcast, or watch a documentary on ASD to learn more? What does your partner think? What's the mental block that keeps you from listening to your partner or pursuing the diagnosis? For the NS partner, what keeps you angry with your partner even after learning about autism and neurological differences?

CHALLENGE: Read an article or book on ND relationships. Check off as many traits as you can on the ASD checklist. Have your partner also do the diagnostic checklist on your behalf and schedule time to compare notes and have a discussion. You may need to have multiple and ongoing conversations about this.

EXERCISE 2. LEAN ON YOUR SUPPORT SYSTEM

For the NS partner, do you have needs or interests that are difficult to satisfy in your relationship? Are there constructive emotional and social support options outside your relationship that you can build on? Are there any issues that you feel need the direction of a professional counselor?

CHALLENGE: Dream a little! Choose an activity that you've always wanted to try. Find a friend with whom to give it a whirl or take a class and make new friends! And repeat.

EXERCISE 3. EMBRACE YOUR DIFFERENCES

Ask yourself: How important is it to me that my partner perceives and lives in the world in the same way that I do? What can I do to accept my partner's differences? How can I shift my thinking and feelings regarding some of my partner's weaknesses or unusual traits?

CHALLENGE: Practice acceptance by having a daily inner dialogue listing all of your partner's strengths and stop when your mind takes you down a negative path of criticism and complaint. Memorize and reflect on the positive aspects of your partner's traits daily, make it a habit!

EXERCISE 4. HAVE A BEGINNER'S MINDSET

Ask yourself: Do I see myself more as a lifelong student or am I constantly showing off how much I know even without meaning to? Even if you think you've done everything you possibly can to better the relation-ship, what else could you do? Start afresh. Have a beginner's mindset!

CHALLENGE: List ten areas in which you believe you can learn something from your partner and watch what happens.

EXERCISE 5. FINE-TUNE YOUR PERSPECTIVE-TAKING SKILLS

For the ASD partner, ask yourself: When was the last time I made my partner's preference my priority? Do I get my way most of the time, or do we both have equal influence in the outcomes of our decisions?

CHALLENGE: For one day, track all of the thoughts you think about yourself. Can you switch your thoughts to your spouse and reach out to them instead? Text, call, or go find them wherever they are. Think about how to help your spouse get what they want.

EXERCISE 6. STAY HUMBLE AND CURIOUS

Ask yourself: When my partner talks, what am I focusing my thoughts on? Am I intrigued by my partner? Which do I value more—feeling right or relational connection?

CHALLENGE: Make a list of ten things you want to know about your partner and share this with your partner at your next date night. Let go of your preconceived notions, practice curiosity, and have an open mind.

EXERCISE 7. RELY ON TOOLS AND STRATEGIES THAT WORK

Ask yourself: Am I open to cultivating some solutions that would work for us as an ND couple? Research and discuss some of the tools and strategies that work for ND couples. For the autistic partner, take the initiative here.

CHALLENGE: Consider taking up a meditation practice, speak to a psychiatrist if medications are needed, and make a deal to negotiate and agree to the best solutions for both of you when problems arise.

EXERCISE 8. SCHEDULE FUN AND DO IT OFTEN!

Do you typically view your differences as obstacles or as adventures? What are some hobbies, games, restaurants, or activities that you effortlessly enjoy together?

CHALLENGE: Ask your partner if you can join them in one of their activities that you typically avoid. See if you can treat the experience like an adventure! Next time, you take a turn and pick a novel and fun activity that you can both partake in. Recall some of your fondest memories as a couple. Pick one of them to "recreate"—revisit the location, or try the activity again.

EXERCISE 9. SEEK OUT ASD-SPECIFIC COUPLES COUNSELING

Are there any issues that you feel need the direction of a professional counselor? You don't have to view couples counseling as a chore. Many couples pursue counseling for a few sessions and then taper down to a monthly rhythm and sometimes only as needed.

CHALLENGE: Take a blank notebook and write down the issues you might want to address with an ASD-specific couples counselor. Have your partner do the same and share the list with each other. Sit together and send an inquiry email to the counselor of choice. Keep the notebook and take it to your first session.

EXERCISE 10. EMPHASIZE A CULTURE OF ADMIRATION AND GRATITUDE

What do you love about your partner? What about your life together are you grateful for?

CHALLENGE: Take a pen and paper and make a list of all of your partner's traits that you most admire. And then make another list of all of the things about your relationship and life that you're grateful for. Share these with your partner and keep them around where you can see them every day so that you don't forget. Refresh the list at least once a week!

Let your love story begin...

Acknowledgments

This book would not be possible without the success stories of the neurodiverse couples interviewed. My deepest appreciation for all the couples that recounted first hand their journeys that led to the growth and change in themselves and their relationships. As a couples counselor, to have the inside scoop, so to speak, on these neurodiverse relationships is my great privilege and good fortune.

I'm grateful to my publisher Jessica Kingsley Publishers and publishing editor Sean Townsend who agreed with me regarding the need to highlight the love stories of autistic adults and their partners that are not only white and cishet, but also those who are from diverse cultures and backgrounds, including LGBTQIA+ communities.

Many thanks to Emily Seymour, my assistant, for interviewing many of the participants in the book and for her diligent transcribing of the recorded interviews. This book wouldn't have been possible without

her great help every step of the way in helping move the project forward. I'm thankful to my editor Bethany Grove, for her contributions to the editing process and finishing touches to the book. Bethany, you brought your warmth and valuable insight to this work, so thank you for that.

Deeply grateful to my husband, Deepanjan, and my daughter, Arya, for putting up with my long hours on the laptop and for the sacrifice of family time while I was busy working on this book. Deepanjan, thank you for reading through many sections of the book and for your valuable feedback. Without your taking on so much of the family responsibilities and childcare, I wouldn't have felt the freedom to pursue this book. An honorable mention must go to our families for their unwavering love and support. As always, my gratitude to the SGI-USA Buddhist community for being my spiritual oasis.

Once again, I would like to thank all the couples who agreed to be interviewed for this book and shared their stories so that multitudes of neurodiverse couples around the world could be encouraged and find hope on their own journeys of love and relationship. Thank you because without you, this book would not be possible!